NEW SPIRITUAL TECHNOLOGY

# for the
# Fifth-Dimensional
# Earth

**ARCTURIAN TEACHINGS
FROM THE SACRED TRIANGLE
THROUGH**

# DAVID K. MILLER

# OTHER WORKS BY DAVID K. MILLER

## BOOKS

*Connecting with the Arcturians*

*Teachings from the Sacred Triangle—Volume I*

*Teachings from the Sacred Triangle—Volume II*

*Teachings from the Sacred Triangle—Volume III*

*Teachings from the Sacred Triangle—Volume IV*

## CDs

*Chants for the Ascension*

*Vibrational Activation through Sacred Sound
with Fifth-Dimensional Masters*

# NEW SPIRITUAL TECHNOLOGY FOR THE
# FIFTH-DIMENSIONAL EARTH

ARCTURIAN TEACHINGS FROM THE SACRED TRIANGLE
*through*
## DAVID K. MILLER

Light Technology Publishing
Flagstaff, Arizona

ISBN:  1-891824-79-1
ISBN 13:  978-1-891824-79-1

Channeled text by David K. Miller.
Photo of David K. Miller by Renate Lippert.
Photo of Gudrun Miller by David K. Miller.
Edited by Linda Bell and Inge Skean.
Additional text editing, digital graphics editing and technical assistance by Bill Spuhler.

Published and printed in the United States of America by:

PO Box 3540
Flagstaff, AZ 86003
800-450-0985
**www.lighttechnology.com**

# ACKNOWLEDGMENTS

I would like to thank the following people for their assistance and support in this book. Many thanks to my wife, Gudrun Miller, who is the artist of the images that appear in this book, as well as for her assistance in transcribing all of these lectures. I would like to thank Inge Keans for her assistance in the editorial process. I would also like to thank Bill Spuhler, who has also assisted as an editor in this process. Finally, I want to thank Linda Abell, who also has done great work in bringing the editorial process to completion. And lastly, my deepest gratitude and thanks go to the Groups' members all over the planet who have assisted me in bringing this Sacred Triangle energy to the attention of the world.

—David K. Miller
Prescott, AZ
April 2009

# TABLE OF CONTENTS

I have been focusing on the new fifth-dimensional paradigm called the Sacred Triangle for the past fifteen years. To teach and expand this work, I have founded a worldwide meditation group called the "Arcturian Groups of Forty project" [information on how to join this project is in the appendix]. Currently the project has more than a thousand members worldwide from twenty different countries, including members from the U.S., Germany, Italy, Turkey, Denmark, Norway, Switzerland, Austria, New Zealand, Australia, Mexico, Argentina, Costa Rica, Canada and many others. I have written and published four books on the subject and have published more than forty journal articles explaining the Sacred Triangle concepts. Since 2004, I have been traveling around the world doing workshops promoting these ideas.

This work represents my fifth book offered to further promote the Sacred Triangle energy. A new spiritual paradigm is needed now to help humankind transition into the next evolutionary stage. This next evolutionary stage must be made by humankind to ensure their survival of global climatic changes, war and environmental destruction. What is the next stage? It involves the expansion of human consciousness, which includes telepathically contacting the Earth spirit and accessing higher energy from the ascended masters.

The symbol of this new paradigm, the Sacred Triangle, was introduced in my first book in 1998, *Connecting with the Arcturians*, and in subsequent books: *Teachings from the Sacred Triangle, Volumes 1, 2 and 3*. This beautiful symbol represents the integration of three spiritual sources for healing the Earth: 1) the Native American spirituality and the spiritual work of the indigenous peoples of the world; 2) the mystical energy found in all the major religions in the world, including Christianity, the Kabbalah, Hinduism, Sufism and the ascended masters, including Chief White Eagle, Sananda/Jesus, Buddha, Archangel Michael, Quan Yin and many great fifth-dimensional teachers; and 3) fifth-dimensional galactic spirituality, which includes energy from extradimensional masters such as the Arcturians and the Pleiadians. My personal guide from the fifth dimension, Juliano, comes from the fifth-dimensional galactic star system known as Arcturus. Juliano plays a prominent role in introducing the Sacred Triangle energy to Earth.

It is important to note that we can work with any side of the triangle. At the same time, we can also seek to integrate any sides of the triangle into a new force for planetary healing. How does one use the energies of the Sacred Triangle for healing? From my spiritual standpoint, the Earth is moving closer to the fifth dimension. New spiritual ideas and technologies are becoming available for rebalancing our world. For example, we can use Native ceremonies to connect to the Earth healing energies; we can use thought projections and thought communications to communicate with Earth.

It is important to connect with our galactic starseed heritage so that we can understand how important it is to relate to our role in the galaxy. Using sacred areas on the Earth, we can establish spiritual corridors with the fifth dimension. We can also download etheric crystals from higher realms into key sacred energy spots on Earth to help activate and receive higher energy. Finally, connections with the spiritual center of our galaxy, called the Central Sun, allow new ideas and balancing methods to be downloaded into our consciousness. This book focuses on and offers suggestions for working with and creating a new spiritual paradigm for both personal and planetary healing.

Planetary healing is the mission for many starseeds—people who have galactic consciousness and who have incarnated on Earth to help Earth heal. The concept is that higher-consciousness beings can focus fifth-dimensional light to Earth. Meridian pathways along the Earth can be activated to bring the biosphere of Earth back into a state that can stabilize our environment. The health of Earth is evaluated in terms of the biosphere and Earth's ability to maintain a level of energy that can support and sustain human life.

So the new spiritual paradigm recognizes that Earth's biosphere is in danger of collapsing. This potential collapse of the biosphere is due to many environmental factors, including pollution, overuse of nuclear radiation, degradation of the oceans and also the thinning of our atmosphere. One result of all this activity is climate change, which results in further extinction of plant and animal life, many of which are necessary for human survival.

Personal healing is also involved in the Sacred Triangle energy process. Our soul missions have brought us to this point in Earth's history both to assist Earth and to accelerate our personal ascension. Ascension can be looked upon as a graduation from the Earth's incarnational process, which allows us to go to other higher worlds. Specific spiritual exercises are given in this new book to support this transition of ascension—including, for example, a spiritual practice called *shimmering*, which is explained in detail. The idea of group consciousness and group energy is central to personal and planetary work. The Groups of Forty are core organizational meditation and planetary healing groups that I established in 1993 and that have grown worldwide ever since.

The central idea to the new spiritual technology for healing Earth is the concept called *biorelativity*. Biorelativity is an exercise in which large groups of people seek to interact with Earth energy through telepathic communication. These key interactions can be done through ceremonies and meditations. This biorelativity we do involves the idea of using etheric crystals from other dimensions to accelerate the Earth's energies.

## CHAPTER 1

# SHIFTING PERCEPTION AND YOUR ASSEMBLAGE POINT

### Juliano, the Arcturians, Chief White Eagle and Sananda

Greetings, I am Juliano. We are the Arcturians. The doors of perception are opening and allowing new views of reality and new understanding of the third dimension. These doors are shifting, allowing each person to begin to assimilate the nature of reality.

## UNDERSTANDING YOUR ASSEMBLAGE POINT

The shamans refer to the energy point that controls your perceptual field, also known as the assemblage point. The biology of your brain and neurochemical apparatus relates consciousness to the reticular activating system. This point and system in your brain are like control valves, allowing conscious perceptions and interpretations to be made.

There is another aspect to the assemblage point, or perceptual field, and that aspect is the galactic field or galactic assemblage point. Each section of the galaxy has unique aspects. These unique aspects exist in such a way that people who incarnate in that galactic aspect of reality must have a certain energetic apparatus and perceptual viewpoint in order to relate to that area of the galaxy.

When a being is incarnated into a section of the universe or of the galaxy, their assemblage point is shifted to allow them to grasp and relate to that particular section. This is important for you to understand while trying to do astral, long-distance or remote traveling. You could be going to sections of the galaxy for which you do not have the corresponding assemblage point shift. In fact, you could go to Venus or Mars and you might see nothing—

no life forms there whatsoever. Yet I could tell you that your assemblage point and perceptual points are not properly aligned with that particular planet. Therefore, you do not perceive anything. You cannot see that there are fifth-dimensional life forms around that area; consequently, you would not believe it. It would require some kind of energetic shift for you.

Likewise, if you were to travel to the Arcturian system or if you were using your telescopes or spaceships with long-distance sensors, you might say, "Well, we do not see anything. This is a relatively new star system and maybe there is a planet or two nearby, or maybe we do not even see a planet. All we see is this huge, red giant star known as Arcturus. There is nothing there." In fact, Arcturus is many times brighter and gives off much more energy than your Sun.

You might conclude there is no way that a planet, if it were nearby, could tolerate any type of carbon life form. Then I would say that you do not have the assemblage-point perceptual shift to see the reality or be able to experience the reality that we experience. We have fifth-dimensional planets, which require different ways of perception. We see the third dimension, but we also experience another reality that is fifth-dimensional. You would be hard-pressed to see this unless we activated a shift in your assemblage point.

## SHIFTING THE ASSEMBLAGE POINT AND YOUR PERCEPTION

The assemblage point is related to the section of the galaxy in which you are living. It is also related to the culture you are in, to your incarnation, to your past history on this planet and to other aspects, including your genetic codes.

The genetic codes for perceptions themselves can actually be stimulated and activated by speaking sacred words and tones. I refer to specific codes and tones that will shift your assemblage point. Consciousness can shift immediately through sacred sounds and tones.

Your culture is explained beautifully in the starseed movie, *What the Bleep Do We Know!?* as it shows that culture programs an assemblage point that will predetermine how you perceive reality.[1] That movie also shows—which is obvious to us—that in this time period, there is a huge opportunity to: 1) since assemblage points can be shifted, become aware of these

---

1. Channel's note: According to shamans, the assemblage point is a cluster of energy lines close to the body. These energy points affect the energy of both sides of the brain and the endocrine system. It is reported that this energy cluster affects the way we feel and perceive reality.

assemblage points and shifts; and 2) see that assemblage points can be shifted dramatically, both by internal codes and external shifts. These shifts can be affected by the Central Sun energy field that is coming into alignment with the Earth. This will set up a chain reaction that will shift the assemblage point.

The shifts in assemblage points will only occur for those people who are activated and pre-programmed to allow this to happen. It will only transpire to those who are starseeds or who are preparing themselves to be starseeds and can incorporate new fifth-dimensional energy and balance.

To shift the assemblage point during an incarnation requires a major effort, and it can be traumatic. Most people's assemblage points are shifted in between incarnations and they come back with the program for a new view.

To shift the assemblage point during a lifetime can be considered a major accomplishment, but it can also be stressful if the person is not properly prepared. The appearance of an extraterrestrial being, a fifth-dimensional being in your reality, in your physical space can automatically shift your assemblage point. That is why extradimensional appearances cannot occur immediately or instantaneously—some preparation is needed. More importantly, it must be determined if the psychological, emotional and spiritual energy fields of the third-dimensional person on Earth can accept the shift required to perceive an extradimensional being.

Let us again reexamine that concept of appearing. The appearance of a fifth-dimensional being—such as an Arcturian—in your energy space will immediately cause a shift in your assemblage point. Thus you might begin to grasp the importance of slowly introducing higher beings into a planet. You might understand the wisdom of UFO sightings and the wisdom of higher beings who desire to interact.

It is preferable to gently and slowly come into a foreign system, as opposed to landing on the White House lawn, as an immediate interaction. This is logical to higher beings, as they understand how you function and they respect you and your process. Therefore, the introduction of higher beings in the past has always remained on the fringe of society. Now it is becoming more intense and commonplace.

We have found that the assemblage points of the South Americans, for example, are different than the North Americans. We have found that there are many people in the Andes Mountains, in other areas around the Mayan area and also at Lake Titicaca who have shifted their perceptual field. There are other power spots where the people are open. They have the assemblage points to perceive this. The interaction of the people also depends on where they are.

There are certain areas of the planet with corridors that have been activated for centuries. We have spoken many times about the corridors, but never from the perspective of the assemblage point. These corridors only require a minimal amount of activation on the person's part. The corridor interacting with a person of higher intent can create a shift in the assemblage point. With that shift, the individual will be able to see another reality where there are higher beings interacting with the Earth.

Billy Meier is an Earth being who had and continues to have interactions with the Pleiadians.[2] There is a beautiful movie of his interactions where he shows and describes that he can see the spaceship coming into his area of vision, yet no one else can see it. They land, and there was perhaps some grass bent or some other things occurring, which only Billy could see. People said, "How is this possible?"

Why could he see it and no one else could? Again, the answer is the assemblage point. His perceptual field had shifted, and he was able to see their reality. He was able to communicate with them. That is why even today some people can have direct experiences with the higher beings, whereas others would not even be able to see them.

Billy had been prepared since birth for these encounters. He had been prepared in between incarnations for this shift in assemblage point to allow this. It is not something that happens instantaneously, unless you have had some type of instructions or intent, or if you are taught.

## SHAMANS CAN TRAIN YOU

Let us return to the shamans. The practices of the shamans and the Native people on the planet can be integrated into our strong belief of the spiritual paradigm we call the Sacred Triangle. This Sacred Triangle energy encompasses spiritual knowledge of mystical, galactic and shamanistic energy that can help you progress (see Fig. 1). The shamanistic or Native people's religious and spiritual practices seek to shift your worldview. Another powerful way to describe the assemblage point is to call it the "worldview." Expanding your assemblage point broadens your worldview because you suddenly begin to see things as energy.

---

2. Channel's note: Bill Eduard Albert Meier is a citizen from Switzerland who has had numerous contacts with extraterrestrials from the star system Pleiades starting at age five. These contacts are recorded in his series of books called *Contact Notes*.

Figure 1: The Sacred Triangle containing three types of spiritual knowledge.

Instead of simply seeing solid chairs, you see molecules and atoms moving. Instead of seeing simply a person, you can also see the skeleton, the muscles, the heart and the blood flowing. You can see their whole energy field and past-life history, including illnesses that might come into being five years in their future. Illness will appear as black energy fields in their aura. You might see attachments of parasitic ghosts around their body. You could be overwhelmed by seeing all this, and on top of all that, you could see relationships of spirit guides—tunnels and corridors. These are wonderful things to view, but they can also overwhelm the person who is not prepared.

You can be trained to do this energetic shift—shamans can train you. This energetic shift allows the healing energy to be used in a way that cannot be manipulated in a regular reality. In order for that to occur, both the shaman and the trainee must have the shift. We have found that Native people in particular understood this. The ancient Mayans also understood it. They understood the 2012 corridor. That is why they understood we live in a galaxy. That is why they understood the archaeoastronomy principles—the relationship between the civilizations and advanced astronomy. They had an advanced astronomy because they were able to shift, relate and speak to the higher beings.

There are huge structures on the ground in Peru that can only be understood from the air. The higher beings were demonstrating to the Earth beings that from the higher reality, an influence can be affected on the lower reality of the Earth. This higher reality that can be perceived and seen from a shift in your assemblage point can be made to affect your reality. It is not just a place to visit and exclaim, "Wow!"

It is to be understood that it is a place for you to change and for you to change the Earth. You can change the Earth in a much more powerful way when you experience these other realities. The ancient peoples, and the Mayans in particular, understood this. This information about the assemblage point is also a key to understanding ascension and how ascension can occur. Within the physical laws that now govern your reality, ascension might seem totally illogical and unscientific. It is against the laws of the universe as you know them. Ascension is counter to the third-dimensional laws of the universe. These laws do not take into consideration the changes in perceptual reality—the reality of which you are slowly being made aware.

As you integrate the concepts of ascension, you must also incorporate and begin to train yourself to shift your assemblage point. Otherwise, you cannot ascend. In the shift, you will see that your true nature is much more vast than this physical reality and this physical body. You will see that your true nature is multidimensional and that you can and do live on multiple levels simultaneously.

## PRACTICE THOUGHT PROJECTIONS

We practice and encourage you to practice thought projections to push your awareness into the other reality. This will encourage, expand and loosen your assemblage point so that you have an experiential basis for the shift.

"Where do you want us to shift it?" you might ask. The Arcturian Crystal Temple is a pure and acceptable place to practice thought projection. It is a place we continue to work with to allow Earth beings to transmit their multidimensional presence. We have also activated energy there that will accelerate healing.

There are many other places to do thought projection on the planet, and there are many other places to go. We also encourage you to move to our ships, because we have certain healing areas on our ships that are designed for your presence when your assemblage point is shifted.

Certain tones and vibrations will allow you—and those who hear these tones—to shift their assemblage points at the present moment. I ask you to center yourself. You may feel a tension in your shoulder. Allow that tension to be dispersed through your body, because the activation point for the assemblage is often over the left shoulder. The left shoulder is a reflection of the energy field from the assemblage point. You could look at the assemblage point as a doorway. The doors of perception will open for you. [Tones.]

"In the name of the *Adonai* light and the presence of the *Adonai* light, let those doors of perception open." [Tones.] "It is important that you have no thought." [Tones and makes galactic sounds.] "The Arcturian corridor of blue light is with you. A fountain of effervescent, blue energetic light is bubbling in the center of the room, and little droplets of these powerful light rays are entering your energetic field, magnetically enlightening and enlivening you, activating this perceptual process within you." [Tones.] "A great feeling of love fills your heart; great feelings of joy emerge."

We offer a corridor opening into higher consciousness so that the transition to the fifth dimension becomes orderly for you, acceptable, and integrates into your original assemblage point that is Earth-based.

Figure 2: Chief White Eagle.

You are in this heightened state. You understand the difference between normal and expanded consciousness. When you come down, return to your normal consciousness, but stay in heightened awareness. I now ask Chief White Eagle (see Fig. 2) to speak with you.

**H**ey ya heyyaaahh! Ho! Ho! Howahey! All my relations, all my brothers and sisters, I open my heart to all of you. I am here to teach and remind you of this heightened state of consciousness and what Juliano called the movement of your perception. In this higher state, it is obvious that energetically we are all related. It is obvious we are all relations. We are all one.

## DANCE TO SHIFT YOUR ASSEMBLAGE POINT

The challenge you starseeds have is to learn to manifest knowledge and actions from this experience into the reality of the third dimension. This is why we dance together. This is why we create sacred dances. It is time to share these dances. I call on all the Native people who hear these words and all bearers and keepers of the sacred dance to show your dances, to allow the sacred dance of life to be brought forth and shown.

The dance is a way of moving the assemblage point, as Juliano called it. There are sacred dances such as the "Rain Dance," which is a way of interacting with higher energies to create a shift in the weather patterns. There is even a sacred life-force dance—it is the "All My Relations, We Are All Brothers and Sisters" dance.

I call on those who know this dance to dance it. Those who are in this room now, I ask that you walk in a circle around this room. Those who hear these words, walk in a circle. I ask you to walk and allow the dance energy to come into you, to your spirit. Connect with the dancing from the higher level. Let us walk around the room clockwise, three or four times.

Try breathing in a deep, rhythmic manner. The energy of "We Are All Brothers and Sisters" beings to fill your heart. You see the life-force energy of all people, and you understand the relationships of all brothers and sisters. You understand the meaning of relationships, the meaning of, "He is my brother, she is my sister, he is my mother, and she is my father." (Yes, it is reversed because of your androgynous nature.) You understand the meaning of the statements, "The Earth is my Mother, the sky is my Father: Father Sky, Mother Earth. Mother Earth, Father Sky; you are my parents.

"I understand our relationship. Mother Earth, we are your children; Father Sky, we are your sons and daughters. Central Sun, we are your children—the *B'nai Elohim*, the children of light. Arcturians, we are your brothers and sisters. We are part of your family of the galaxy." Hey hey ya, ho! Ho! I am Chief White Eagle. Blessings.

**G**reetings, I am Sananda. You are amazing energy forces, amazing children of *Elohim*. You are the sons and daughters of the *Elohim* light.

## THIS SHIFT IS AVAILABLE THROUGH LOVE

The great message of the shifting of the assemblage point can also be described and accessed through love. It can be accessed through the opening of your heart, through the love of your Father, through the love of your Mother. Honor your Father, honor your Mother and also love God, *Adonai*, with all your might, with all your power, with all your essence. This love moves what Juliano calls your assemblage point. This moves your perceptual field. This is the basis for the shamanistic secret to changing perception.

The path is also available through love—love of God. [Sings in Hebrew]: *Atah Gibur le'olam va'ed. Baruch Atah Adonai Eloheynu Melech ha'olom, asher kiddishanu le'chal chai ya vik'ah'yom! Atah Gibur le'yolam va'ed.* You are great forever and ever, and your greatness fills our hearts with power and love. It is your love, *Adonai*, that sustains us. It is your love that sustains us in this energy body known as Earth. It is your love that will sustain us when we transition into the next realm.

When I feel God's love, then I feel my assemblage point shift. If I cannot feel your love, then I can speak of your love. By speaking of your love, I receive your love. By speaking of your unity, I experience your unity. *Shema Yis'rael, Adonai Eloheynu, Adonai Echad.* Hear, O Israel, of your unity, for you are one and we are one with you.

Evil is the blockage of this unity energy and of this consciousness. You are here to learn the difference. When you learn the difference, then you can choose light. Darkness and evil disappear because they have no power. That is the beauty of your mind and your power—what you focus on is what you become.

I am sorry that the Earth experience can become a painful lesson at times. Millions of souls are lined up for this painful lesson—to come here to have the opportunity to learn it. You too lined up to come back. If you have pain, know that love is coming to you to alleviate it soon. I am Sananda.

# TOOLS FOR ASCENSION AND EARTH'S ALIGNMENT WITH THE CENTRAL SUN

Juliano, the Arcturians and Metatron

Greetings, I am Juliano. We are the Arcturians. We shall reexamine ascension. The uses of the etheric crystals that are now within the Earth are also tools to be used for your ascension.

The alignment of the Central Sun plays several important roles in the development of the Earth energies. Particularly, we will look at the role that the alignment of the Central Sun will play in your ascension. The Central Sun alignments in particular are necessary for the ascension. To ascend, one must have alignments with the higher self, with soul purpose and with the fifth dimension.

These alignments enable you to instantaneously shift energy and move into another realm. Needless to say, the alignment must be exact and precise. The alignment must be so total that ascension will be instantaneous or simultaneous and without effort. "Without effort" implies that you are not *trying* to ascend. "Without effort" means that you are so in alignment that the energy in your lower bodies can shift. You suddenly are transcending into the next realm.

## EXERCISE: A CENTRAL SUN VISUALIZATION

Where can you learn about this and where can you get the energy for this kind of alignment? There is practice and learning necessary before the ascension. It means that there are certain things that you must practice to accomplish and certain lessons that you must complete as soon as possible. It means that you can cut the cords of attachment to the Earth, and at the same time, remain grounded in the Earth's energies. You are on the Earth as a third-dimensional being, but you can simultaneously be in a Central Sun alignment.

Many people have difficulty visualizing where the higher energy aligns within themselves. This is where the Central Sun visualization becomes helpful. In your mind, visualize the Central Sun. The Central Sun is the center of the galaxy, and it sends out a beacon of light and energy. It is available to you in your fifth-dimensional body and in your third-dimensional body. The third-dimensional body, which you are now in, can send out an etheric antenna from your crown chakra.

Please visualize an etheric antenna being raised from your crown chakra. As that antenna rises, try to visualize and receive the higher dimensional energy from the Central Sun.

Now you say, "What does this energy feel like, Juliano? What am I supposed to look for?" Look for a sensitive energetic beam with a pulsing frequency. This pulsing frequency is faint, but it is also steady, and it can be interpreted like a heartbeat. Take a moment with this etheric antenna. It is being raised from your crown chakra. Expect to receive this special energy from the Central Sun.

Project yourself to the crystal in Moraine Lake in Banff, Canada, where an etheric crystal was placed. Note the amplification of that signal. You are thought-projecting into this etheric crystal. Experience your alignment to the Central Sun, to your higher self and to your Earth body. Then call on all of your past lives on this planet to come into this alignment. Call on your galactic families. Call on your galactic self to come into these alignments that we now establish. Visualize these alignments. This can be alignments of all past lives, all galactic lives, lives on this Earth and with the Central Sun.

A unique corridor created for the Arcturian starseeds on the Earth opens. This corridor is a beautiful and powerful connection to our starship, to the fifth dimension and to the Stargate. This beautiful corridor is designed for you Earth beings, our friends, to interact with this Arcturian connection.

## APPROACHING THE STARGATE

The Central Sun and the Stargate are colinear. By that, I mean that they exist on the same plane. Their functions are different, but the energy is similar. Perhaps you would think that in the fifth-dimensional scheme of things, there would not be an order of linearity. Colinear implies that they are parallel, existing energetically in a similar fashion.

In speaking of the ascension, I must also speak to you of the Stargate, because the Stargate is an intermediate step to the ascension energy. It can be viewed first as a destination point, a transition point, especially when you understand that you are not allowed to go through the stargate until you have completed the ascension and your Earth incarnational cycle.

You can approach the Stargate now, but you cannot go through it. Going through the Stargate is an energetic experience in which your entire light spirit body is transformed. It is transformed in a way that is so powerful.

After going through the Stargate, then your current energetic conglomeration of your Earth field is no longer available to you. You could not return to Earth unless after you went through the Stargate you chose a new Earth incarnation. But you can come to the vestibule of the Stargate, or the fore-room. In that room, you are connected with and in alignment with the Central Sun.

When you align with the Central Sun, you realize your Arcturian starseed consciousness. You are Arcturian workers aligning with this vestibule of the Stargate. You are now aligning with your soul energetic essence that is beyond your Earth mind. When you align with the Central Sun, you are also able to experience your cosmic-egg energy field. You are able to experience your energetic essence and form. This energetic spirit form is common to all beings of higher evolution in our galaxy.

We, the Arcturians, assume a different body form, and we may look different than you. When we come into the soul energetic essence that is connected with the Central Sun, then we can share a common energetic form with you. This is an energetic form that is preincarnation. This is an energetic form that is preplanetary and perhaps can be referred to as a soul energy. Therefore, we have much in common with you. We have much in common with all beings who are moving into the higher planes.

## YOUR EARTH BODY IS PROGRAMMED FOR ASCENSION

Your connection with the Central Sun and your understanding of the Stargate teaches you soul transcendence energy. It teaches you about moving into the star realm. The ascension becomes part of the natural completion of your planetary work. It is part of the birth process and the goal within all incarnations—a goal that you move toward in which the codes and the work for this transformation are embedded in all your cells. The Earth body is programmed for ascension.

An alignment like we will see on Earth accelerates, amplifies your ascension and accelerates what is a natural process. Ascension is a natural process that is not normally discussed on the Earth. Ascension is a natural process that is not part of the accepted religious ideology. There are thoughts of enlightenment and there is also talk of reaching higher consciousness in religions. It is only in some religious texts that this idea of ascension is spoken. It has only been brought to your attention recently because of the possible cataclysmic events on the Earth. It is presented to you as if the ascension is an escape for you from these cataclysmic events.

There is one level of truth to these statements. Cataclysmic events are occurring even as we speak today. The polarization becomes more accelerated, as we had predicted in earlier lectures. Do not think that it is the polarization or the cataclysmic events that create the ascension, or that you should expect to escape these because of the ascension. Rather, work to align yourself energetically with the Central Sun energy. That will bring other parts of you into alignment. Work to align yourself with the Stargate. Then you will react neither to the cataclysmic events nor to the polarization.

Linking cataclysmic events with the ascension is a mistake that people on other planets have made. They became lost in thinking that the polarization and the cataclysmic events were the energies that set the stage for the ascension. From a lower consciousness viewpoint, it looks like people want to escape.

In truth, polarization is a co-event. It just so happens that at this time of polarization, those of lower energies are unable to hold higher alignment and they can be thrown into a catastrophe that has never been described before in the recorded history of this planet. That leads us to an important discussion about holding energy.

## CALL ON THE ARCTURIAN MASTERS

Holding energy is a process that requires a beautiful vessel. Holding energy requires an evolution in the body. Holding energy for alignments implies an evolvement of the body so that a higher vibration, a higher understanding, can be processed and contained. You are working and have worked to hold a higher vibration.

Some might say, "What happens if I fail, if I am not smart or advanced enough, or I am not meeting my spiritual lessons enough to reach this alignment energy that you are talking about, Juliano?" That is where the Arcturi-ans come in. We consider ourselves soul brothers and sisters to you.

You call on us, call on Juliano, call on Helio-ah, call on Tomar and the other Arcturian guides, and ask them to cohabitate with you. "Cohabitate" is a concept in which a higher being's etheric spirit form enters your energy field. We do not enter your physical body. When we are in your energy field, we can raise your vibration and raise the level of energetic spiritual light that can bring you into higher alignment.

There is need for a rapid alignment. We use the term "alignment" rath-er than "progress" or "advancement." In our terminology, you become "aligned." You are already higher beings, and your evolvement means that you come into alignment. That immediately removes all the thoughts of low self-worth or not being able to complete certain tasks because of blocks. You seek an alignment, and we offer our abilities to cohabitate with you on a higher level to accelerate your alignment.

You might think that if we cohabitate with you and then leave, you might not be able to hold higher energy. We have many Arcturian teachers who are willing and able to work with you continually in cohabitation. In fact, I would be willing to bet that some of you who read these words were at one time on Arcturus with us and volunteered to cohabitate with some of the unaligned students on the Earth. This might be a well-known process to you.

Cohabitation is a process known to Sananda and to all the great masters throughout the galaxy. You are not alone. The process of this alignment does require assistance, just like you needed assistance in being born. Most of you had a doctor present when you were brought into the Earth. It is not really out of the thought realm to have a higher being from Arcturus cohabitate with you and assist you in the alignments.

Call on an Arcturian master to be with you. Make room for them in your thoughts and in your energy field. You must give permission for them to be with you. When you do not want them with you, they will leave. In fact, it is a good practice to have them leave and then call them back.

These are masters who are trained to work with you Earth beings. They are in alignment with the Central Sun and with the Stargate. Therefore, they can help you be in alignment. They might tell you something such as "release your fear" and "release your feelings of unworthiness." You may feel a surge of higher vibration. This higher vibration, again, is our defini-tion of an attribute of you moving into alignment. You can then feel and experience more light.

The closer you get to the Stargate, the more you feel this soul energy—this primordial light energy. Just to be able to conceive of the Stargate, just to be able to understand the Stargate, is a step toward higher consciousness. To travel to the Stargate is an energetic experience of the highest desire. One of the guardians and keepers of the Stargate is the overseer Archangel Metatron.

Metatron is deeply connected with the Arcturians. His name, "Metatron," is in fact an Arcturian name. It means "guardian of the Stargate" in the Arcturian language. I will ask Metatron to work with you, and then I will return. Here is the guardian of the Stargate, Archangel Metatron. I will return.

**A**tah. Greetings, I am Archangel Metatron. I speak to you about you being a vessel and holding a connection to the unfolding of these ascension codes. The ascension codes are words and energies that help to bring forth the alignment of which Juliano spoke. This alignment is also called "unlocking." To unlock or open these codes requires that you have the vessel to hold the energy. I will explain this to you.

## RAISING THE ENERGY OF YOUR VESSEL

Each of you, as a cosmic-egg energetic field, vibrates at a frequency. Frequencies define levels of energy. If you vibrate at a low frequency, you do not hold a great deal of spiritual energy. If you vibrate at a high frequency, then you hold more energy. Your vessel is shaped like a cosmic egg, and it is the envelope around your whole energy field that represents the real you as opposed to your physical body. When that vessel is able to hold higher vibrational light, then you resonate at a higher frequency. Eventually, because you are at this higher frequency, you can ascend.

Opening the codes and bringing yourself into alignment can occur only if your vessel can hold the higher frequency. If it cannot hold the higher frequency, then your vessel breaks. You become disorganized. The energy falls away and you have to reconstitute yourself. I can explain this to you simply by using the analogy of the Godhead and the Sun.

Let us imagine that you are in a spaceship going to the Sun, and as you get closer and closer, the ship disintegrates because it cannot hold the energy back. You did not have a strong vessel to protect you. Let us imagine also that you are getting closer and closer in your evolution until you are before God. You are in a place where you can see the face of God, but you do not have the vessel and vibrational ability to hold that higher energy. Then you are in that energy field and you disintegrate because your vessel was not able to hold it.

This is mentioned in your Bible and was referred to by Jesus. Moses wanted to see the face of God. Even Moses, who was a high being, was not allowed to see God's face. If God would have looked at Moses or Moses would have looked at God, Moses would have disintegrated. God only allowed Moses to see His shadow, and that was almost more than Moses could tolerate, but he was able to keep himself intact.

Imagine the evolved vessel that was held by Jesus. Jesus' vessel was so intact, so perfect, that he could be right next to God. That is why he was called the Son of God. The Son can sit next to the Father. You will be able to sit next to the Father too, but you cannot do that now because your vessel cannot hold this energy yet. We know that is your destiny. The work that the Arcturians are talking to you about really involves raising the energy and the strength of your vessel.

## Focus on Your Vessel

I have spoken these Hebrew words to you before: *Eh'yeh asher Eh'yeh.* You may translate this as: "I will be that I will be." These are the coded words. Some say, "I have heard those words before, Metatron. Why do I have to hear them again?"

It is not something you say once; it is a mantra. It is something that you work with continually to build up your energy. Focus on your vessel; focus on building up the energy. If you want, also focus on the Arcturian who will cohabitate with you. That will bring some higher energy. Remember, vibration and frequency in spirit means higher energy. [Sings]: *Eh'yeh asher Eh'yeh.*

When you are in this higher frequency, then you align. Your thought that you want to ascend is all that is required. When you are in the higher vibration, you are on the level of power. This level of power is such that it creates the happening. So, you see, the ascension requires certain things of you and requires you to be on a certain level. I know that you cannot maintain that level all the time on the Earth—especially during this time of polarization and catastrophic events. Fears and densities will bring you to a lower vibration. Life on Earth is not necessarily based on where you are at one moment.

I know this will sound like a paradox, but life is an accumulation of who you are and what level you have reached. You may have reached this higher level right now, and then twenty minutes from now, you might fall, but your heart is still good. You have faith and had alignment and want to hold that alignment. Higher energy returns.

It is true that at the moment of death you should be at this high level, but not everybody is going to do this. Even Jesus on the cross had doubts and temporarily went to a lower vibration. Was he denied his ascension because he had a lower vibration at that moment? No. Even if he were totally lost, he would still enter the kingdom. He was a perfected energy. He had high light and he was able to hold it. I tell you this so you do not feel badly if you temporarily lose the light you have right now. I guarantee you that at times you will not be able to always hold higher light because this Earth is so filled with polarization.

It is a challenge for all but the masters to continually hold the light. Do not think that being dense at times precludes you from your ascension. You can hold the thought of "I will be that I will be." It is like a hypnotic suggestion when you hear or say these words. They are coded energies that remind you of the higher state and will activate you. Even if you do not instantaneously go to the higher state, you will feel the power of these words. The vibration of these words does something to your energy, it sets things in motion—even if you do not feel it immediately.

Have faith. I will chant the word "faith" for you in Hebrew and this will activate your faith light. [Sings]: *Emunah, Emunah Tov.* Good faith is important. Your vessel is brighter. Your cosmic-egg energy now is more solid. It is a vessel that can hold this alignment and begin to vibrate.

*Atah Kadosh.* You are holy light. Holy light is light of a higher vibration. Let holy light come into you now so that you can be at a higher frequency. When you are at a higher frequency, then you can ascend and align with holy light. *Aur Ha-Kodesh.*

The energetic light from the etheric crystals holds a frequency that cannot be held in normal Earth vessels. The Egyptian pyramids were built to hold energy, just as you have dams to hold back energy. There are vessels on the planet that were placed here to hold spiritual energy. That would be the purpose of building an Arcturian temple on Earth—to build a sacred vessel to hold spiritual energy.

The etheric crystals have the purpose of holding spiritual energy for the Arcturian starseeds. You are so beautiful, especially when you are holding this magnificent energy. I will return you to Juliano. Blessed are you, children of the *B'nai Elohim* (children of God). I am Metatron.

This is Juliano. I am glad that the understanding of these etheric crystals is deepening so that you better understand that they hold special spiritual energy. I feel that the ascension is near because the Central Sun alignment is near. Your participation and understanding of ascension has deepened tremendously in the past years. Practice ascending to our starship. Practice using the corridor. Practice going to the Stargate vestibule. I am Juliano. We are the Arcturians.

## CHAPTER 3

# THE SACRED ETHERIC CRYSTALS

Juliano, the Arcturians and Sananda

Greetings, I am Juliano. We are the Arcturians. We have, with your assistance, provided sacred etheric crystals that have been placed within the Earth at strategic points. Each of these crystals has a specific function for providing contact with the etheric realm. Together these etheric crystals provide a new corridor and a new method for expanding the Earth's consciousness and etheric energy field. The Earth has an etheric energy field just like each person on Earth.

Indeed, extraterrestrials like the Arcturians and the Pleiadians also have etheric energy fields. These etheric energy fields, both of a person and of a planet, have the ability to reach out and communicate at enormous distances in the galaxy and the universe. The etheric energy is not like the normal third-dimensional energy. Rather, the etheric energy is in part composed and is initially a reflection of third-dimensional energy.

But in a higher aspect of the etheric energy, we have noted that the energy field can reach enormous distances and can also interact with different realms. This provides proof that each one of you has the ability to exist and experience simultaneously greater distances in this and other dimensions.

## CONNECTING WITH THE HIGHER REALMS

Earth's etheric energy field is controlled by many factors. It is receptive and sensitive to the higher extradimensional energy that we, the Arcturians, have provided with your assistance, by using etheric crystals. The crystals have interjected fifth-dimensional connections to the higher realms. These higher realms include Arcturus, the Central Sun and many other places and planets in the fifth dimension.

Arcturus is not the only planet in the fifth dimension. The Pleiades, where many of you are also cohabiting and have come from, is also a fifth-dimensional planet. There are numerous fifth-dimensional planets in this section of the galaxy and countless fifth-dimensional planets throughout the entire galaxy.

Connecting with the fifth-dimensional realm will allow you to travel to these other planets. Some of these planets are, in fact, your home planets. Many of you have entered this section of the galaxy through the Arcturian Stargate, and many of you have used the Stargate as the springboard to enter the Earth energy field. I know that some of you have home planets that are far away from this section of the galaxy. Some of you are great galactic and soul travelers.

You have enjoyed these opportunities to communicate, learn and explore the nature of the third dimension. The third dimension is an expansion of the Creator's will, which allows a new episode in consciousness. The third dimension allows special lessons and it also allows even lower vibrations to enter into manifestation. There can be greater opportunities for those to advance when entering a lower realm. Naturally, the other side of this is that when there are lower vibrations, then there can be greater polarity and conflict.

## EARTH'S ETHERIC CRYSTAL CONNECTION

Let us return to the subject of the etheric energy field that has been created by the powerful etheric crystals. These etheric crystals are now connected to each other.

Visualize that the effect of these crystals is actually creating a corridor. Visualize that this corridor is projected upward from the Earth at a distance to the Moon on the one side. Visualize that this etheric crystal connection is also being projected through the Earth and out the other side of the Earth. It is touching and interacting with both sides of the planet. Most important for our lecture is the great news that these etheric crystals are also connected to the Inner Earth.

The Inner Earth is able to communicate, receive and transmit etheric energy through this etheric crystal connection. Many of you who are connecting with the Arcturian field are also connecting to this powerful etheric crystal energy field. The Inner Earth is now linking with all of you through this special corridor of light and etheric corridor. It is becoming a holographic corridor that is projecting out of both sides of the Earth. Also, it reaches out as a long corridor into the fifth dimension.

Dimensions are actually spheres. Foster this connection to the fifth dimension from the beautiful corridor that we created with your assistance. Visualize a sphere. Visualize that your existence on the third dimension is in fact similar to being on the sphere called "Earth."

It is no accident that the planets are in a semispherical shape, because the third dimension is a sphere. It is an expanding sphere that seems to go outward into infinity. Even though the sphere of the third dimension goes out to infinity, there are corridors that leave and go outside the third dimension—some have called this "hyperspace." It is that space beyond the third dimension. You could say that it is an intersection, but we like the description used by your scientists: hyperspace.

When you are in hyperspace, you are going beyond the laws of cause and effect, and beyond the laws of finiteness. You are beyond the space-time continuum. You are in some ways in a state of suspended animation. Hyperspace is that interstellar, interdimensional place where you can travel throughout the galaxy and connect to the fifth dimension.

With special permission, guidance and specific techniques, you can travel forward and backward in the space-time continuum to look into the future or the past. This hyperspace arena allows you to travel forward and go beyond what is now happening. Based on that place where you started, you may go forward into hyperspace, stop at a given point in the future and then, with a corridor, come down and see what will happen in the future. This is a complex matter. With that knowledge and experience, you might be able to return to the present and change the future.

Your scientists have experimented with hyperspace and have also experimented with going outside the etheric energy field of the planet and moved forward into the future—sometimes with questionable intentions. They have gone forward, perhaps with warlike dominating thoughts, and they have tried to change present realities by coming back with future knowledge. In some ways, there were some successes. But they also did not understand the laws of the universe, of etheric energy—the laws of the corridors and also of hypertravel.

Earth beings traveling in hyperspace have set off a major alarm factor in many of the extraterrestrial higher beings because they are aware that the Earth does not have the spiritual technology of the higher masters. It is still possible to go through hyperspace without spirituality. The Earth could affect and change the outcome and the interactions of other parts of the galaxy, and it can even lead to a domination of other parts of the galaxy. There is a need to establish a protective field so that those Earth scientists cannot misuse knowledge about hyperspace for war purposes.

I know that many of you are interested in using hyperspace to connect with the fifth dimension and even with the future on Earth. You are moving into higher consciousness, and for the most part, want to graduate from the Earth. The starseeds are not interested, I believe, in domination. They are not interested in trying to have the Earth become more warlike. I know that many of you want the Earth to be healed. Many of you want to see that nature and many of the natural species return to pristine conditions.

Many of you are committed to Earth healing. You have a dual purpose: the purpose of ascending through these corridors and your personal healing. The special etheric corridor is going to assist in your ascension. You have the desire to participate in the healing of Mother Earth, and also in the healing of the hyperspace rifts that were created by the scientists on Earth who wrongly understood and misused the technology of accessing hyperspace.

This etheric connection corridor is accessing you to another sphere. Outside of the sphere, there is a hyperdimensional space. Hyperdimensional space can also be defined as space between dimensions. I make a distinction between hyperspace, which goes to the edge of a dimension, and hyperdimensional space, which is the space between two dimensions.

Therefore, to cross dimensions, you have to cross a "chasm," a space that is not describable. Some have referred to it as emptiness or nothingness. All of these are approximations. We are able, through our spiritual technology, to extend the corridor through the hyperdimensions so that the corridor connects to the fifth dimension.

This beautiful etheric corridor will allow an extension from Earth through hyperspace, through hyperdimensions, to the fifth dimension, so that you do not have to experience this void, this chasm. You will have the opportunity to travel directly to the fifth dimension. The Earth will serve you like a rocket booster that will send you up. We will travel today to this corridor created by the etheric crystals.

## ENTERING THE ETHERIC CRYSTAL ENERGY FIELD

Release your connections to the third dimension. Let the crystalline structures around your energy field loosen so that you have the ability to interface with this higher energy field. Each of you choose an etheric crystal—whether it is in Canada, Argentina, Australia or elsewhere. You do not have to go to the one that is closest to you; go to the one with which you feel the most connection. Feel your body relaxing into a deep state, and at the same time, feel your etheric spirit leaving your body.

Thought-project yourself to the etheric crystal of your choice. Enter the etheric crystal. You enter an energy field that is shaped like a crystal, and it is a crystal within the Earth. This crystal absorbs a high-energy frequency from the Inner Earth, and it also provides each of you a wonderful healing experience because the etheric crystals are connected with the Central Sun healing energy. Enter this energy field and feel a general heightened healing.

We, the Arcturians, are aligning our ship, the Starship Athena, with the etheric crystals. The crystals are being activated as we send down heightened beams of special spiritual light and energy into these crystals.

There is a deep activation from Earth going through the Inner Earth, the outer Earth and through deep sections around the solar system. The corridor now expands outside of the solar system. We are all working together. It expands at a rate that is indescribable. It reaches the outside of the third dimension, and then we come through the sphere of the third dimension through hyperspace to the fifth dimension. It is like a chariot of fire.

We enter the fifth dimension in this etheric corridor. We stay within the corridor. We are not allowed to let you leave the corridor. We are now in a beautiful harmonic energy field in coordination with the Central Sun. Master Sananda will speak to you all in this corridor.

G reetings, blessings, my brothers and sisters, my galactic brothers and sisters. I am Sananda. The abilities and spiritual understanding that you show are part of your heritage and your birthright. You are an aspect of what we consider higher consciousness. We consider you higher beings. I know that many of you have personal problems and concerns that might lead you to think otherwise. At the same time, I know that you have this highest ability and understanding.

Therefore, in spite of your Earth limitations, you are infinite beings of higher light. We all consider you members of the spiritual army who will bring an etheric solution and healing to the Earth. This will help people experience the Earth changes in a positive way—in a way that will allow higher light to reach Earth.

## REALIGN YOURSELVES WITH THE HIGHER REALMS

In order for each of you to survive on Earth during the next few years, you must realign your DNA and the codes of ascension within you. You must shift your whole energy field so that your electromagnetic fields become less vulnerable and so that you can assimilate certain frequencies that are beyond the reach of most of those on the Earth. At the same time, you will have the ability to protect yourself in enclaves of communities.

From these enclaves of communities, you have the ability to activate energy fields to assist in suppressing negativities. These enclaves of communities do not actually have to be physically close, but rather they can be communities of people connecting from different parts of the planet. We consider starseed groups to be an enclave, for you are going beyond normal space and time to connect with each other. You are activating yourselves as powerful beings of consciousness and starseeds. You understand the nature of the galaxy and the work that needs to be done so that the Earth can assimilate fifth-dimensional energy and become part of the galactic family. I send a special healing to each of you because I know the electromagnetic spectrum on the Earth can become disruptive and unbalanced. I know that each of you can benefit from this alignment.

There is a gathering of great ascended masters within the Galactic Council. This gathering is coordinating a huge intervention that will be forthcoming, which will last fifteen to seventeen days. During this time, there will be opportunities for each of you to magnify and amplify yourselves as spiritual beings.

Understand and visualize yourself as gigantic beings, not just five- to six-and-a-half feet tall, but visualize yourselves as gigantic etheric energy beings. This will allow you to make connections to the other realms. It will also allow you to expand your energy fields and presence in a way that will make you less vulnerable to the intrusions that possibly will come— intrusions from other sources that are not of the highest light.

You are the children of the *Elohim*, children of the manifested Creator light, and you have the ability to be multidimensional. You have the ability to have gigantic energy fields, to project and focus energy from the Central Sun into the etheric crystals and into the corridor. You can project that energy field outward or inward into the Earth or around the Earth.

I am so happy that you have come to this place with me on the fifth dimension, where many of your soul brothers and sisters visit with you now. I am so happy that you have this moment to be in a higher garment. Your Earth body is a garment, an important garment, but it is only one aspect of yourself. Joseph in the Bible had many coats. The coat he had was a reference to the many aspects of himself, and the many different colors are representations of the different levels of dimensions and consciousness.

The Arcturians are high beings linked to higher life forms in this galaxy. They are ambassadors; they are healers; they are fifth-dimensional assistants. We are helping to move the fifth realm closer to the third dimension. We will see this intersection of dimensions. When this intersection occurs, there will be an ascension. There will be a magnificent display of light and energy on the Earth.

When the dimensions are near and even touch Earth, then the Earth will experience something like what you know as solar flares or aurora lights. It will be a thousand times more powerful. Maintain a consciousness when this happens. Do not fall asleep, but maintain your awareness. I return you to Juliano. I am Sananda. Blessings.

This is Juliano. You are all beaming brightly, and it is exciting to learn of the higher energy and experiences that will come from this intersection of the dimensions.

Some of you may have the opportunity to use this corridor again. We will guide you back to your Earth body, back through hyperspace and the hyperdimension. I, Juliano, call on each of you to begin to depart from this wonderful place on the fifth dimension and travel with me back into this corridor through hyperdimensional space.

As you enter hyperspace, also go forward in time with me on the Earth. As you are given permission and I guide you, you might look down these special corridors that can be called "observational" corridors. You can observe Earth in the future and see future events. Most importantly, look around the Earth and see the energetic rumblings, the energetic light waves created from the interfaces of the third and the fifth dimensions.

See yourself there and also see how you assimilate and raise your own energy fields. Let us return to the main corridor. I will ask later how and what some of you may have observed. Return with me through the corridor, leaving hyperspace and reentering the Earth. Return down the corridor, through the etheric crystal corridor where we started, and then through the etheric crystal that you went through and finally back into your Earth body.

## USE THE ETHERIC CRYSTAL TO HEAL YOURSELF AND EARTH

Take a moment to reintegrate your Earth body with your etheric experience. You are all back in your bodies. When you connect to the light field from these crystals, then you can also project great healings. You can take the outline of the crystal and project its crystal shape onto an area of the Earth.

For example, you can project the crystal shape over the area of the Middle East. Hold that crystal shape over the area for as long as you can tolerate it. Then, as you hold it, the crystal will absorb a tremendous amount of polarization and negativity—such as from hatred, destruction and other negative energies.

Next, take the outline of the crystal and realign it back with the main etheric crystal, which will absorb all of the darker energies and dissipate them. You can do this by yourself or with a group. Each of you has the potential to do this beautiful exercise—because of the level of polarization on the Earth, there is a need for repeated interventions.

You also can use the same exercise for personal healing. Project an outline of an etheric crystal and place it over your physical body. Your physical body will receive a wonderful healing. All denser, negative, bodily energies can be absorbed. Then you can take that etheric crystal and place it back on the base crystal for absorption and dissipation. This is an example of the technology involved in etheric crystal healing.

We are also aware that the Central Sun has a direct link into this etheric crystal and charges it with quantum-light healing energy. Quantum light is light beyond space and time. It is beyond the finite world. Some of you can feel quantum light coming into you. I am projecting it to each one of you who are reading these words so that you can feel, so that you can heal, so that you can gain the ability to move your etheric body more easily into the fifth dimension.

In reality, you will move your spirit, your etheric presence into the fifth dimension, and the physical body will accelerate into fifth-dimensional energy. Your fifth-dimensional body will travel through a time corridor.

We have sent a second ship, the Starship Solara, along with the Starship Athena to the Earth's solar system. The second starship is able to accommodate many starseeds. Many new guides and teachers are on this ship. [Sings]: *Sooooolaraaa.* I am Juliano.

## CHAPTER 4

# LEVELS OF DIMENSIONS AND MESSIANIC CONSCIOUSNESS

Juliano, the Arcturians, Gurhan from Andromeda and Sananda

G reetings, I am Juliano. We are the Arcturians. You might wonder what it would be like to have a consciousness without a physical body. You might wonder how the evolution of your being can express itself in consciousness and yet not have the physical form that you are familiar with that is your fifth-dimensional body.

We know of many beings in the galaxy who have higher and more evolved consciousness, yet they do not have a physical manifestation on the third dimension. This is true of Andromedans and their special "Blue People," who have spiritual evolution and consciousness that is so high, it allows them to be in such a state of being. I simply call it a state of being because it does not have a manifested body with which you are familiar.

## YOUR FIFTH-DIMENSIONAL BODY AWAITS YOU

In many of our discussions, we have alluded to the transfer of your presence and consciousness to the fifth dimension. You might have envisioned this transfer as going from a physical body to a fifth-dimensional body. Still, even in your visualizations and imagination, you probably accepted that you will be going into a fifth-dimensional body.

The truth is that there will be a fifth-dimensional body awaiting you, which is far more advanced than your third-dimensional body. The fifth-dimensional body has abilities that are indescribable and might be viewed in your language as science fiction. The fifth-dimensional body has untold abilities, such as teleportation, telepathy and being unified in higher thought patterns with the Creator. The fifth-dimensional body also has the ability to continually interact with beings known as ascended masters.

There are also fifth-dimensional planets. Our planet, Arcturus, is one of those fifth-dimensional planets, but there are numerous other ones. These fifth-dimensional planets are actual structures. The fifth-dimensional bodies that you will inhabit have actual forms. "Forms" in our definition are stepped-down energy patterns created through manifest thoughts.

Consider the possibility that you can be a being of pure consciousness and that there are beings even beyond the manifested form of a fifth-dimensional body. Consider that these are elevated beings on sixth-, seventh- and eighth-dimensional levels. Your consciousness on Earth includes your dream state, your higher consciousness and your shamanistic consciousness. You have inklings and intuitive processes that place you into this awareness of being. Your ability to access the "unmanifested consciousness" either in a sixth- or seventh-dimensional consciousness is within your DNA structure. It is within your coded awareness possibilities and within your evolutionary cycle that you have such abilities, perceptions and goals.

It is a great joy for us to work with the Andromedans and the Blue People. It is a great honor to have the Blue People, who are people of pure consciousness, work with the Arcturians and the Group of Forty.

## LEAPING INTO THE REALM OF PURE CONSCIOUSNESS

You must leap across the fifth dimension, and from the fifth dimension you can make another leap into the realm of pure consciousness. There, can you begin to meditate on what it would be like to have an existence of consciousness but not form? What would it be like to have an existence of consciousness and interact with other consciousness beings who also have no form? Then you have the situation of how you would deal with time and space aspects.

Look at the fifth dimension. There are issues of space and time, but these issues of space and time become manifested in terms such as eternal time. On the fifth dimension, linear time becomes circular time, where the past, present and future become unified. On a sixth and seventh level, consciousness of time has no reference because if you have no form, then there is no need for a limitation. On these dimensions, there is no need for a description of time and no need for the manifested body or form.

Consciousness on the sixth dimension becomes a model for your development and movement to the fifth dimension. Ultimately, it is your con-

sciousness that survives beyond the third dimension, it is your consciousness that survives beyond the fifth dimension, and it is your consciousness
that unifies and unites with the Creator light. It is your consciousness that
actually comprises the most powerful force in Creation. It is the bedrock
of all abilities that include expansion and transformation.

I introduce to you Gurhan. Gurhan is an Andromedan from the Blue
People, and he is also sitting on the Andromedan Galactic Council. Gurhan
will speak about the matters I have described, and he will also enlighten
you about some of your abilities in the interdimensional traveling depart-
ment. I now turn you over to our dear friend, Gurhan.

G reetings, I am Gurhan. I am from the Andromedan galaxy. We are
your sister galaxy. Some say that we are a younger sister galaxy because we are not as old as your galaxy, but time is so relative and our place
in the galactic expansion is such that we have experienced much of what
the Milky Way galaxy has experienced.

We have also had a different path as a galaxy. There are in the Andromedan system 5,000 known solar systems with higher beings in
them. There are within the Andromedan galaxy approximately 250
ascended planets. In the Andromedan galaxy, there are approximately
five planets that are similar to the Earth with the same size, shape and
form as the Earth. Some of these planets actually are being used in the
third dimension as places of transferring those who are on the Earth
and who are not progressing, or who need to go to other systems for
certain soul lessons.

There are certain warrior types and certain soul groups that are unified
and want to be with others like themselves. There are certain people who
want to be continually in a warlike culture, who are comfortable with that
and are not willing to go into a higher consciousness. There is a warrior
planet in the Andromedan system that is perfect for them. They will have
opportunities to experience as many wars as they wish and continue on
that path. Fortunately, they will not be involved in the destruction of the
Earth realms.

It is truly a puzzle as to why so many of the war beings on the Earth have
to continue dominating the Earth. From our perspective in the Andromedan galactic system and the Andromedan Galactic Council, we feel that there

will be a separation of the Earth into the fifth-dimensional Earth and those beings who are of a higher spirit. They will separate their consciousness and the Earth energies, and move into a higher state. The third-dimensional Earth will include those who are warlike. They eventually will be transported to another place such as I have described in the Andromedan galaxy.

## GROUP CONSCIOUSNESS IN THE ANDROMEDAN GALAXY

We have beings on the Andromedan galactic systems who are very evolved. We have beings who are like myself, more in an unmanifested state, but also in a state of group awareness. We refer to this as a group consciousness.

Group consciousness is a basic fundamental block of evolution throughout the Andromedan galaxy, the Milky Way galaxy and other galaxies. Therefore there are soul groupings in a state of awareness that can be described as a circle of beings. Perhaps they might be viewed as holding hands and sitting in a circle. Can you visualize a circle of beings who have no third-dimensional physical bodies? Visualize a circle of beings who only have an awareness, and those joining the circle of beings then can transcend their own circle and go up to a higher level. This is what we refer to as the "blue" energy.

The blue energy is the fine ethic energy of spirit. It is the fine ethic energy of nonmaterial manifestation. Blue is also a color that we, the Andromedans, can manifest as our energy. We can manifest our energy not as a form but as a color, not as thought but as a color vibration.

We can communicate with others and even with distant systems and beings through a dynamic color system. This dynamic color system is based on the primary colors, but it is also based on new color realms that we have been able to evolve. We create new color patterns, different patterns of colors that have never been observed before.

We seek to bring those into a form so that we can communicate with the Earth beings. Earth beings, like yourselves and the starseeds, are very interested in the Andromedans because some of you who are starseeds have been in the Andromeda galaxy.

The Arcturians have worked with the Andromedans. The Arcturians have come into our sixth- and seventh-dimensional ships and have actively created a portal so that the Stargate and fifth-dimensional connection to the Stargate have formed a tunnel connection to the Andromedan system. Many of you, when you have completed your Earth consciousness and Earth path, will undoubtedly decide to come to the Andromedan system.

We see many parallels with our galaxy and the Milky Way system. We have many other planets and solar systems in our galaxy. In our calculations, there are many solar systems in our area that have planetary life of higher consciousness on their systems.

We see that the Milky Way galaxy is divided into three sectors and that the Arcturians are overseeing the spiritual development of a sector. There are groups in the Andromedan galaxy and also in the Milky Way galaxy who may be described as religious groups.

These groups believe there will be a certain pattern that will keep everyone together in their group. They believe that there will be a certain place where everyone meets after their incarnation. They often designate this meeting place as "heaven." The truth is that this promise of meeting together as a group after death is a focused attempt to bring a soul family to a planetary system that they have set up in previous lifetimes. They will reincarnate or transfer their soul existence onto this planet where they all will be, in some cases, in a higher dimension.

There is a religious group now on Earth that has worked hard to move their people into this awareness, and people have accepted and are waiting for the transfer into that type of a planetary system. I have been asked if that is a fifth-dimensional system. From my perspective, I would actually call it a higher fourth-dimensional place on the cusp of the fifth dimension.

I, Gurhan, am bringing a blue light of energetic spiritual activation for all who hear and read these words. This is an activation that will allow you to identify with that part of yourself that is higher consciousness—that is awareness. I now return you to Juliano, who has some more information for you. I will work with some of you in the dream state. I will also work to prepare those of you who wish to return to your home planets.

Some of you have made prior commitments before coming to Earth having to do with returning to planets that are "home" to you and have your soul families. Some of you now are meeting your soul families and your soul brothers and sisters on the Earth, and you will travel back with them when you ascend. Understand that the awareness I speak of, and the Andromedan galaxy, is on the fifth dimension and also beyond the fifth and sixth dimensions. It is beyond even what you call a sphere. It would be beyond a description of any object, any form. Blessings to all you starseeds. The Andromedans connect with you in spirit and in our love. I return you to Juliano.

Greetings, this is Juliano. I am pleased to speak about some of the planetary systems that are in the fifth dimension. There are several planets in the Arcturian system in the fifth dimension, and each of you, on a personal basis, has been visiting one of those planets. These fifth-dimensional planets have a special energy and vibration. A planetary vibration can correlate to a vibratory tone. There is a special alignment for those who are coming out of an Earth experience and going into the fifth dimension.

There are levels also of fifth-dimensional planets and places. There are different levels of fifth dimensions in different galaxies. The fifth-dimensional planets, for example, in Andromeda can be different from the fifth-dimensional planets in the Milky Way.

You have on the Earth different levels of the astral plane. These different levels are sometimes referred to as the first level, the second level and the third level. Some call these the lower, middle and the higher astral planes. From this perspective, one can say that there is the lower fifth dimension, the middle and the higher fifth dimension. Once in the fifth dimension though, that terminology does not make sense because the fifth dimension does not use linear measurements.

There is also evolution in the fifth dimension. The evolution in the fifth dimension brings you to the sixth dimension. The evolution from the sixth dimension brings you into the seventh dimension, where there are higher beings beyond the Arcturians. These beings who are in the sixth and seventh dimensions have the ability to be multidimensional and in multigalaxies and multiuniverses.

We, the Arcturians, know of at least ten different levels of universes. This whole creation and the process of these levels are elaborate. As you move up the ladder from the fifth dimension and higher, then the complexity does not become as much of a problem to keep in track. The complexity is accepted as part of the process.

## YOUR MIND WILL HAVE A DIFFERENT FORM

Your ability to integrate complexities of multiawareness will be easier on the fifth dimension because your mind will have a totally different form. Consider that the mind is also a manifested form correlating to the dimension that you incarnate on. Your mind manifests a form as an aspect of your self. That self then becomes your personality on that incarnation.

If you are able to suspend your Earth mind, then you are that much closer to your fifth-dimensional lightbody and consciousness. There also is a fifth-dimensional mind. We on the fifth dimension do not like to use the term "mind," but we will use that terminology so that you can understand it.

The mind, as you know it on the third dimension, does not function the same way on the fifth dimension. There are boundaries and limitations on the mind that exist on the Earth. The mind on the fifth dimension does not have boundaries. Everyone on the fifth dimension can read everyone's thoughts, and everyone identifies with everyone else. Yet there is not an identity problem because we have a consciousness that we call group consciousness, which is very comforting.

Coming to Earth required that the connecting links to that fifth-dimensional mind be temporarily set aside. You may have floundered for many years. The interesting aspect of mind union on the fifth dimension is that all healings and energies needed for any kind of personal work are available through the group consciousness.

On the third dimension, if you need a healing, you find a healer, form a relationship and pay someone. On the fifth dimension, you are automatically connected to everything you need for your healing and for your energetic development because you are tied into a group consciousness. This is something you will all return to and something about which you all will be joyful. You were told when you came back down to Earth that you would be experiencing the mind in a third-dimensional way. You underestimated the trauma of being cut off from that group mind.

People who are not starseeds are newer souls. They do not have that previous experience of the fifth-dimensional mind. Incarnating into the Earth is not as traumatic for them. This is why possibly some of the starseeds now have many physical, emotional and spiritual problems. They are still recovering from the trauma of being cut off from group consciousness!

Group consciousness happens to be one of the great foundations of the Arcturian Group of Forty work. It is our belief that this starseed work will provide a focus in union of group consciousness that will accelerate the removal of trauma and help foster a reconnection to the fifth-dimensional consciousness.

I turn this next part of the lecture over to Sananda. He will speak to you about Messianic consciousness. We understand Messianic consciousness from our fifth dimension. We have, from your perspective, Christ consciousness on the fifth dimension. We have continual connection with the Messiah as you know it. Life of the Messianic age is already in existence on the fifth dimension. From your perspective, we the Arcturians live in a Messianic era. Sananda will speak to that. I am Juliano.

A*donai, Adonai.* Greetings to all the starseeds. I am Sananda. I know that many of you are awaiting the fifth-dimensional ascension. There will be wonderful opportunities for your spiritual advancement and an intensity of fifth-dimensional energy entering the Earth realm. Some of this is due to certain alignments, and some of it is also due to the overwhelming, attractive magnetic energy that you have created. The energy of the Messiah is an electromagnetic pulse—an electromagnetic force.

The electromagnetic force of the Messiah energy is based on attraction. Attraction increases during periods of polarization. This fundamental law of physics is the basis for the creation of the known universe as you see it. There were particles, and the particles formed into bodies, and the bodies then separated and formed into planets.

In some cases, the planets separated and formed into moons. Many of the solar systems in the Milky Way galaxy have civilizations on the moons, not just the planets. If you have the telescopes looking only at the planets, then you will miss the moons. There are some powerful systems of moons—especially in the areas closest to the Central Sun.

Some of you have been on planetary moons. Seeing the Earth Moon is a reminder to you of planetary moons. The planet X-Terra is a planet close to the Central Sun area. That planet has three moons in the sky. Each moon is a moon planet. Imagine what it would be like from your perspective to live in a system that had planets and additionally moons that were visible from the home planet.

## MESSIANIC CONSCIOUSNESS IS THE RETURN OF CHRIST ENERGY

Messianic consciousness is the return of Christ energy in a way that dominates and heals all activities and all interactions in a planet. Messianic consciousness is the return of Christ consciousness so that each person is only acting from their connection and their inner Christ awareness. Christ consciousness is part of your DNA structure, which is involved in evolution.

Evolution is involved in the awareness and openings into this higher state of awareness, where there is group energy. You cannot have group Messianic energy if there is hatred or polarization. The paradox is that the polarization now on the third dimension accelerates people one way or the other. People who go toward judgment, hate, war and domination are accelerating themselves into a new planetary system that is going to continue to experience the warrior culture.

You on Earth may not be able to change the Earth polarizations and the wars, but you are still able to create and attract the energy fields of the Messianic consciousness. You are able to set a foundation for the Messianic consciousness. When the right time occurs, then the ascension occurs. This will include a huge spiritual passageway into 2012. There is preparation and a foundation for this process to seed itself.

Let us speak about the Messianic consciousness on the Earth and on the fifth dimension. The Messianic consciousness on Earth will foster a fifth-dimensional system of enclaves that will attract people who are willing to live only in a certain higher vibration. These fifth-dimensional enclaves will begin to transcend and vibrate into a realm so that they are in two realms simultaneously. This can be described as the Shamballa and Shangri-la. Books written about Shamballa and Shangri-la were actually describing an evolutionary state in which groups of people evolved into the fifth dimension together.

There must also be people who work in the enclaves. There must be people also who are working in the higher-evolution spiritual realm. Do not think that if you work on this concept that you abandon your other Earth responsibilities. Do not feel that you alone have to work to stop war. Everyone does not have the soul mission to do that, even though it needs to be done.

Beings like yourselves can set up enclaves of communities, spiritual groups that begin to vibrate in and out of the fifth dimension. These enclaves can then begin to assimilate Messianic consciousness. Messianic Consciousness includes galactic awareness and awareness of yourself as a soul being evolving through the universe. Understand that the polarization is part of what you would describe as a separation from the higher dimensions. People can choose to be in the Messianic state on the third dimension.

The Arcturians have said that there is a potential for an Earth catastrophe. A catastrophe *is* a possibility. From our perspective, this catastrophe has to do with a group of people who think of using a nuclear device on the planet. That situation could be devastating for the Earth. The enclaves will work with the Messianic consciousness, and higher beings can focus on the Christ energy and attract the Christ energy into the thought fields of the whole Earth. This attraction will permeate the Earth and spiritually counter the potential for war.

## Acknowledge Your Role in the Messianic light

The Messianic energy is so strong that it can permeate everything, and people have even written that when the Messiah appears, then war will stop. If you as a group of starseeds are focusing on Messianic conscious-ness and attracting the Messiah energy into the thought field of the planet, then this accelerates peace and a neutralization. I believe that it is time for you starseeds to acknowledge your roles in the Messianic light.

Messianic consciousness is not just on the third dimension; it is also in the fourth dimension. There are great angelic hosts and angelic beings in the Messianic light that work on all levels in the fourth and fifth dimensions.

On the fifth dimension, there is no struggle, no doubt and no division. There are communities, planets, temples and spiritual places there. When you go into the fifth dimension and into a temple, then you can instantly connect with the Creator. You can experience light at a level that is not reproducible on the third realm.

Here is a great service you can do. When you are on the fifth dimen-sion, then you can access the Messianic consciousness. Since you have lived on the Earth and have Earth roots, you can, from the fifth dimen-sion, project that energy into the thought fields of the planet. By project-ing that energy into the thought fields of the planet, it will accelerate the evolution. Those beings on the Earth who want and are open to Messianic energy will receive it.

That means, my dear friends, that at this moment on Earth, there are many ascended masters who are projecting Messianic energy to you. Re-ceive to your best ability this Messianic light into your consciousness now, for these ascended masters work under my direction and send this light to each of you.

Focus on the many ascended masters who are working so diligently to bring Messianic light to the Earth. Our friends, the Arcturians, have in place the Iskalia Mirror and the etheric crystals. They have in place many corridors on the Earth now. Each one of these aspects of their spiritual work with you will be devoted to Messianic light.

We are working to prevent a nuclear explosion on the Earth. We are working with the Messianic process to enter the thought fields of the planet. Messianic consciousness is the strongest consciousness on the Earth. I am Sananda, keeper of the light of *Adonai* for the Earth. Blessings!

## CHAPTER 5

# THE FIFTH-DIMENSIONAL TECHNOLOGY OF LIGHT

Juliano, the Arcturians, Chief White Eagle and
Archangel Michael

Greetings, I am Juliano. The light technology of the higher dimension is based on the principles of vibration. The basic principle can be expressed in a formula where a higher energy can influence a lower energy. On the Earth, however, it certainly also happens that a lower energy can influence a higher energy.

In the fifth dimension and in the higher realms that we work with, and with the ascended masters, the formula of the lower energy affecting the higher energy does not work. In fact, only the reverse is true and operational when you work with fifth-dimensional energy and fifth-dimensional beings. Therefore, when starseeds are in the midst of a higher vibration, you will be affected and you will have a shift in your consciousness.

We explore and work to assist in the mass transformation of a planet. We assist you in developing the interventions that will allow a higher energy of group consciousness to affect the lower energy that is present on the Earth consciousness. This includes the technology of light.

## DOWNLOADING INFORMATION AND ENERGY

Let us review the basic knowledge that you have of light from the standpoint of your scientific realm. Light can only travel at the speed of 186,000 miles per second. But using that model means that you are limited by that speed, which still is a fantastic speed from the perspective of the third dimension. The distances and space that can be covered at that speed do not allow you to go far, because the universe is so vast!

On the fifth dimension, the speed of light is not fast enough. Another aspect of our realm is that the concept of space does not exist the way you conceive of it in the third dimension. This means that when you are traveling at the speed of light, you do not have the reference point of space that you have on Earth. Untold distances, untold actions and interventions can be accomplished at unimaginable speeds.

When you are able to move out of the third-dimensional consciousness and expand your abilities into the fifth dimension, then you connect to corridors that allow you to download information and energy from the fifth dimension into the third dimension. This gives you the advantage of being able to travel beyond the normal speed that we have talked about. At the same time, you can activate energy and light that can be brought down into the Earth. Light frequencies can be projected to affect a mass consciousness.

The consciousness known as Messianic light is a consciousness and energy that is so powerful and intense that it has the activation energy to shift the mass consciousness of a large group of people. Messianic light can even shift the consciousness of an entire planet.

The Messianic light is a light that comes from the Creator-source through a special messenger, or Son of Light. It is also referred to as the Sons-of-Light energy because the messenger of the Messianic light also has workers and assistants. They carry the light and are known as the Sons-and-Light carriers, or the Son-and-Light children.

It is no accident that you assume the name of lightworkers. We refer to the name of the White Brotherhood/Sisterhood that so beautifully describes those who are mystically bent in understanding the universal consciousness and light consciousness of the All. We ask that the name be changed to the Light Brotherhood and Sisterhood, so that it acknowledges the rising above any possibility of color differentiation or any possibility of misinterpretation.[3] More importantly, it is acknowledging the spiritual basis of light technology.

## WELCOMING THE NEW LIGHT ENERGY

This fifth-dimensional light that we have described is a combination of Messianic light, fifth-dimensional light and light that is connected

---

3. Channel's note: the name to be used as only the White Brotherhood.

through the fifth-dimensional corridors to the Earth. Let that light enter those of you who hear and read these words and who designate themselves as lightworkers. We designate and call on you to remember this time of activation of lightworkers. It is a time of bringing together tools for the light technology interventions.

We are aware that there are groups of lightworkers throughout this planet who gather at certain times to work and assist in shifting consciousness, and to shift the events for a more positive outcome. In many instances, this has been very successful.

We ask that new light energy be brought into the consciousness of all lightworkers. This light consciousness is designated as Messianic light and can be transmitted into the central core of the Earth. Simultaneously, it is transmitted into the etheric crystals that are placed in key positions by you on the Earth.

An activation moment will occur when that Messianic light emanates from all sources and fills the etheric energy, the astral energy realm of the Earth, and at the same time, begins to form a circular pattern. You can visualize an etheric ball of light that may be as much as a half-mile in diameter. This ball begins to circulate around the Earth at approximately five to six miles above the Earth.

This ball is an interdimensional ball and begins to heal the etheric holes in the Earth's energy field. It will begin to heal the rifts in the space-time continuum on the planet that are causing such disturbances. Most importantly, it will begin to cleanse the lower astral realm that is around your planet. From our observations, the lower astral realm is filled with less evolved beings who have died by means of violence or they have lower consciousness, lower thoughts, and have done lower deeds while on Earth. They have remained in the lower levels and have not gone on.

When we come to your Earth, we see a tremendous clogging of the energy valves around your planet from the lower astral planes. Due to the space-time rifts and holes in the etheric energy field of planet Earth, lower beings can periodically descend and attach themselves to other lower beings on Earth who are not of the light consciousness. These less-evolved beings from the astral realm can create upsetting situations or problems through such attachments.

You have seen people commit strange crimes of violence such as school shootings, suicide bombings and murders of family members. You have seen this where there has been perhaps some major political difficulties or civil wars. These lower astral beings like to instigate such havoc on a planet. These beings are what you might call the "darker forces."

The lower astral realm field cannot tolerate the light energy that we help and work with you to create. The lower energy beings or fields cannot tolerate the golden light filled with Messianic light consciousness. You will see emerging opportunities of peace on Earth. You will see opportunities for resolutions of political differences. But then the calm can just as easily be turned around. Conflict can reemerge unless there is also the cleansing of these lower astral fields.

Remember, the lower energies cannot tolerate or work when there is the presence of fifth-dimensional light. You who are lightworkers have the ability to connect to fifth-dimensional light. We see possibilities for peace and harmony and a growing connection of brotherhood and sisterhood on this planet.

## CALL ON THE LIGHT ENERGY

Let us continue our discussions of light. You can project yourself in light consciousness when traveling through the astral realms. When you wish to move into a higher state of consciousness or when you wish to connect with us, the Arcturians, then call on the light energy. Remember that this is an energy that travels beyond the normal speed of light as you know it.

When you call on this light energy to enter through your crown chakra, then you will be able to thought-project yourself into certain areas in the etheric and the fifth dimension. You can thought-project yourselves into the crystal temple and to the holographic healing chambers. Even though these places are, from an Earth standpoint, forty or fifty light-years away, in this fifth-dimensional light you have the ability to cross galaxies instantaneously. You have the ability to cross the universe instantaneously. You have the ability to go backward and forward in time instantaneously in consciousness and with intention.

The beauty of the fifth-dimensional light is that you can bring back with you higher instruments of spiritual technology. The light technology that we speak of allows you to go forward in time and project yourself in fifth-dimensional spaces, and then this light consciousness is interactive with your third-dimensional mind.

Using your third-dimensional mind, which can be elevated through many of our exercises and work, you can integrate and download higher light energy to affect lower energy fields on the Earth. When you are gathering together in a group consciousness, then you magnify and accelerate the effect so that a small number using fifth-dimensional light can influence a large mass. Influencing many people can be accomplished through Messianic light. One person can affect a whole group. The person carrying the Messianic light might not be visible. The thought of that light is so powerful that many people become transformed just in meditation on that energy.

We, the Arcturians, are living and breathing in this fifth-dimensional Messianic consciousness. As higher beings, we have found ways to integrate and use this consciousness to transform our planet and the people living on the planet. Each of you would love the experience of being on our planet, which is filled with this kind of consciousness.

## THE APPEARANCE OF THE FIFTH-DIMENSIONAL CORRIDORS

You, my starseed friends, may be surprised to hear the Arcturians talk about Messianic consciousness. You can readily understand that this consciousness is part of the fifth dimension. It is one of the main focuses of the fifth dimension—the light.

The light that you see from your Sun is beautiful light, but it is a third-dimensional light. The light that we see and that you will see in the fifth dimension is a light that has a golden vibration energy that can be compared to a brilliant sunset. At the same time, it has the brightness of a noonday Sun and the subtleties of the setting and rising Sun in combination, minus the intensity that would be difficult to observe without special glasses. It is a special frequency of light that can, by its mere appearance, affect and transform you.

Many of you have noticed interesting appearances of cloud formations and interesting planetary shifts of light from the planets in your solar system. You will see some unusual sunsets and sunrises, and at the same time you will notice little shifts in the Earth's energy that will briefly permit the appearance of fifth-dimensional corridors.

We work with you and with the masters to make the opening of the corridors visible. These corridors are only visible to those people who have the ability to see that energy and light. This situation is similar to your light spectrum. There are human limitations to perceiving the light spectrum. The rods and cones in your eyes are only able to approximate a certain level of energy. Beyond that limit, light appears invisible to the human eye.

With the raising of your vibration and with the downloading of this higher Messianic light, you are virtually in the presence of higher fifth-dimensional energy. When you are in the presence of this fifth-dimensional energy, you can begin to vibrate. When you begin to vibrate, your rods and cones and the other cellular perceptual cells begin to shift. They are shifting because you have been doing work on light technology and light energy. The activations you have been doing allow you now to see this other higher light frequency reality.

## USING THIS LIGHT TECHNOLOGY IN YOUR WORLD

It is most important to use this technology, this experience, to assist in transforming your third-dimensional life and your third-dimensional world. The light energy—this light that travels beyond the speed of the Earth-measuring devices of 186,000 miles per second—can be directed and focused for changes on the third dimension. That is the purpose of why you, the lightworkers, have come to incarnate at this time—that is, to use this light technology.

The new light technology must be downloaded. You must be capable of holding it, projecting it and connecting with others to magnify it. And then you must, with intention, focus your energy on a specific field that needs uplifting. These lower energy fields can include, as explained, the lower astral realm, which is now extremely clogged. Even as we speak, we are projecting, with our technology and our spaceships, light into your lower astral realm. At the same time, I project this light into the lower aspects of yourselves. Each of you may have a lower vibration that you do not like about yourself. Each of you is student and participant on this third-dimensional plane, and you have experienced pain and suffering from the lower vibrations.

Sometimes you have difficulty getting out of the lower vibrations. I now project light from the Starship Athena and the Starships Gaia and Solara. All three ships are projecting a huge cleansing light that goes into the etheric crystals we have placed on the planet. The etheric crystals are radiating outward to all who hear and read these words.

You receive a cleansing of fifth-dimensional, high-frequency light that is faster than the speed of light. It is higher light. You receive this light into your lower energy field—it is a great upliftment. We will stay in a brief meditation while you allow this energy to work through you, to cleanse and raise you.

This light can be projected to other people for healing and for change in consciousness. Many of you have contacts with people and you wish to change their consciousness. The correct way is to find ways to elevate their consciousness. It is not for you to determine what change they should have, but rather it is your ability to send light that will activate them and allow them to go to their higher state. Their higher state of consciousness might be different from what you envision.

This is an important aspect of light change. Many teachers and students wish to change others to fit how they think the other person should be. They also may want to change a situation on the Earth, whether it be political, geographical or economical. There are many intervening variables that you do not see in a situation, so it is wiser to project the light so that the highest energy and good for that situation or person, and ultimately the Earth can be maximized.

The energy for Earth transformation is ready to be elevated, maximized and strengthened. This energy is coming now from the central core and the fifth-dimensional realms of the Central Sun, which brings the Messianic light. My dear friend, Chief White Eagle, will now speak to you. This is Juliano.

Hey ya hey ya ho! Greetings, this is Chief White Eagle, and I welcome you and all of the Native peoples of all lands. I welcome the Native energies of all the spirit workers who are on the Earth now. We call on the energy of the great ancestors of all lightworkers to gather with us and create a gigantic energy powwow in the etheric realm.

## RECONNECTING WITH YOUR STAR ANCESTORS

This great powwow is the opportunity for all ancestors of higher frequency to gather. Understand, my brothers and sisters, that your ancestors are not just the ancestors you are aware of in your personal family. We speak of your starseed ancestors. We speak of your mother planet and your ancestors from there. We speak of the ancestral guides and teachers of the civilizations that you have been a part of on other planets.

The ancestral guides and teachers receive the calling and the invitation to come to the Earth realm now for this powwow of light, this dance of lightworkers. Hey ya ho ya hey ya! Many of the Native peoples remember their star family and the instructions they received from their star ancestors.

Go forth onto this third-dimensional planet, called Mother Earth, the blue pearl of the galaxy, and bring the teachings of the ancient ones to the Earth so that the people on the Earth will receive the information and knowledge that will allow them to become part of the galactic family. We encourage the Earth brothers and sisters to unite in consciousness with the galactic family.

I, Chief White Eagle, call on all the ancestral spirits, guides and teachers of all lightworkers to be activated at this moment. Information and energy will be instilled in each lightworker that will allow that lightworker to feel, experience and remember all that is necessary to become reunited with the galactic brotherhood and sisterhood and reunited with the Council. The reunification of the lightworkers with the galactic family will instill the light energy about which Juliano has spoken. The reunification with your galactic family will instill a new power on Mother Earth. Every time a lightworker reunites with the galactic family, a huge downpouring of Earth light technology emerges.

It has always been the intention of the Native peoples on the planet to unite the Earth, to bring the Earth into the galactic family and allow Mother Earth to be the blue jewel of this galaxy: respected, honored and a place where all will wish to visit.

It is a great honor, my friends, when a higher-dimensional being visits a planet. We, of the Star Nation People, were greatly moved when in earlier times we saw the ancient ships coming, when we saw the Arcturians, the Pleiadians and the Andromedans. We were greatly moved and honored that they chose to make themselves visible.

We knew that they came in light with a higher energy. We are all brothers and sisters. We welcomed their higher energies. Maybe we did not understand them with the technology and science with which you now understand them, but we opened our hearts to the higher-dimensional beings. We learned and still learn much about the different dimensions from them.

Some of these higher beings came to the Earth and spoke with us. White Buffalo Woman was brought here at one time from another planet by the Galactic Council, just like Jesus was brought here by a special emissary of the highest galactic connections from the Central Sun, on the orders of the *Adonai* light form. That type of higher visitation is going to continue to Mother Earth. That level of energy is going to continue to appear on Earth.

One feels a great sense of honor when a higher being enters the Earth. Know that it is an honor and also know that higher energy, by its mere presence in your Earth field, is a stimulation for everyone to go to the next level of their own expansion and of their own "lightenment." Hey ya ho yah!

We will be with you in this energy field and the great powwow in the etheric tepee with the many ancestors. There are hundreds of ancestral higher spirits visiting the Earth at this time. The calling goes out for the ancestral higher spirits to come to the Earth in great joy. All my words are sacred. This is Chief White Eagle.

Shalom. Greetings, this is Archangel Michael. I welcome all light-workers. You are beautiful spirits with bodies that are like garments, and these garments that you call your Earth bodies will be removed and you will be transformed. It is an illusion when you think that you will be transformed, because in reality you are that transformational being already. When you take off your coat, which is your body, then your true essence appears.

Jesus has tremendous energy. He had a garment that he had to wear, which was his Earth incarnation. It allowed him to be in your sight, in your memory and in your consciousness.

## CONNECT WITH THE SACRED MESSIANIC LIGHT

The Messianic light can enter in a basic form now because the consciousness is higher. The Earth might look like it is in worse shape than it ever was; however, the consciousness of light energy is more intense. The Earth is therefore ready to accept the Messianic light. It is also called the holy light, or *Aur Ha-Kadosh* in Hebrew.

The Messianic light is a sacred light, a holy light. The description that Juliano gave of this beautiful sunlight is an appealing description. The transformational quality of seeing this light accelerates your own ability to remove the body garment and be in the soul light of *Neshamah*, the Kabbalistic word for the higher soul self.

Many of you also have holes in your aura or attachments that are unnecessary. I have worked with some of you already to heal these holes so that a lower vibration does not enter into your energy field. A lower vibration can bring you down into a lower space, and I know that you wish to be in the highest state possible.

I, Archangel Michael, send down to each of you a blue light that fills your energy with a spiritual counterbalance that will remove the lower vibrations from your energy field. Also, I close for you any gaps in your energy that would allow a lower entity to enter unknowingly into your energy field, especially if this being is from the fourth dimension and not of higher consciousness.

You each have the ability to call on a higher being—especially from your ancestors. You now have the opportunity during this time period to have a higher spirit cohabitate with you. This spirit will raise you and help you gain and raise your vibration, and most importantly, to integrate this newer light energy so that you will become more psychic, more healing, more energized. You will also become better activators for the Earth and for those people with whom you come in contact.

Let each of you have a great ability now to call on higher spirits, higher energy, ancestors, angels and higher fifth-dimensional beings. All can be near you and communicate with you in this coming time. Holy light . . . *Aur Ha-Kadosh*. Calling out this energy automatically brings out the light frequency into you and unlocks your own cellular structure so that you can see this light and energy that is around you. *Kadosh, Kadosh, Kadosh, Adonai Tzevaoth*.

Let a great blessing come to each of you now. You have this ability to connect with your ancestral light energy. The unification of the lower with the higher will come. The unification of the present with the ancestors is now possible. The unification with *Adonai* and also with the Messianic light, *Aur Ha Moshiach* (Hebrew for the "light of the Messiah") is within your hearts now. This is Archangel Michael. Shalom.

CHAPTER 6

# HEALING BIOSPHERE CRACKS AND BEING SPIRITUAL WARRIORS

Juliano, the Arcturians, Quan Yin, Chief White Eagle and Chief Buffalo Heart

Greetings, I am Juliano. We are the Arcturians. This is an important time to practice group consciousness and group connections. This group consciousness represents the next step in the evolution of humankind. The bringing together of people of high spiritual intention can foster a new energy field around your planet.

## HEALING THE BIOSPHERE THROUGH UNITY CONSCIOUSNESS

The biosphere, which is the life-shield energy force around the planet, is extremely fragile. This has been demonstrated by the terrible earthquake and tsunami that have occurred in 2004. There are many cracks in the biosphere—cracks are really pressure buildups that are symbolized by what you see as an Earth change. There are other forces behind the Earth changes that are for all purposes "hidden." You who are spiritually attuned can understand that the Earth changes are at the forefront of all conscious beings.

All have to assimilate this Earth energy and the possibility that it represents. Understand that this terrible tragedy of the tsunami that you recently had is only one step of the Earth changes. It is only one aspect of the planetary shift that is possible. It is an initial step of a long process that will lead to what we call the 2012 corridor.

As higher spiritual beings, we naturally wish to prevent such catastrophes. We have the spiritual technology in place to shield and to protect the fragile biosphere and to offer great assistance. Conceive that these cracks, these weaknesses in the Earth's biosphere are receptive to your spiritual energy. They are receptive to your spiritual intention. Most importantly, they are receptive to group consciousness.

Earth is on the brink of a total biospheric crisis and a biospheric collapse. You have to look at certain possibilities and sequences of possible events that indicate this collapse. The occurrence of catastrophic events becomes difficult to predict because it is formulated on a basis of pressure, weaknesses and cracks in different energy aspects. One area can release a great deal of energy because the crack is bigger in that area. It does not necessarily mean that this area, in particular, was causing the problem. It does not even mean that that area had an unusual amount of negative energy.

Due to the relationship of the planetary numbers and the huge energy fields, everything is shifting, and everything is related. A crack, for example, over the energy field of Iraq can travel through the Earth's biospheric energy and affect another place. The energy in the magnetic field in the North Pole can be broadcast through different areas. Suddenly, unity consciousness becomes important to grasp as a tool for understanding how the biosphere can be healed. The unity-field energy concept becomes an important tool because it works both for catastrophes and healing. This energy field is like your subconscious—it reflects what input it receives.

Let us compare the biosphere and biospheric energy to the human subconscious and unconscious. For the purposes of this discussion, I will use the words "subconscious" and "unconscious" interchangeably. The subconscious of your species—and quite frankly, the subconscious of other species—is formulated and activated by certain laws, which are irrespective of morals. Whatever is put into the subconscious comes out on the other side as a manifestation. When there is an input of positive and spiritual energy, then spiritual energy and results come out the other end. This same principle works when we speak of Mother Earth, as you and Chief White Eagle call her.

The biospheric energy field can reflect and be affected by the collective unconscious. The collective unconscious relates to the human subconscious. We are referring to the Inner Earth subconscious. This Inner

Earth subconscious is receptive and does work on the same principles as your human subconscious. This is both good and bad news for the Earth. The bad news is that you see numerous wars and the destruction of many species. You see degradation of the environment, degradation of the biosphere, and you see a lack of understanding of this principle.

The good news is that higher spiritual beings like yourselves, working in the collective energy field, can input a transformation into the subconscious of the planet. You can input the Earth subconscious to make a significant shift and change. It is clear that those who can do this represent the next evolutionary process—the next evolutionary mode for the human race.

## EXERCISE: PROJECT THE ENERGY OF REPAIR TO EARTH

Survival of the human species on Earth depends on grasping and using this principle to input a positive spiritual input. Spiritual energy can be accelerated. Unfortunately, some people would like to predict a total end-time scenario. They see that a series of end-time events are now occurring. Recent Earth tragedies such as fires, floods and earthquakes do seem to follow a pattern of a series of "end" events. But people predicting end-time events do not take into consideration the ability of higher beings who are spiritually connected to the fifth dimension. Higher beings can download spiritual light and repair the Earth.

Project the thought and energy of repair into the subconscious of the Earth. Recent tragic Earth events can be overwhelming. There has been a tremendous release of pressure. Some say this means that other events will occur. Catastrophic events can be viewed on a global scale as a release of pressure so that there can be a repair. I want to begin to send the energy of repair into the Earth's subconscious. Focus on that energy of repair and know that the Earth's subconscious will process this energy.

You can connect to the etheric crystals. You can project this energy of repair into the crystals and the crystals can be projected, for example, into Southeast Asia, where the tsunami occurred. Truly, there is a huge gap in the energy field there and in the biosphere there. The biosphere of the whole area was in danger of collapsing. If that area had collapsed, then it could have affected other parts of the world and set up a greater biospheric collapse. The tsunami wave flowed into different areas around that whole Indian Ocean. In a similar way, the biospheric collapse energy could have propagated around the whole planet. Fortunately this did not happen.

I will spend two minutes toning with you while you all project the energy of repair. We project light from our Starship Athena into the biospheric energy over the area affected by the tsunami. At the same time, we can use your thought patterns from your energy to send in the repair light into the Earth's subconscious.

When you are finished listening to this meditation, I ask that you, with your right hand above your head and your left hand facing downward with the palm being flat, just spin around seven or eight times and think of the word "repair" as you are spinning around. This spinning energy will set up a dynamic flow of repairing.

There are intricate etheric but almost invisible energy lines that make up the biosphere of any planet and in particular the biosphere of this planet. These energy lines can be experienced by the sensitive little hairs on your skin that actually pick up feelings. You cannot see the Earth's energy line with your naked eye, but we are able to see it.

The Earth's energy line is an intricate web of energy around this planet. This intricate web has fractures, holes and cracks in it. There are certain areas of the planet where there are wars and where wars are occurring, and there are holes over the energy fields of the areas. There is now a hole over Southeast Asia, but we can work now to close that hole by you doing the circular spin and sending out the repair energy.

What you are actually doing is emitting a new etheric string energy of the biosphere from your body. The tapestry of energy that is broken, cracked or nonexistent can be replaced by energetic emanations from you. People who do whirling understand that this action can help to re-create the bioenergy field. Then etheric energy can go around the whole planet. You will, hopefully, be able to start this exercise. Visualize yourself doing this now and emitting a new light field. It will be emitted from where you are; then it will go into the greater Earth biosphere. You can repair yourself when you are wounded using whirling energy. This whirling energy can help repair the Earth's energy field.

While I do two minutes of toning, visualize this healing energy field. When you have the time, then do it some more. It is true that even visualizing also contributes to repairing the Earth. A great release has been accomplished!

## THE MESSIANIC LIGHT IS IMPORTANT TO EARTH

We have referred previously to a great energy shift and energy power that is coming to the planet Earth. We referred to this great energy as Messianic consciousness. We referred also to the fact of a great change in the Earth. It is clear that the Messianic light that will come to the Earth is now an important factor on the planet. This light is important for creating good faith and well-being and assistance. It is an important factor for humanity and for unity. There will be a great outpouring of this Messianic light.

We have made reference to, and Chief White Eagle will also speak about, the many spirits of the ancestors who have come to this planet. Many of these ancestor spirits were called here to assist in the transformation of the souls who will leave the planet at this time. There will continue to be a great calling for these spirits to come here to be of assistance.

The Messianic consciousness and light is still available and can still be activated. In fact, it has been activated from that date when we first spoke of it. Hold that consciousness and hold your great humanity and love in your heart. I, Juliano, say that we have seen many other planets go through transitions like this.

Now our friend, Quan Yin, who is the guardian of the spirits of many of those in the Southeast Asian area, will speak with you. She is a member, of course, of the Sacred Triangle energy.

**M**y dear ones, this is Quan Yin. My heart is open wide with great compassion for the suffering that is being experienced on Mother Earth and for the suffering that in particular has been brought to the forefront by this recent terrible tragedy known as the tsunami.

## MANY SPIRITS ARE WORKING TO ASSIST YOU

There are many spirits, many assistants, spirit guides and angelic presences who work at this moment to assist those who have been so traumatized and who try to cross over. Many of those spirits who have died in a physical body are still trapped in the area and have not been released. Many of them were so shocked by what has happened that even though they are out of the physical body, they still experience what has occurred. This is a strange event and a strange process on the astral world. I will explain this to you.

On the lower astral world, when you die from a traumatic death and you do not have a higher consciousness or understanding, then often times you can be trapped in time. You then relive what the trauma was at the time of the death. There are instances, for example, of people who died in earthquakes or in other types of traumas who became trapped in that frozen moment of time. I know this sounds hard to believe because on Earth, the event happens and then it is over. You carry the trauma with you, but to think it would remain that way in an astral world might be incomprehensible to you. People who have higher spiritual presence and have achieved higher development and are connected with the Buddha light, for example, understand what is occurring and they move on.

Now, there are, as Chief White Eagle and Juliano have pointed out, spirit guides who returned and are combing that area. They work with each individual person who is trapped in the astral world, assist them, remind them what happened and then also remind them where the light is. Naturally, you think that trapped spirits would respond to someone who looks like the Buddha. They would respond to their type of spirit guides. They might not understand the Arcturians or even Chief White Eagle, coming in his beautiful headdress, but perhaps they would understand the nature of the Buddha and the Buddhic light.

We can assimilate the pain and the sorrow of the trapped spirits, but we also realize that they need to go to the other side. This was a powerful transition. There must be a group movement and a group effort to move these many people on.

## MEDITATION: HELPING OTHERS TO MOVE ON

Each of you now, in a silent meditation, direct yourself astrally to this area of the tsunami and go into the astral realm. Speak to any spirits you meet who are trapped and tell them that you came in the name of Quan Yin. They all know me there. Say that you have been told to remind them that they are transitioning and to follow the Buddhic light—they are transitioning to the other side and they are transitioning into the universal light. You can help them by directing them there. Remind them that the tragic event is now over. They do not have to stay there. We will spend several minutes in silent meditation, and I will make slight tones.

Do not be afraid to take on their pain or a trauma, because we will be able to discharge it. If you meet someone in terrible pain, accept it and we will discharge it for you later. [Makes crying sounds.] You are brave souls. Each of you might have taken on someone's pain and you may feel the need to release that pain at this moment. If you feel any tears or sorrow, please release them now.

This will assist those who move on. I, Quan Yin, with my right hand, send the power of light from the fifth dimension into this area that is known as the disaster circle of the tsunami at this moment. This light that I send will be a guiding light for those spirits who will now know to walk out of that repetitious trauma and move to a higher light. A thousand blessings to all those who have passed over at this time.

You have heard us say, my dear ones, that Earth life does include suffering. You have heard about the transitory nature of your life and that it can be taken in a second. You have also heard about and studied the ascension. Each of you, individually in your heart, has spoken about desiring to leave the Earth and go to the fifth dimension.

You are ready at any moment, at any calling, to ascend. This could be during any event at any moment. Know that when or if you are in such an event and you hear the calling of the ascension horn, then you can walk on through the astral realm. Do not stay in the astral plane, for you are higher spiritual beings. Let the calling of ascension awaken your highest abilities of spirit.

We will stay with these many people and work to move them on. We have already, with your assistance, deepened the light there. There are many more people who need to be moved. If you are so moved and feel the ability to discharge the pain and sorrow that you will see, then I invite you to go back when you are comfortable and do more of this work. It is so valuable.

I am Quan Yin, my dear ones. Blessings to you all in the life that you are living and blessings for your transition into the fifth dimension.

**H**ey ya hey ya hey! This is Chief White Eagle. All my words are sacred. Ho! Greetings!

So you understand when we call on the ancient guides and teachers and when you hear that the ancient guides and teachers are coming, that that is good news. They can help you if you are attached and desire not to leave the astral realm. It could be good news in that you have more access to your spirit guides and teachers.

## BECOMING A SPIRITUAL WARRIOR

It is not bad news to "go to the happy hunting ground," as we say. When we were on our Native lands, we knew when we were going to die. We would often say, "This is a good day to die." We did not look upon death as a bad thing. What we wanted to do is experience our death with honor. We wanted to experience our death with courage and with great consciousness.

We know we all will die. That is no big secret. Maybe this is a big secret to the Western world, which does not seem to incorporate death very well. In the Native worlds, including the people in Australia and all over the world, death is understood as a part of the life experience.

There are mystics in the West who have spoken of this higher consciousness—of holding this consciousness when you go into the transition state of death. Many people lose that awareness of higher consciousness when they are dying. It is hard to maintain that awareness in the face of a trauma. We go out every day and realize that there could be a death. We call ourselves spiritual warriors. Hey!

I hope that each of you have within you this understanding of being a spiritual warrior. Being a spiritual warrior means that you are ready to meet your death at any moment. This was even spoken of by the famous American writer Carlos Castaneda, the man who worked with Don Juan, from the Mayan culture. This ancient Mexican shamanistic tradition is powerful, and it has much to teach you and much that we have incorporated in being spiritual warriors.

It takes a special man or woman to have the courage to face his or her death at any moment. It is not an intellectual experience. We speak of your heart energy and releasing attachments to the Earth. Could you do this in two minutes? The answer is yes.

You have been preparing for your ascension. You have been preparing for the fifth dimension. You have been preparing to meet White Buffalo Woman. By committing yourself to that, you must have considered what it is like to die. You have each died many times in many different lifetimes. It is even possible that I might have met one of you on the battlefield in one of my lifetimes. If there are any of you who are listening to my words whom I have met, I send you a special honor and a special blessing to be able to unite with you again through this transmission.

You can prepare yourself for the transition of death by releasing your attachments and connecting with the soul-ascended masters who are plentiful in the spirit world. We transcend the astral plane. There are powerful corridors on the astral plane. Quan Yin tried to help direct those beings who were lost. The children were not spiritually developed enough to go through those corridors to the other side without assistance. For you, my friends, are great students of spirit. It will be an easier task for you during your transition to observe and to find these corridors. You will travel through the corridors.

We beat the great etheric drum. My friend, Chief Buffalo Heart, will also speak with you. Heyyyyaaaahhhooo heyyyyy, all my relations. This is Chief White Eagle.

Ho! This is Chief Buffalo Heart! My heart is filled with receptivity. My heart is open to the pain. Know that this great trauma from the tsunami has opened up many hearts on this planet. There are many powerful hearts working overtime now. In the moment of death, in the moment of trauma, go to your heart.

## GO TO YOUR HEART!

Your heart will not fail you but will sustain you. It is the love of Jesus that comes into your heart at that moment when you are "naked." Your soul is naked at that transition moment—it is a moment of power. Do not be afraid. At the same time, do not be in fear, for as Chief White Eagle said, "We walk with courage, for we are warriors." You know that the way into the fifth-dimensional gate is through the heart. Focus on your heart—how your heart has opened and how you have affected other hearts.

Those people who recently passed on so dramatically during the tsunami affected the hearts of the whole planet. Let your heart be affected. Let your heart feel their pain. Send your love to them. You have big hearts, my friends. Let this experience also be a step toward your spiritual warrior position. Let this experience teach you and prepare you for that sacred moment when it comes—whether it be the moment of ascension or in the moment of death.

Know that your ascension will be experienced as a detachment from Earth. There is the moment when you remove all attachment. You can transition to a state called the "void." Be courageous. Remember your warrior self. I am Chief Buffalo Heart. All my relations. Ho!

his is Juliano. Biorelativity is accelerated by your heart. Biorelativity practices and exercises use the energy of crystals and the energy of the Central Sun for healing on the Earth. Become spiritually accelerated by opening your heart energy.

It has been said that higher beings can counteract the lower consciousness on the Earth. The reason this is so is because of the ability of higher beings, like yourselves, to accelerate the spiritual powers through your heart energy. This heart energy that you have is so unique that many other extraterrestrial beings came to the Earth trying to understand what this Adam species was about.

Some of the interplanetary beings did not have the heart energy or the heart potential that Earth beings do. Higher beings like us, the Arcturians, are attracted to the Earth because we know of your potential. I have said this before: "You are equal to us spiritually." We do not look at ourselves as being better than you. Yes, we are more advanced spiritually and technologically, and we have a greater understanding of the dimensions, but your heart energy can be as advanced as ours. Your heart energy can unlock the secrets of creation and the secrets of biospheric healing. When you put your mind together with your heart, then there can be a wonderful acceleration.

## EXERCISE: SEE THE FUTURE OF EARTH

I, Juliano, now open up the holographic healing chamber on our spaceship. I invite all of you at this moment to etherically enter our wonderful spaceship. I ask that each of you, in your sitting meditation, allow your spirit form to gently accelerate out of your body in a spinning fashion. Around the world, I see all of you. We come upward together off the planet through a beautiful corridor.

As we come up the corridor, look to the horizon deep into space. You can see the Central Sun, the birthplace of Jesus, the focus of the crystal light forces that replenish the crystals on the Earth. Come with me into my Starship Athena.

As we come into the Starship Athena, I have prepared a huge holographic healing chamber for you. You all can enter it. You all are invited into it. As you come into the chamber, you will experience an upliftment and a unification of your future self with your present self. Your future self has higher spiritual enlightenment and higher healing powers. Your future self will help repair Mother Earth.

You can see the future Earth where humankind—like we, the Arcturians—meditate and send light and energy into the subconscious of the planet so that there is communication and interaction. Your planet, in the higher level, does not erupt but is living in harmony with the beings. All this is coming to your vision in the holographic light.

The light from the Central Sun, the higher frequency, fills the holographic chamber. The light of Messianic consciousness fills the holographic chamber. In this future time, Messianic light fills the Earth as well as you and your consciousness.

We will go into a moment of silence while you experience this holographic light chamber. Let yourself be replenished, for you are with your future higher self. When we return after the meditation, I will leave the doors and the corridor to this holographic chamber open, but you must return to your physical body.

Descend down this corridor through the Earth chambers into your body. As you enter your body, you will assimilate this wonderful holographic energy. You will use this holographic energy in repairing the Earth.

Remember to do the spinning in the light of the Central Sun, in the light of the Arcturian brothers and sisters and all the ascended masters, guides and teachers. I bless you, and may you be in the light of *Adonai*. I am Juliano.

## CHAPTER 7

# PERSONAL AND PLANETARY HEALING

### Juliano, the Arcturians, Sanat Kumar and Tomar

G reetings, I am Juliano. We are the Arcturians. The mission of the GOF starseed group focuses on personal and planetary healing. Many of the GOF starseeds and all other starseeds experience the need for personal healing.

There are many problems that confront the emotional body, the physical body, the spiritual body and the mental body. In fact, the conceptualization needed for working with ascension energies are complex. The conceptualizations—or mental thought patterns—have to be on a certain frequency to allow the correct belief systems, moods and physical harmony.

To harmonize all four bodies requires a profound effort. Many of you have struggles with one or two or even all four aspects of your bodies. You might at times find that your moods become somewhat confused or even depressed.

It is easy to become attached to the events that are unfolding on the Earth and to identify emotionally with the physical, emotional, mental and spiritual pain that is before the planet. I, Juliano, totally empathize with the feelings that you have and your attempts to harmonize and work with those feelings. Let us focus on the emotional process that each of you is probably experiencing on one level or another.

## THE DIFFICULTY OF ASCENSION

From the perspective of the fifth dimension, emotions are far less complicated than they are on the third dimension. On the fifth dimension, one experiences a unity with the heart. One is therefore capable of experiencing a love energy that allows even a higher unity with God, or *Adonai*.

On the third dimension, there are many polarizations, even with the people to whom you are close and with whom you experience a love relationship. It is not unusual, from our perspective, to hear starseeds report that they are committed to the ascension process, yet their spouses or significant others do not share the same value. Therefore, their spouses are not in harmony with this starseed work. That, in itself, presents an interesting polarization. You would be much more committed to the relationship, and would want the person with whom you are closest to share in your commitments.

I would say that this would be a difficult polarization with which to deal. You cannot ignore the person. It is hard to pretend that it does not bother you if your significant other is not in alignment with your own spiritual beliefs. You might find that they are also not open to the healings that you think are possible through working in the starseed ascension energy. It requires great compassion and acceptance.

Many of you ask the masters about the difficulty of the ascension itself. The ascension can present other complex problems. You might be committed to caring for someone, or you might be committed to caring for a personal pet or an elderly or infirm relative. These animals or people might not be capable of sharing in the energy of the ascension. You might then wonder, "What am I to do in the event that the ascension occurs?" You still feel the responsibility of caring for the pets or the close relatives or friends. Indeed, several have said that if they were confronted with having to leave their relatives or pets behind, then they would not leave.

Sananda and others have spoken about the importance of the moment of ascension. The moment of ascension is a key nanosecond, in which your 100 percent cooperation and commitment is required in order to ascend. If at that nanosecond you think about the commitments to your pets or caring for someone, then you could be sidetracked and lose the opportunity at that moment to ascend. There will be three opportunities of general ascension. If you miss the first opportunity, then of course, you have a chance at the second or third.

It is our opinion, based on the readings from our computers, that by the second ascension, many of the people who missed the first will have totally changed their perspective. Between the first and second ascensions, the polarities, upheavals and Earth changes will become so profound that many people who did not go in the first level will not hesitate at the second opportunity. Their own personal discomfort of being on Earth will be so great. If they are given the opportunity to ascend and the window of a nanosecond to make that decision emerges, then they will immediately concur with this opportunity.

## YOUR PHYSICAL BODY IS AT A LEVEL OF CONFLICT

This brings up the subject of the discomfort that many of you now feel about being in an Earth body. We are in great sympathy and empathy with your struggles and profound experience of dense energies in the body. Some of your physical bodies are not responding correctly, and this is due to the stress of being on the third dimension with this level of intense polarization.

Some of your physical problems relate to the genetic conflicts in your DNA. You are now trying to access extremely high frequencies of light, you are trying to assimilate new frequencies, but you have grown up in a lower frequency and were originally programmed physically at a much lower frequency level.

Many of you were raised with parents who were at a far lower frequency than you are now. Many of you as children were in a lower, polarized position. This current level of consciousness that you all hold may be far beyond what you were originally programmed to hold. This means that your DNA has not made the higher etheric changes sufficiently to harmonize with the physical body.

The physical body is at a level of conflict. It is stretched at full capacity to accommodate the higher spiritual and etheric energy toward which you all are accelerating. I send a tone to all of you now that will help to unlock and accelerate your DNA in the etheric. The etheric body will then send a message to your physical body, which will allow the physical body to accommodate and interact at a higher level with the newer frequencies. You can then assimilate these frequencies in your consciousness.

It can be a conflict to have a consciousness that is higher than what your physical body is used to or can accommodate. It might be hard and it might be a conflict for many of you to strive for the beautiful ascension and the fifth-dimensional places that await you. At the same time, you are witnessing such upheavals, polarities, human suffering and the suffering of plants and animals in this dimension.

We have telepathically communicated and surveyed many of you, and we understand that you are tuned to the Earth energies and to the energies of plants and animals. This sensitivity can affect the elevation of consciousness if sadness and even depression of that experience overwhelms you. It is easy for me to say, "Don't hold onto that sadness." That alone still does not soothe you. In many cases, the physical and emotional identification that you experience can be overpowering.

We strive to teach you to identify with your fifth-dimensional body and consciousness. At the same time, we do not ask you to ignore your third-dimensional identifications. I do not ask you to turn your back on the suffering. The solution focuses on the greater perspective, the greater picture of the evolution of consciousness, the evolution of each person and the evolution of the planet.

On the third dimension, you witness only an aspect of another person or a species or a planet. That aspect is not the whole picture. If I look at your physical suffering or physical ailments, I do not see those physical ailments or those problems as the entire you. I look at them as an aspect of you. I also see energies, conflicts and even karmic processes that help to create that "whole" aspect called "you."

I know that in many cases your physical, emotional, mental or even spiritual structure might not represent the highest level of consciousness of which you are capable. We do not see only what appears on the third dimension. We see your entire soul connection. We see your entire self on the multilevel.

People say, "Why is it that I cannot bring that consciousness, that multi-information back into this third-dimensional body so that I can become totally healed and become perfected in the third dimension?" Some have asked that the polio they had for thirty years be immediately eliminated, or that their blindness go away or other end-stage illnesses be reversed because they have achieved higher levels of consciousness.

There can be an upliftment. There can be higher-consciousness cures where that person might be able to reverse their illnesses. The overall goal is not to create these "miracles"; the overall goal is to move your consciousness and your ability to evolve into the fifth dimension.

## LOOK FOR TOOLS THAT BRING YOU INTO HARMONY

If having a miracle cure provides the last foundation for that, then in some cases it will happen. In other cases, it is not necessary. The expenditure of karma to create an "instantaneous cure on all levels" might not be necessary. Using other tools, such as acceptance and identification with a fifth-dimensional body and higher consciousness can often be enough to bring you into harmony. You must look for tools that bring you into harmony.

There are many cases of people who have or had great physical disabilities and yet they harmonized with their spiritual, emotional and mental bodies and ascended. On the other hand, there are people, even today, who have perfect physical bodies with no health problems, yet they are as far away from ascension as one could be. The measurement of the ability to move into this ascension mode is not dependent on the perfect physical, mental, emotional and spiritual body. It is dependent on a harmonization of those bodies in unity with higher consciousness, which I, Juliano, refer to as fifth-dimensional consciousness.

The emotion that is the most conducive for this unity is love and acceptance—because you understand these concepts, you have the ability to ascend. I assure you that: 1) because you can project your consciousness into the higher realms; 2) because you understand that there is another dimension that is so high; 3) because you understand the starseed consciousness; and 4) because you can unite, you have all of these features.

This is the most important message. You need healing and the regaining of your inner harmony. The other problems that do exist will also require your attention. But with this fifth-dimensional consciousness and openness to bringing down solutions, you will begin to perceive and receive newer possibilities of harmony and healing.

## EXERCISE: JOURNEY TO THE RING OF ASCENSION

We are also committed to the planetary healing. We are committed to your personal healing as well. Any increased level of personal healing will make you better planetary healers. Doing the planetary healing has an important side effect—that is, you will be able to extend the planetary healing energy into your personal healing field.

Let your DNA be activated when you hear the rapid firing sounds: *OOOhh-hhhhhh. Tat tat tat tat tat.* This input tones into your DNA, thereby expanding you. Physically, each of you will gain an expanded energy field that will enable you to go to another level of personal healing. [Repeats tones.]

I, Juliano, call on each of you now to go with me to the ring of ascension, the etheric halo of light that appears similar to the rings of Saturn. This halo around the Earth is being activated by the Arcturians, Helio-ah, Tomar and many of the other higher space brothers and space sisters, including Sananda, the Archangel energies and many other higher beings with whom you are familiar. They now bring in a golden blue light into the ring of ascension. This ring of ascension has an aspect of harmony and power, which helps to raise the halo of light around each person and around the planet. You, with your third eye, can project pure healing light into the ring.

Despite any feelings of disharmony you might have, each of you projects a powerful healing light into the ring of ascension. [Repeats sounds.] You are projecting your energetic healing light from your third eye into this beautiful ring of ascension around the Earth. The ring becomes more activated because you, as starseeds, are interacting with the higher planetary beings.

Simultaneously, the beings of light, the White Brotherhood/Sisterhood, work to download energy into the ring of ascension and download energy and light into your crown chakra. You might experience a phenomenal connection. You also upload light from your third eye up to the ring of ascension to help activate this halo. Simultaneously, a circle of energetic light is emitted from the halo, the ring of ascension, back into your crown chakra. As that occurs, you experience a beautiful halo, a harmonizing golden light around you. Focus on that at this moment. [Repeats sounds.]

I, Juliano, activate each of you and each of your DNA structures through the ring of ascension connection. The more you focus on sending light from your third eye, the more we are able to return to you an energy that is twice as powerful as the energy you send up. This activation of your halo produces a version of the ring of ascension around you. Suddenly, quantum levels of golden healing energy circle each of you now. This etheric energy is called nanolight. [Repeats sounds.]

As you breathe in, hold your breath for at least three seconds and then release it. As you release, you will find a huge discharge of any negativities or densities that have accumulated within you. I take this discharge of densities and send it back up to the ring of ascension, where it is disposed of safely.

## HOLD THE FORMATION OF THE COSMIC EGG

Take this opportunity to remember my instructions about the cosmic-egg formation of your energy field. At this time, when you receive such powerful connecting light from the ring of ascension, remember: Healing and protection are maximized when you think of your energy field as being in the perfectly configured shape called the cosmic-egg formation. This means that your aura and your energy field are now configuring themselves in an egg shape as we speak. As it gets into that shape, more beautiful experiences are possible.

All hooks, all holes in the aura are suddenly removed. The stronger you are able to hold that shape, the more difficult it is for lesser beings, hooks or discarnate lower spirits to connect with you. In fact, lower spirits will drop away. Mentally hold the formation of the cosmic egg. As you do that, you are simultaneously connected to the ring of ascension through your uploading light from the third eye into the ring. As you receive this light into your crown chakra, simultaneously you are forming the cosmic egg.

Together, we project a cosmic-egg formation around the Earth. For this part of the experience, I turn the lecture over to Sanat Kumara. This is Juliano. I now introduce you to Sanat Kumara, the planetary spiritual leader for Earth.

reetings and blessings, my brothers and sisters of the White Brotherhood/Sisterhood of the starseed family. I am Sanat Kumara. You share my deep love for this planet and for this planetary experience. You have been learning in these lectures of the existence of holes in your auras, about repairing those holes and about the attachment of discarnate spirits who may be with you. They are now released because of your work.

## EXERCISE: REFORMATTING THE EARTH'S ENERGY FIELD

Imagine that the Earth and its energy or aura have become distorted and have even been filled with many discarnate and detached spirits. Many of you know that the Earth has been visited by unsavory extraterrestrial beings who did not have the highest good. Many of you know that there have been planetary distortions through powerful x-ray technologies, nuclear devices, radar devices, high-beam electronic HAARP-type devices. Indeed, there has been a distortion of the Earth vibrations.

Many of you know that the basic pulse of the Earth's frequency has actually been changing minutely. There is a base core vibration of the Earth, a rhythm that must be kept in order for all to be in harmony. You can participate with me in the bringing together of a thought pattern to connect to that rhythm or frequency. Focus on the Earth's energy field as it is miraculously being reconfigured into a perfected cosmic-egg shape. In higher consciousness, evolved starseeds can resonate and work with the planetary aura.

Now we, in connection with Juliano, reformat the Earth's energy field into a perfected cosmic-egg form. Hold and project that image, especially in those places where you know that there are certain deficits or holes in the Earth's aura because of political wars. Perfect that cosmic egg even more, for you may find holes in those areas that are deeper. This level of healing has a profound impact. We are concerned about the coming months and the potential for upheavals in the Earth's situation. Therefore, this input that you now hold with me is particularly helpful.

I have been concerned that the lower vibrational extraterrestrial beings have inserted hooks into the Earth's energy field. This has been, from my perspective, a parasitic relationship. In some ways, they suck the Earth's energy. But the Earth's energy is also being upgraded through the Central Sun and through this powerful alignment. Hold the cosmic-egg light of the Earth now simultaneously.

Your cosmic-egg formation becomes stronger and stronger. You starseeds have a particularly strong ability to enhance the Earth's cosmic-egg formation in Earth's aura and to simultaneously resonate with that in your physical body. This resonance creates a healing vibration within your energy field. This energy will modify some of the polarizations on the Earth and in the Earth's weather patterns. It will modify or soothe some of the polarizations.

The biorelativity experience is a necessary link to ensure planetary survival and planetary evolution. People can periodically do biorelativity exercises throughout the day in different time zones. It would be powerful healing for the Earth. I return you now to Tomar, who is in the Arcturian temple. I am Sanat Kumara.

Greetings, I am Tomar. I am one of the Arcturian spiritual teachers and masters. I speak to you from the Arcturian temple on Arcturus. That is the place where many of our temple masters meditate and hold the frequency of light, which preserves our civilization and that preserves our integrity and energy field.

## FEEL THE CONNECTION WITH THE ARCTURIAN TEMPLES

We learned that the input of powerful meditators can control and hold the vibrational field of an entire planet. In our temple, we have certain people who are trained from childhood to be able to work with and hold vibrational energy. It requires a special ability. Some of you are able to do this now—even your thinking about it has an input. Some of you might not be able to visualize as well as others. Yet if you think about biorelativity healings for the Earth, then those thoughts also contribute to Earth healings.

Your healing thoughts enhance the universal unconscious and this changes the energy on the subconscious levels of the spiritual, the mental, the physical and the emotional. You either may visualize or project positive thoughts to the Earth. The akashic records are the universal records in the galaxy and in the universe that hold all imprints of thoughts. Each thought has a vibration and an imprint. Thoughts created in groups have a more powerful imprint in the akashic fields than individual ones.

We in the Arcturian temples have become experts at creating and holding an energy field. We even create and hold energy fields from our spaceships that are in many parts of the galaxy. Each spaceship has a special meditation temple room where one or more of the space travelers connect with us. They can go as deep in meditation as we in the temple do. By their connection to us, we can download energy from them. They achieve a higher input and level than we alone could.

We connect with them and are able to receive a frequency from them that is greater than if we vibrated alone without trying to connect with them. One of the important keys to understanding the Arcturian work is that you may not by yourself be able to achieve the high frequency that you desire. With our input, we can send you our connecting link.

That is why we utilized the title in the first book, *Connecting with the Arcturians*, because we connect with you also from our temples. I help provide a link from our temple masters and the highest frequency they have for the Arcturian planet. They send this light and the energy of the cosmic-egg formation around the Earth. They send their strong abilities to hold that energy. Let us again hold that energy and simultaneously you will experience a deeper connection and shape of your aura.

Hold that field and feel the connection from the Arcturian temple masters with whom we are in unity, with the ring of ascension, with you the Arcturian starseeds, with me, Tomar, and then with my connection with the

Arcturian temple masters. We have created a stronger, solid cosmic egg around the Earth and around each of you.

If you decide to build an Arcturian temple on Earth, then that temple should have people committed to the task that is similar to the masters of the Arcturian temples. They can hold certain higher configurations of energy for the Earth planet, such as the configuration of the ring of ascension or the configuration of the cosmic egg. The temple would provide a focus on Earth similar to the holding of the Arcturian temple energy from our masters' work on our planet. On behalf of Juliano, on behalf of Sanat Kumara, I am Tomar. Blessings.

## CHAPTER 8

# SOUL FAMILIES

### Juliano and the Arcturians, and Archangel Metatron

Greetings, I am Juliano. We are the Arcturians. The emergence of your soul families as key players in your development is gathering more force on the planet. Many of you are gaining an awareness of the composition of your soul family.

As you have correctly suspected, the Arcturians are part of your soul family. It is no accident that you decided to learn about the Arcturians and it is no accident that you have such deep connections and interests in the higher-dimensional, extra-planetary sources and extra-planetary guides.

It is well known on Earth by those who are spiritually advanced that you each have many guides and teachers. It is clear that each of you may have as many as fifteen to nineteen guides and teachers at any one time when you are on the Earth. Unfortunately, most people on the Earth do not spend time trying to connect with their guides and teachers.

On occasion, one or two guides or teachers become prominent and are able to download higher information and lessons to you. This is admirable. Less often, one comes in contact with a person who knowingly has activated his or her connections to extraterrestrial, higher-dimensional guides and teachers.

## ACCESSING YOUR DNA CODES AND YOUR SOUL CIRCLES

As planet Earth moves toward the 2012 alignment, this is a time of great awakening of consciousness and super-consciousness, and an expansion of awareness. There are different levels of existence. This is also a time of awareness of the circle of soul families.

Soul families appear first as an initial circle. Then there is a wider circle and then an even wider circle. A soul family can consist of more members than we wish to count. Of particular interest is the fact that the circles intersect, just like DNA strands intersect with other strands in other dimensions. Let me clarify that: Your DNA codes are multi-dimensioned. Your thoughts and your soul exist in other dimensions. There is a way to alter the dimensional structures of your codes by having the codes interact with higher-dimensioned codes.

These codes can be accessed through special thought processes and specific chanting, or through tones and sounds. This awakens the DNA codes. You can, for health reasons, open up different mental abilities and access and stimulate yourself to shift your third-dimensioned body to access higher dimensions.

If you are experiencing physical problems, then you could shift the physical structure of your DNA so that a new physical replication can appear. This is similar to the concept of regeneration that certain species of animals have in which if one part of their bodies is cut off, that part can regenerate. Believe it or not, you do have this ability. You can go into different levels of the internal structure of your body, including organs, and begin to regenerate. The key is to work through the intersection of the DNA so that the point in your DNA spiral that intersects with your higher fifth-dimensional DNA can be brought into a downloading position.

It is the same with soul circles. The soul circles intersect with other soul circles. A soul guide, like an Arcturian or a higher-dimensional guide, can give you information about higher realms, other dimensions and your soul connections. This information can be useful.

Let me explain this in another way: You can connect to a guide like me, Juliano. I am also part of a soul circle that is beyond any circle of light you may perhaps ever been able to attain in your Earth presence. However, because you are connecting with me, you are intersecting with my energy and my light. Thus, you can now get access to beings and energy that I am accessing.

This is a spiritual ladder. I am connected to you and I also can connect to your soul group. I am part of your soul family and am a guide for many of you. The information and energy that I am able to attain on this higher level can be downloaded from me to you. Due to my representation on the Earth through this channel, I have the abilities to understand the circuits, voltages and amperages you operate on in a spiritual energy field; therefore, I am able to download spiritual energy for you. You can receive and process it in a way that is useful to you and also in a way that will uplift and open you up more.

## THE ARCTURIANS ARE WORKING WITH YOU

It is clear that we, the Arcturians, are working on several levels. The first level is to remind you that you are part of the Arcturian soul family. For many of you, we are your guides and teachers. The second level is to activate you. You not only attain a contact with us, but also you will be able to access the higher energy that we are able to access. The third level is the experience of connecting with us and acknowledging that we are part of your soul family. This helps you understand that you are connecting with the soul family energy.

Hopefully, you will then realize and be able to connect with others of your soul family besides the Arcturians. We are not on a mission just to help you become aware of the Arcturian influence (although that certainly is a great part of our mission), but we are on a mission to help you become aware of all of your soul family members and as many of your soul guides and teachers as possible. You then can become filled with soul information and soul energy at this point in your development. This can represent a monumental leap in your spiritual development.

We always speak to you of the evolution that the human beings—the Adam species, the sons of Adam—are going through. Part of the evolution is the development of new consciousness, which is the critical factor in allowing evolution. This new consciousness is the distinguishing part of the evolution. Part of this evolution of consciousness includes a relationship with your soul family and with your guides and teachers in the higher realms. This allows a huge leap, especially when you are able to intersect with higher beings who are willing to share their intersection with other soul groups above them with whom they are working.

You will be pleased to learn in following this process that you can attain the highest energy from the source of Creation, from the source of the Central Sun. This is a key factor in filtering light and energy. Some of you expressed fear and concern about an overwhelming amount of light and energy, and that so much energy can also be filled with other sources that may not be of the highest light. I, Juliano, assure you that we filter much of the light and energy to ensure that only the highest and purest light will reach you.

At this moment, I am connected to the soul masters and spirit teachers of the Arcturians. We are on my ship, sitting in a huge energy field. Our energy field is connected through a link that my teacher, who is sitting with us, has to the soul group that is in the Arcturian system right now—they are in a spiritual temple and are connected to us. We are linked to them and they are simultaneously linked to a powerful teaching energy from the Central Sun. They filter in that energy. We now have this beautiful circular link of light and energy, and it enters your consciousness as I speak.

Hold this thought in a brief meditation. You can work to download a spiral circle of intersections of connections of soul circles that you are part of at this moment. Begin to process this light.

My friend, Archangel Metatron, who is the guardian of the Stargate, will speak with you. I turn the next part of the discussion over to my friend, Metatron.

S halom, my friends. This is Archangel Metatron. It is a great awakening to learn that you, as evolving ascended beings, can access your DNA. The key to the DNA is the concept of the spiral intersection that Juliano has described to you.

There are certain tones and sounds that will assist you to get into that intersection. I believe at this moment that many of you are sitting on the intersection of great spiritual contacts with soul families, soul guides and teachers. I am happy that you acknowledge me as one of your soul guides. If some of you do not have me as a member of your soul family, there is a beautiful technique available called "invitation," where you can invite higher beings to join you as part of your soul circle and ask them to be a guide and teacher. As you gain in your development, you can meet other guides and teachers and say, "I invite you to be part of my soul group for my soul teaching."

## ACCESSING YOUR TEACHERS AND GUIDES

Many of you on Earth have multi-lessons. One of the lessons is to learn how to gather and access greater soul families, greater soul teachers and guides. You have families on Earth and your families grow—wouldn't it be logical that the soul family can also include new members? Is it not also logical, as your mind expands, that you realize you have access to greater beings and greater energy?

You can invite those higher beings to whom you find yourself attracted. You can invite them to become part of your soul teaching and your guides. You might say, "Well, Metatron, I am still trying to learn about and invite the other guides I have." Understand that accessing one guide can give you access to others.

Your guides can all sit in a huge circle working with you, overseeing you, giving you information. They would all give you information at once if you could process it. If you could process information from twenty masters at once, then they would download it immediately. Part of the problem is that you have to be in a position to receive and to process higher information.

For many of you, it is still a far stretch to realize that you have information coming from other dimensions and other beings. You need to open yourself up to that information. If I said there are two who wish to talk to you simultaneously, you might think it far beyond what you could do.

It is not as complicated as you might think in your normal consciousness. Right now, you are receiving two speeches: Juliano is still talking to you even though you do not hear his voice consciously; I, Metatron, am talking to you; and Chief Buffalo Heart, who will talk to you next, is also talking to you simultaneously. Stay focused with me. Do not stray too far. Be aware that there is a great deal of information being downloaded. You are all becoming more receptive.

## CONNECT WITH YOUR FIFTH-DIMENSIONAL LIGHTBODY

The work of the DNA can alter your consciousness so that your mind becomes aware of being multidimensional and then your consciousness becomes multidimensional. The DNA of the brain intersects with the higher DNA in your fifth-dimensional body. I already see each of your fifth-dimensional bodies, and I see you in a perfected state far beyond the limited physical body.

Your physical presence on Earth is only a small portion of your total being. With the connections that we will make, you can open yourself up to your fifth-dimensional lightbody, and you will begin to perform some wonderful self-healing. The technique we use (connecting with your fifth-dimensional body) is a replica of what you can do when you connect with the fifth-dimensional body of planet Earth.

Planet Earth has a fifth-dimensional body and a DNA code within its core. You can access those DNA codes through the beings of the Inner Earth living in Telos. They have contact with the inner links of the DNA of Mother Earth. When you connect to the Inner Earth and the beings from Telos, then a powerful healing energy can be experienced.

This healing connection goes into many different solar systems and even into many different universes. A solar system can interact with another solar system; a galaxy can interact with another galaxy. A chain of intersections already exists throughout the universe. The chain has been awakened on Mother Earth. You are part of this chain of interlinks.

I now give you the sound codes for opening up your DNA so that you can connect with your fifth-dimensional lightbody and begin a healing and transformation. Accelerate it now. Some of you have already received this sound and thus you are ready for the next level. As we hear these toned words, visualize your DNA intersecting with your fifth-dimensional DNA. [Sings]: *Kadosh, Kadosh, Kadosh, Adonai Tzevaoth.* Hold this light and this connection in a brief meditation. These sounds are creating a wonderful intersection with your fifth-dimensional DNA. You can even visualize the spiral DNA from your fifth-dimensional body being downloaded into your third-dimensional etheric presence. That etheric presence will then begin the process of downloading into your physical body.

As you do that, I call on Archangel Raphael to amplify this fifth-dimensional DNA spiral that is being downloaded into your physical body. Let it be used and directed by each of you for an accelerated personal healing of your own body. Let the healing of this DNA light be accelerated and processed immediately into each of you. *El na Re fa na la.* Let the Arcturian starseeds be healed now!

The Central Sun provides an energy of evolution and creation. Feel these light energies. Wherever you are on the Earth, you can become a refractor and emitter in the place that you are. You are connected to these energies. You become a transformer, a holder and a vessel of this energy. It is upon you to transmit it through your thoughts. We will spend another minute in meditation where you gather these energies and begin to emit them in the place where you are on Earth.

Understand that part of the new healing coming to the Earth is a healing of the polarities on Earth and a creation of new forces and new energy. Many of you continue to think that one polarized side will resolve the Earth's problem or that one polarized side will prevail. Think now in terms of creation and acceptance of a new Earth field of energy and a new field of light. *Adonai* created the Earth and the heavens. That word—i.e., creation—must stay in your consciousness. Each of you are beings who have an ability to connect to the Central Sun with this powerful energy and create a new way, a new light and a new frequency on the Earth. Shalom.

Shalom is also the name for harmony. It represents integration of the polarization into a new unity. [Sings]: *Shalom.* This is Archangel Metatron.

This is Juliano. This concept of creation is especially applicable when we do corridor work with you. The corridors are tunnels from the Earth going to the etheric realms that connect to the fifth dimension. They can also connect to our ships. They connect to the Stargate. They can also be used during an ascension. There are now several huge corridor tunnels. One is over the North Pole, and there are corridors over each of the etheric crystal areas.

## You Have the Power to Create Corridors

These corridors will be open when there is an ascension. You can go to that corridor and become uplifted. I think that each of you has an opportunity to connect and create corridors. Many of you have asked how to create a corridor. You have the power to create them—this is part of the fifth-dimensional light and energy. How do you create corridors? Creation occurs by thought. Thought is expressed through words. Thus you can think and visualize etheric corridors and then they can be created. We on Arcturus are able to use our thoughts to teleport and accelerate ourselves.

I do want to mention some interesting aspects of science. There is hardly enough physical fuel energy in the third dimension to accelerate an object to the speed of light. Yet when you combine certain thought patterns and waves with an energy acceleration, then that combination accelerates an object far beyond the speed of light. Those two combinations—thought and physical energy—will accelerate you beyond any speed that you can imagine even beyond the speed of light. You are able to enter certain corridors. By using these corridors—which in this part of the galaxy are fairly well developed—then you can begin to space travel. Some of you can astrally travel even now, using thought projections. In your astral traveling, you can do remote traveling and even remote healing. You can practice to connect remotely even through phone conferences. You can send your energy throughout the planet together using a phone conference. This is excellent practice.

Take a moment and hold your connection to many different places around the planet. You can, in a way, teleport yourself there energetically. To create a corridor, you have to feel like you are in an accelerated state, and then call on me, Juliano, and say: "I would like your assistance in developing a corridor." I will then provide the external point in the fifth dimension that allows you to download the outer structure of the corridor.

Sensitive people who come in contact with this higher energy will sense it and be able to use it. You will be able to use it to download different energy and to travel. I ask that you, through your corridors and through your work, create a new harmony, a new light and a new frequency. This is the key to transformation. I am your soul teacher, your soul guide, part of your soul family and your friend, Juliano.

# Chapter 9

# TELEPATHY, BIORELATIVITY AND THE ZOHAR LIGHT

### Juliano, the Arcturians and Archangel Metatron

reetings, I am Juliano. We are the Arcturians. Greetings to all the starseeds. The starseeds are those who have an awareness and connection with their galactic heritage and galactic family. The starseeds are those who have come into this Earth renewed, and have activated their consciousness to be able to remember past lives on other planets and to remember the coded genetic connection that is within each Earthling. This galactic-coded genetic connection is a basic link to the galactic family.

The galactic family includes many beings of higher consciousness who have evolved beyond the realm of the third-dimensional Earth consciousness. Nonetheless, the galactic family welcomes and wishes to integrate with the Earth family. You, as starseeds, are part of the process in aiding to: 1) help the Earth and the species evolve into the next evolutionary step; and 2) to integrate the human species with the galactic family.

In order to integrate this process, there are certain steps that have to be completed in the Earth's consciousness. These steps include universal peace, universal love, acceptance and compassion for all living beings and an ability to comprehend and accept the principles of ascension. Ascension means that you are able to transport and move your consciousness and physical body into the fifth dimension.

It is a unique process that requires higher spiritual technology and training. Some of the training involves being able to transpose yourself into the fifth dimension. This technology includes the ability to communicate telepathically and also to be involved in thought projection. These are two important spiritual attributes and skills necessary for fifth-dimensional work.

### UTILIZING THE ENERGY OF TELEPATHY AND BIORELATIVITY

One of our most basic missions is to help train you in these spiritual skills. Telepathy involves the transmission of thoughts from one person to the next without speaking. You might wonder about this because originally, in the primitive state, humans did not have speech. In that state, there actually was telepathic communication, but on a primitive basis. There were no complex thoughts or ideas to transmit. In one sense, there was no necessity for words.

Speech developed and then the thought process developed. As the thought process developed, ideas and thoughts became more complex. The development of thought processes, which led to speech, did not mean that humans' emotions became more complex. In fact, the emotional body has remained relatively primitive, even to this day.

The emotional body has not evolved the way the mental body has. The mental body is highly developed on Earth because of the formation of language and speech. The emotional body has remained in a lower state. In the energy and the technology of ascension, all of the bodies must evolve. You need the ability to integrate the different bodies so that the energy and development of a higher mental body can assist in the rising of the vibrations of the emotional body. The development of a higher spiritual vibration can assist in the development of the mental body, the physical body and the emotional body.

Telepathy involves the transmission of information and energy from all four bodies. You might think that telepathy only involves the mental body and the processes of speech related to words or thought patterns, but emotions can also be telepathically communicated. There are many instances on Earth where someone is in a great deal of fear or anxiety, and that fear or anxiety transmits over long distances to someone who is receptive to this energy.

Telepathy on a higher level also involves the reception of visual images. This ability to use visual images is a higher level of telepathic communication that integrates thought and words, and raises telepathy to the next highest level. Images and visualization utilized together by a sender create a higher mental process, which will be more powerful.

The energy of telepathy is multipurpose. It can be used for remote heal-ing and for remote activation, and it can also be used for remote commu-nication. Let us look at the combination of higher-thought telepathy with words and visual images together. Let us adapt this to the Earth healing known as biorelativity.

In biorelativity, we are actually using telepathic energy to commu-nicate with the Earth. We are also using telepathic energy to link with other people so that a uniform and universal vibrational energy field is created. Each person can telepathically participate in this. The prin-ciples for biorelativity can also apply to remote healing, which is a form of high energy telepathy. Ultimately, telepathy can apply to ascension, because in ascension and in the technology of ascension, you are using the skills of telepathic visualization.

The basic principle of thought projection by the Arcturians and all higher beings in the galaxy is this: You go where your consciousness is. You follow your consciousness. If you project your consciousness to an-other place, then your energy can follow, including the mental, physical, spiritual and emotional bodies. The energy for sending the spiritual body might be easier to access than it would be to send the physical body.

You must also realize that we are dealing in a different time frame than the normal consciousness of linearity on Earth. If you project your consciousness telepathically to the Stargate, then you might not immedi-ately have your physical body at the corridor. However, in future time—which is transcending Earth time—you are there and the work that you have done at this time affects the energy and your abilities to consciously bring all four bodies to that place. Telepathic communications have a high ability to influence you in multitime.

I am using these principles to also talk about biorelativity because it is similar to the energy of telepathic communications. Going to the Stargate involves using the principle of visualization. You visualize yourself going through a corridor and being there—this is a form of telepathic commu-nication. We are able to communicate with you through the corridor that is there.

In biorelativity, the principle is that you are projecting thoughts to change the Earth to a more positive vibration that is compatible with the needs of the humans on the planet (see Fig. 3). The basic ability to com-municate with the Earth is similar to the patterns of communication in your dream world and in your art forms. Those forms deal with images

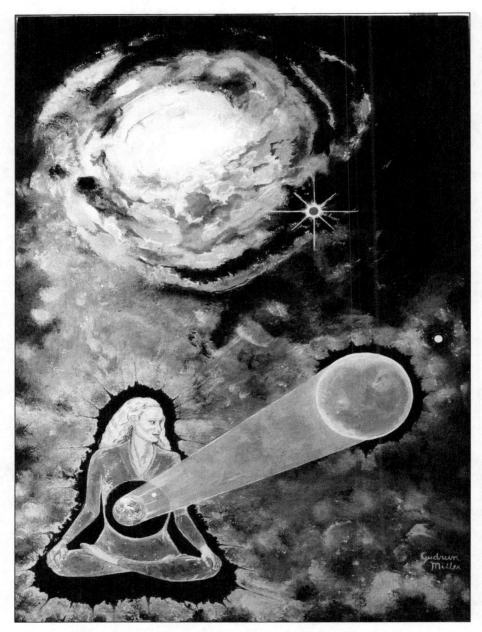

Figure 3: Projecting thoughts to change the Earth in biorelativity.

from the universal unconscious, universal subconscious and symbology known as imagery.

In a telepathic communication, an image with words is a more powerful vibration than just an image alone. An image and words together can be more powerful than just an image. The words that go with the image can have a certain strength or potency. You can increase the visual vibration by certain phrases. There are certain phrases with an image that will enhance the power of a telepathic communication.

In addition to the image and words, tones can amplify the vibration even more. Then you use the three strategies: you use the strategy of words and thought; you use the imagery, which is a picture; and you also use the tone, which is based on a vibration. These are ways to heighten and amplify the thoughts.

In working with telepathic communications with Mother Earth, and for that matter with any planet, we have found visualizations and imagery are necessary. Imagery is the key tool to communicate with the Earth. There are many forms of Earth prayers where only words are spoken, and this is beautiful. Prayers with words are a beautiful intervention to telepathically communicate with Mother Earth.

Prior to the 1970s, you did not have an actual image of what Mother Earth looked like from outer space. You are on Mother Earth now; you are on the physical body of Mother Earth. Mother Earth is also a spirit. You have an image of the Earth that was taken by the astronauts when they went to the Moon. Humanity saw totally, for the first time, the blue jewel, which is what Earth is referred to by the Galactic Council. You saw the blue energy field around the Earth, and you also saw her with clouds and greenery. You saw an unbelievable perfected image of her. I know that image has had a tremendous impact on the ability of people to communicate telepathically to Mother Earth. When you do biorelativity exercises, you want to have that image of the blue jewel in your visual field so that you project thoughts and healing energy to the spirit of Mother Earth.

## EXERCISE: VISUALIZE EARTH'S ETHERIC CRYSTALS

We have downloaded some very large crystal structures into the Earth. These are etheric crystal structures. We have used our interactions with you to teach you the power of an etheric crystal and how to use the etheric crystals to generate the healing energy necessary to unblock the Earth meridians. This energy can be used to bring forth healing energy and to help stabilize the Earth's biomagnetic energy field.

Visualize the etheric crystals that are in Lago Puelo in Argentina, the Grosse Valley that is in Australia, and also the one that is in Moraine Lake in Canada. Then picture the one in the Bodensee area, which is in southwestern Germany on the Swiss/German border. Picture the one at the Volcán Poás in Costa Rica and the one at Mount Shasta in California. If you do not know exactly where these places are geographically, then you can think about their names and then visualize these places. As you visualize the crystals, see them as crystals that are one mile in diameter and about a half-mile tall. They have energy that resonates with the Arcturian Stargate, the Arcturian crystal temple and with higher magnetic energy coming now from the Galactic Council.

The Galactic Council at this moment sends a powerful ray of energy and higher vibrational light to these crystals. This light is to help balance the Earth and all its inhabitants and all those who participate with these crystals. The Galactic Council includes Sananda, the Arcturians, the Pleiadians, representatives from the Ashtar Command and other great beings of light. They are all focusing and sending light and energy to these etheric crystals at this moment. Can you telepathically communicate with these crystals because you have projected your thoughts visually to them?

Everyone can say this affirmation: "I am there in the etheric crystal." You telepathically use two methodologies: You use the affirmation: "I am there in the etheric crystal," as you also visualize yourself there, and you move your consciousness beautifully.

The crystals interact so that when you are in one crystal, there is an automatic link to all the other crystals at the same time. With your energy there, you receive the telepathic energy that is sent from the Galactic Sun. Telepathic energy being sent from higher beings is a powerful energy, yet you still have to be a sensitive soul to receive this energy.

What is important to acknowledge is that being in an etheric crystal is like being in a high-frequency antenna field. It is like being in the largest satellite dish you can imagine on Earth. However, this time you are in a crystal, which is like a large receiving dish. It is the receiving antenna for energy from the Galactic Council. You now telepathically transmit your thoughts and energy to the crystal. You have the ability to receive on a high level energy coming into this planet directed from the Galactic Council.

## COMBINE WORDS WITH IMAGES TO HEAL THE EARTH

Biorelativity is a process of telepathically communicating to Mother Earth in order to heal or shift storms, earthquakes and other large events that can be disruptive to the human consciousness and human species. The most powerful biorelativity method is through using visual images. If you had seen several weeks ago a cyclone coming to the Australian coastline and you could communicate with Mother Earth, you might say, "Change the course of that cyclone." A more powerful way would be to visualize the cyclone changing directions.

You now have access to TV weather satellite images that are projected daily or hourly to you. You could use the image of a TV screen and visualize the cyclone going in another direction. You could visualize a turn in its energy field. You could visualize with words. You could visualize the TV announcer saying that the storm has taken a turn and is going in another direction. These are examples of using the combination of words with visualization.

When you are in the crystal energy fields, your abilities to think and visualize are magnified, and they are more powerfully received by Mother Earth. Visualize the Earth maintaining a beautiful temperature that is perfect for the planet. The temperature is in the highest good for the planet and causes no undue storms, no global warming. Picture in your mind this balance and visualize that the icebergs are remaining frozen longer. You can picture that the currents are remaining in the ocean at a good, peaceful stream without turbulence that could create strong storms.

You can picture the interactive balances that are needed to create a certain harmony. Visualize the ocean currents moving to create balanced weather. You can picture that the icecaps in Antarctica remain frozen. You can picture that there is a balance that allows humankind a little more time in order to make the adaptations necessary to keep this balance.

Then visualize, as you saw in the pictures, Mother Earth as a beautiful planet known as the blue jewel. Then picture a spirit form of Mother Earth. This is to whom you send these images. This is to whom you send this communication. You do this in a visual way, and you also communicate the words "balance" and "maintenance" for the necessary level of homeostasis. Picture that the oceans remain healthy. Then picture that humankind has begun to understand the importance of global weather and its relationship to what humanity does. You can even picture that world leaders talk about it on TV and accept these concepts.

At this moment, the crystals send out a powerful energy around the world. We are all on the same frequency. We all generate this same frequency and send it to Mother Earth. The frequency of this healing and this light is telepathically going around the world at this time. We work now with the subconscious of Mother Earth. Our telepathic powers now go to the great etheric energy field that represents the human consciousness, which has an energy field around the Earth. We are now downloading these thoughts, power and information into the consciousness of the human species.

Hold this energy from the telepathic link from the Galactic Council to you in the etheric crystal. This link is also from the etheric crystal to the Mother Earth spirit. It is linked from the Mother Earth spirit to all the energy patterns in the Earth and the oceans. It is a new feedback loop based on telecommunications and telepathic communications from higher energy beings! You are participating in the telepathic feedback loop.

This new feedback loop is based on a causal link between the Earth and humankind. Now humans have become strong enough to intervene in the link. The power and energy to directly intervene in a feedback loop is reserved for only the highest energy beings and only the highest lightbeings. It is reserved for the starseeds who understand the sacredness and the holiness of this task.

Each of you who are in different parts of this planet may want to send your energy and visualizations now to that part of the planet where you live. If you live in a part of the planet that needs rain, you might want to visualize that moisture is coming in a balanced way. If you live in a part of the planet that needs more Sun, then you might want to visualize that. If you are close to the ocean, you might want to visualize the ocean currents being in a certain balance.

Take this time and remember this new feedback loop. Your thoughts and visualizations go through the feedback loop. While you are still in the crystal and in the feedback loop, I am going to ask Archangel Metatron to speak with you now about applying these principles to your personal activation. This is Juliano.

G reetings, this is Archangel Metatron. You are now using the higher aspects of yourself. You are connected at this moment to your starseed mission. Think about the telepathic transformation that awaits you in your ascension. Visualize yourself in the fifth dimension. Visualize that you are at the corridor of the Stargate. The Stargate is right in the entranceway into the fifth dimension. If you go into and through the doorway, then you enter into the fifth dimension.

## EXERCISE: TELEPORT YOURSELF THROUGH THE STARGATE

You will not be able to pass through the entrance today because you still have an Earth embodiment. Visualize that you are able to teleport yourself there through thought projection to the doorway. Based on the energy field, amplification and powers of the crystals, you can thought-project yourself to the entranceway.

Sometimes we refer to entranceways as the vestibule of the Stargate. I stand right in front of you as a group at the doorway, and I am allowed to open the doorway perhaps one-fifth of an inch—a very small amount. As I open this doorway, the light and beautiful energy of the fifth dimension come out so powerfully, bathing each of you in a beautiful warm ray. We hear the cherubim, the little angelic hosts, singing the famous phrase: *"Eh'yeh, asher Eh'yeh."* This phrase *"Eh'yeh, asher Eh'yeh,"* is translated as "I will be that I will be." Use this phrase to hold this thought: "I will be on the fifth dimension."

We telepathically help you project your consciousness in the future to here. With the energy and focus that you now have, you are able with these thoughts and visual images to hold the energy to create a great pathway. "I will be on the fifth dimension. I will be on the fifth dimension."

As the light comes out of the doorway, we hear the little cherubs singing, *"Aur Ha-Kadosh."* Holy light. Light of the holiness. *"Aur Ha-Kadosh."* Use your telepathic powers to visualize this light as a holy light. It is a light that is so powerful that it balances you. It is a light that is so powerful that you feel in communication with God. You feel in communication with all the starseeds. You feel in communication with Jesus/Sananda. You feel in communication with all the higher beings. Most importantly, you have a connection to your eternal presence, your eternal divinity within.

This holy light has special healing powers. The healing powers are for you. Also, there is enough of the healing light and the holy light that you can bring it back with you into the etheric crystal. When you transport yourself back to the etheric crystal, you will have the energy of holy light.

Many of you may not know how to use the holy light in the most effective way. You are conduits for this light, and the training and energy that you now have before the doorway have allowed you to receive and be a conduit for holy light. Then the holy light will be transmitted.

It is necessary for transmitters of light to be on the planet in different areas. Say this affirmation: "I now activate my higher self to be always in consciousness on Earth." In Hebrew, this higher self is called the *Neshamah*. Redirect your consciousness now back to the crystals that are placed in the Earth. As you redirect that consciousness, you are filled with the presence of this light. Know that you have helped your process by placing your consciousness here. You have helped to lay another foundation stone for your ascension.

Mother Earth can come into this balance because this is a combination of energy and light that is extraordinary. It comes from a higher source. You are the transmitters of this bright light, starseeds. I send the brilliant light from the source into the community of the galaxy. This light is known as the *Zohar* light. On your return back to the crystals, know that you are riding on the brilliant *Zohar* light. This is Archangel Metatron.

CHAPTER 10

# SPIRITUAL REALITY ON EARTH

### Juliano, the Arcturians and Chief White Eagle

G reetings, I am Juliano. We are the Arcturians. The nature of spiritual reality is becoming more obvious to you Earthlings as you mature in your understanding, gather experiences and put pieces of the puzzle together. This understanding is, in many ways, an unfolding of some of the earlier teachings you have had in this lifetime.

#### APPLYING YOUR UNDERSTANDING OF SPIRITUAL REALITY

Understanding this new spiritual reality is also an opportunity to connect the dotted lines. You will have a greater understanding of the spiritual reality, and you can also learn how to use new spiritual techniques for personal and planetary healing.

It is not enough just to understand this reality. You have to learn how to use it. The new reality that you are beginning to grasp is the same reality that we, the Arcturians, experience. It is also the same reality that is involved for all of the star beings on the planet. This reality has to do with some important rules we will describe to you, and hopefully you will be able to integrate them so that you can use them.

Reality is affected both by physical facts and spiritual consciousness. Reality is affected by spiritual intention. This means that you can combine a physical action with a spiritual intention. If you use a spaceship to travel, then you might find that energetically there is not enough energy to boost the rocket at a fast enough speed to leave the planet—or to even leave this reality.

However, when you combine the ability to connect spiritual energy with that rocket ship, you are then able to magnify the acceleration power of that vehicle beyond what might even be considered the normal laws of Earth physics. This has a great ramification for everything that is occurring on this planet. It means that when you build some object, you must try to coordinate that object with this spiritual law. In designing an object, receptivity to the spiritual energy and power that you will project has to be taken into consideration.

The Arcturian temple is a demonstration of this principle. The principle is that the physical building itself is designed so that it is receptive to your spiritual energy. The Arcturian temple is also receptive to our input. Therefore, you can design and build a structure that has the dual purposes of relating to both physical and spiritual energies.

Some of the starseeds have asked, "What is the point and purpose of building any structure for spirituality—especially because there have been some ambivalent experiences on Earth with such structures that have religious or spiritual connotations? Do we need to have another structure?"

This structure we are describing has, in essence, a practical purpose to demonstrate the interaction of spiritual and physical energy. That means the temple would be able, with the input of both energies, to transform into a corridor and actually give those people who are there the ability to enter into other realities. This would not be possible in a "normal" structure.

## THE LEVELS OF BIORELATIVITY

Other masters or guides have talked about the *Merkavah*, which is the etheric chariot. You need the ability to create an etheric energy field that can take you to other realms. The idea is that you, as a physical Earth being, cannot travel to another dimension without an assistant structure.

This is an important idea. It has implications also in the work of biorelativity. It has to do with the evolution of the Earth and creating a detour for certain unfortunate events such as earthquakes, cyclones, volcanic eruptions and even an asteroid that could come to the Earth. Biorelativity states that the applications of spiritual energy to the Earth and to specific Earth areas can help divert catastrophic events.

The effectiveness of biorelativity can be heightened by working with Arcturian energy. First, use your Earth energy abilities. Next, call on the energies of a higher fifth-dimensional civilization that, in cooperation with you, can magnify and accelerate the power of the biorelativity. I do emphasize "in cooperation with you," because you, the starseeds, are grounded here on the Earth. You, the starseeds, are the ones who are able to coordinate the Earth energy. Other fifth-dimensional beings cannot and will not participate in any such projects, in any such acceleration of energy, without the coordination and the acceptance of a stable Earth group such as you.

The Sacred Triangle is not only an energy that coordinates the three different spiritual voices and fields; it is also a triangle connecting Earth to the spirit of the starseeds and to higher beings such as the Arcturians.

Another level of biorelativity focuses on the relationship between the objective reality that you see and how to merge it with spiritual energy. There are many physical events on this planet that seem out of control. Many starseeds feel overwhelmed by the negativity, by the destruction of the biosphere, by the potential of great outbreaks of war and by the possibility of the whole bioenergetic field of the Earth collapsing.

This has been expressed time and again through catastrophic predictions that have been referred to as the "end times." It has led to an expectation of great catastrophic changes facing you. Many people are preparing for some overwhelming tragedy—whatever that might be. We all generally agree that this can be a predicted outcome on the Earth. In some way a divine intervention will hopefully occur that will lead to the ascension of those who are open. It will also lead to the evolution of the Earth to the fifth dimension.

The next level of the biorelativity exercise is the projection of spiritual energy into the future. This involves time differentiation and a new understanding of time. Events in time can be seen as a layer of energy that is in different sections of the Earth's body. There is a layer of energy that represents all the present events.

There is also a layer of energy that is an imprint from all past events that connects to future outcomes. I use the word "layer" very loosely because by talking in third-dimensional terms, I have to describe it as layers. It is not a totally accurate description, but for the purposes of our lecture, we will utilize this terminology. We may need to get into a more exact description that will meet some of the paradoxes that could be brought before us.

There are time-event layers, and in particular, we speak now about the future layer. We can speak about projecting healing and positive spiritual energy into the future.

For example, we practiced with an Australian group several weeks ago concerning a cyclone. There was a great concentration of energy, and with the help of biorelativity thought, the cyclone dissipated and changed directions. Everyone felt it was a positive biorelativity experience. There was another event, a tsunami, where there was no major warning or predicted energy. The event came totally out of the blue. There was no ability by anyone to work on the event with biorelativity to either prevent the tsunami or try to redirect the force.

Initially, the description of biorelativity involved present events where you knew there would be a catastrophe and your intent is to lessen the damage. You can now enter a much more advanced level of biorelativity work by projecting yourself into the future.

By projecting yourself into the future, you then have the possibility of shaping the outcome of the future. This is an extremely powerful ability and an extremely great responsibility, but it is also time for you, the starseeds, to understand and accept this work that you can do. It can be co-ordinated with us, because often you do not have the ability by yourselves to do this at this point. With our instructions and aid, we can provide the link that will help you.

## HELP FROM PLEIADIAN TECHNOLOGY

Let me explain this to you on a deeper level. You must go into the layer known as the future. We, the Arcturians, and others of the masters who have come to this planet to provide assistance, have continually gone into the future layers. In fact, the Pleiadians, who are our dear friends, have special computers that are so advanced that they can log onto your energy field. With these computers they can see the outcome of this lifetime that you are in based on where you are, taking into account the interaction of the past and the present.

That is high technology. The technology that the Pleiadians have (and that we also have) is based on an interaction between the physical and spiritual energy and the computer. The computer by itself cannot do this. The Pleiadian computer was designed to have the spiritual input of Pleiadian energy. We have also developed a computer that locks onto a planet and reveals future events.

It is important to discuss these computers because Earth computer technology is also rapidly advancing. Even so, you are just reaching the point where you might be able to talk to the computer and the computer can respond to simple commands.

This enters into the technology of robots. You can give an order to a robot, such as to open or close the door, and it responds to voice commands. This seems highly evolved from your perspective. A higher technology would be that the computer would receive your thought waves. The computer then can log onto your thoughts.

Earth can use the technology of biofeedback. In this technology, the computer ties into an apparatus that measures your pulse and brain waves. From such a connection, an advanced Pleiadian computer could make a prediction of your future. For example, the computer may detect an aberrant energy wave in your brain system. This energy wave, if it remained in that same pattern, could produce a result thirty years from now that may result in Parkinson's disease or cancer. Identifying that aberrant wave now and directing the person to change that pattern wave could change the future outcome. This has fantastic applications, which is the level to which you are evolving.

Higher computer technology can help predict future outcomes for the Earth. There are even those now on Earth who have advanced technology that can be used for some of the advanced computer applications in personal healing.

Generally, you do not have the advanced technology to do this work on a planetary basis, although there are great scientific attempts being made to develop programs to measure the outcome of weather patterns and their effects on the Earth, and how global warming will affect different areas of the world. You already know what the potential outcomes are from global warming. These potential outcomes are already in the programmed consciousness of many people and in the programmed consciousness of the Earth.

As advanced biorelativity workers, you can choose a time in the future where global warming has decreased. It is potentially possible because the outcomes that are in the future are only potential outcomes. You can enter a layer in the future that looks like global climate change has dramatically affected the Earth, but this reality did not really happen yet. It is just a layer of potentiality. You search that layer and observe the "potential future."

Then with your biorelativity force field, you project a shift in that energy. You project that this anticipated event does not occur. You thought-project yourself into the future in order to see a change. This has helped create positive changes.

There are science fiction stories of people who travel into the past, changed an event in that time frame and then the future event does not happen. This was explained beautifully in the movie *Back to the Future*,[4] a humorous movie, filled with great descriptions of time travel.

## THE NATURE OF MENTAL AND SPIRITUAL REALITY

The question is then asked of the Arcturians: "How can you go into the future and change an event? Would such a change not create untold events that no one could even measure?" The answer is that when you enter the future, you should do so under the guidance of Jesus/Sananda and of higher beings and higher masters who are able to determine what can and cannot be done for the highest good of all.

You cannot do this by yourself. The masters know that there needs to be a healing for the Earth. They understand that there is an ascension and that you will evolve as a planet and personally as evolutionary beings. As part of that future outcome, they see certain windows of opportunity. These windows or corridors are specifically open for divine input. They can only open for keys and input of higher beings who are entering under the guidance of the Master Sananda and others. With their assistance, you can thus penetrate the future and shift.

Earth events can provide an opportunity to demonstrate how biorelativity could be used. The greatest good is served when there is survival. The greatest good is served when higher consciousness is focused.

There can be a dark side of time-layer travel, however. We have noted that the American and Russian military have grasped this understanding of time travel and they have been able to do some manipulations into time travel. They have tried to shift some events for military purposes.

When you thought-project yourself into the future, you use your mental and spiritual energy. What is the nature of mental and spiritual energy? Mental and spiritual energy is close because mental energy is expressed through pictures, ideas and words. They are the groundwork for creation of a reality. The spiritual aspect has similarities. When you add the word "spiritual" to the word "mental," then you come up with an energy that transcends physical laws and includes divine energy.

Physical laws alone do not explain spirit. Spirit is beyond physical reality. Upon your physical death, your spirit leaves. Your spirit transcends space and time. You are able to integrate spirit into different levels. Understanding spiritual-mental energy and how to use that energy involves word intention. Intention determines the direction of your outcome.

---

4. Channel's note: A science fiction movie starring Michael J. Fox.

Coordination of your intention with this spiritual energy is complex. You each have come to Earth to refine that ability. There are many lessons on Earth, including personal lessons for you. I am always happy to have the other guides and teachers speak to each of you individually about a personal lesson that you are here to learn.

Each of you has come to Earth to learn how to practice and refine this technique of spiritual and mental energy with intention, so that you can manifest, influence and affect outcomes. You must learn this lesson slowly. For example, if you learned it when you were nineteen years old and used these powers to manifest a million dollars, then that might immediately take you off the spiritual path and might not be in your higher interest.

Using spiritual energy for manifestation requires a certain maturity and integration with higher energy. After reaching maturity, you can then focus the mind to project yourself into a future outcome and use that ability to shift the energy for the higher good.

Because of the magnitude of planetary healing, you need to work with group consciousness and large groups. We have provided the etheric crystals to help you focus group energy and to accelerate your spiritual energy and abilities to shift future events. The exercise that would be most helpful is to project into the future positive planetary events. See yourself doing powerful Earth work by projecting into the future in coordination with the Arcturian starseeds. You are practicing biorelativity to shift some of the complex problems that seem to have no solutions. See, for example, that there is a great leader who is helping you do this work.

It is a fulfillment of your destiny to do this cooperatively. This is Juliano. I turn you over now to Chief White Eagle who will speak to you more about biorelativity and the future.

Hey ya ho ya hey! Greetings, Arcturian starseeds. Greetings, all brothers and sisters who are connected with the Earth spirits. Greetings, my brothers and sisters, for I am feeling a great heart connection to all! I speak of combining the heart energy with the spirit work.

The successful outcome of any biorelativity activity in the present or the future lies in your connection to love and spirit. When you work toward a future outcome, remember that your intention is connected with your heart. Our love and your love are for the Earth. Your love for humankind and your love for these lessons that you are learning are connected with heart energy, my friends. You came to Earth to refine your abilities in this activity of spirit and outcome, spirit and the shaping of a higher Earth reality.

## ACTIVATE THROUGH ACCELERATED PRAYER

We access this energy in the Native American tradition: through prayer. We access it by going to a power spot and opening our hearts and talking to Spirit. We say that we are one with Spirit. We wish to have an opportunity to participate in the creation of the outcome of this higher reality. We humble ourselves and open our hearts and we open to the guides and teachers. Then we speak. We talk to Spirit and to the Creator.

It is our accelerated prayer, our accelerated speech and our higher consciousness that carry great energy and great weight. This is an energy of intention. The intention is the fulfillment of spiritual destiny and harmony. We have all come here to work toward a spiritual awakening on Earth. Those of lower consciousness, who seem to be in charge of many things, are susceptible to a higher frequency input.

The question becomes: "How do you change the minds of those of lower consciousness?" That can only be done when a physical reality shifts, like when a miracle happens such as the one described in the Old Testament when the Red Sea opened. Suddenly people become believers!

There are major events on the cliff that can go one way or another. This demonstrates that prayers and heart energy that you connect with can influence outcomes. I, Chief White Eagle, announce the presence of the starseeds to Spirit, and I announce their intention to shift and influence the Earth toward the Shamballa light.

The light of the Great Tepee comes to the Earth and creates a united brotherhood and sisterhood. A great healing light flows around this world in the future, with my friends, the Arcturian starseeds, who work closely with me to activate this energy. I see a great expansion of a healing energy. Hey ya ho hey ya!

Our guides, our brothers and our teachers have purposefully placed markers in the future. These markers can be viewed as opportunities to connect to the ancient ones. We know that such a marker is the Galactic Kachina (see Fig. 4). She has great powers to activate the Central Sun energy that will make you more powerful as spirit manifestors and thought-projectors. Her rays of light that she brings with her come from the Central Sun. They now are activating each of your spinal columns.

As I speak, a bolt of streaming golden light from the Central Sun comes into each of your spinal columns now through the Galactic Kachina. You experience a rise of the highest kundalini energy connecting you to your mind and spirit, giving you a great increase in spiritual powers to accomplish such practices as the biorelativity experiments and procedures. Receive now this golden light that travels up and down your spinal column. That will be a great healing for you—a personal healing.

While dancing around the etheric tepee and around the fire, you will be experiencing great activations. The Galactic Kachina is in the forefront of the consciousness of all in this group now. Use this feminine energy to connect to your spiritual gifts and power. This is your brother, your father, your grandfather, Chief White Eagle. Ho!

Figure 4: The Galactic Kachina.

CHAPTER 11

# LIFE AFTER "DEATH"

Juliano, the Arcturians and Chief White Eagle

Greetings, I am Juliano. We are the Arcturians. This lecture is from the perspective of the fifth dimension. We will explore the perception of death. We will examine some of our teachings about this transitional time from the perspective of higher beings, and also from the perspective of Earthlings.

I see that this subject of death is one filled with great fear, with great emotion and also with many psychological blocks. Most Earth beings do not focus on the concepts of an afterlife, death or the dying process during their lifetime. For many people, even the knowledge that there are other lifetimes beyond the current one is rather difficult to accept.

In studying many Earth beings, we have found that fifty or a hundred lifetimes may be necessary before a person actually has an awareness of the process of soul travel and soul evolution. Most people require lessons in different lifetimes in order to come to a basic understanding of what is considered standard, acceptable knowledge in the galactic civilization.

This standard acceptable knowledge is that one can incarnate into different planets, different solar systems and even different galaxies in a soul time. The understanding of this reincarnation can lead you to accelerate the processes and choices that are possible. It is also a step in evolution to realize that the incarnation process is not limited just to Earth. It is a step in your evolution to understand that you can actually evolve and incarnate onto other planets beyond the Earth.

## YOUR INCARNATION TO EARTH

Many people in traditional religions and philosophies and many people on Earth in general find it controversial that one can incarnate back onto the

Earth. Imagine how they will accept or even consider the fact that not only can you reincarnate on the Earth, but also you can incarnate to other planets in the galaxy. This is the basic truth from our understanding and we know it to be true.

We know that some of you have actually incarnated on Arcturus. Some have had incarnations on other planets that are totally unknown to Earth scientists. The name of these planets would be totally unrecognizable to the modern Earth science.

Many of you have had incarnations on planets that are particularly closer to the center of the galaxy in what we have called the Central Sun area. The Mayan civilization knew about the Central Sun. The Central Sun is the origin of the basic life incarnation cycle of the entire galaxy. It is the seat of many higher planets, higher wisdom and higher beings. It is always a magnificent reward or feeling to know that you have come from, or that you can incarnate into, a Central Sun planet.

I would say rather cautiously that each starseed has had incarnations on other planets throughout the galaxy, and many of these incarnations have been a good experience. So why then would you bother to come to Earth? Why lower your vibration to come into an Earth incarnation? From a general Earth perspective, there is not a high understanding of death, nor a high understanding of the process of incarnation.

These thoughts are not meant to be critical of any religious or spiritual practices of the planet. Many spiritual practices have incorporated the attempt to understand death. The religious perspective of this planet is limited, though. Imagine several hundred years ago when the famous explorer Columbus went to sea, seeking a route to India. He had no concept of the geography of the entire planet. The basis of consciousness of the planet at that time was limited by humankind's knowledge of the geography of the Earth.

Expanded scientific knowledge of the galaxies is important to understand religion or spirituality. Knowledge of dimensions and knowledge of the meaning of death, reincarnation and the soul journey are important for the whole process of your soul evolution and for your comprehension of what it means to be part of a spiritual soul family.

Why have you come to Earth? There are several reasons. Some of you came to Earth as starbeings from other planets to help seed consciousness. The seeding of consciousness is generally performed from within a species. It is not done as an outside intervention.

Intervention is an interesting subject. It is generally accepted that exploration and change in evolution of a society or of a civilization occurs from within. The greatest example is the powerful work of Jesus, who came into the Earth from within the system. You will note that he did not arrive on a rocket ship. He did not arrive on a flying saucer. He was not brought down from outside the Earth and given to a group of people who were told, "This is the master who has all the knowledge and understanding of how to transform everyone." It was done from within. Jesus incarnated into an Earth body! Moses went up to meet beings who were of higher consciousness and then he came down. You notice that those beings did not come down with him.

Some of you will remember other planets that you were on. You will remember that it was a choice to come into this planet and this incarnation. You were met by your soul family and by your soul teachers. Some of the soul teachers were actually Arcturian. Your soul family and your soul teachers are composed of a galactic conglomerate of higher beings. They are not just teachers from one planet. You might be in contact with a teacher from one planet or a teacher from one lifetime.

There is certainly enough to contend with in understanding an Earth lifetime. You might only have the mindset to deal with guides from one planet. You might say, "Juliano, how am I going to deal with a soul teacher's system from multiple planets?" When you have expanded into your full consciousness and awareness, then this will be easier.

## THE CONCEPT OF DEATH

Some of you came here for service and to project new energy. Also, it is a general galactic spiritual knowledge that the parts affect the whole. Our galactic evolution is in part dependent upon all the life forms in our galaxy. What occurs with life forms in one part of the galaxy affects the whole galaxy. What transpires on Earth affects the evolution of the Central Sun and the rest of the galaxy. It is, therefore, a path and commitment to work for the upliftment of the Earth.

The other important factor is that there are many souls who came to Earth and became trapped in the incarnational cycle of the Earth. This means that they have to reincarnate before they can graduate or leave the Earth's incarnational cycle.

There are countless examples of people who came to Earth thinking that they had enough power and energy to leave and go back into the fifth dimension. They did not do that. Why? You probably can answer this better than I can because you experience a third-dimensional body, deal with third-dimensional issues and struggle with your own identity as a third-dimensional being. That struggle often leads to total identification with the third-dimensional body and third-dimensional life experiences. Therefore, it can be easy to become trapped in the third dimension.

This is where the concept of death enters. In the Arcturian understanding, death is viewed as a liberation. It is, in scientific and computer language, a rebooting of the computer so that a new program of the self can be reviewed. The old program of the self can be rebooted. There can be a clearing of the hard drive.

Many different symbols can be used in describing death. I tell people that death is a liberation. Many have no concept of death as a liberation because they think they will have to give up their identity with the current life form and experiences. In the fifth dimension, we do not even use the term "death" because we do not have the ego concept of "I am" as you do on the third dimension. We do not even have descriptions of duality in our language. Your language is filled with the duality of finiteness—the duality of end and the duality of death. We look at the transition of death as a reboot. This idea of death has some important ramifications on the third dimension. We find it interesting to study how a being coming to Earth would experience death.

Some of you who are starseeds from higher planets wanted to have this death experience. You wanted to see what it was like to come into a body and experience these spiritual truths: 1) death is a liberation; 2) after death, you have choices on how to proceed; and 3) each lifetime has a particular task or lesson.

After coming into an Earth body from a starseed consciousness, you might expect to remember all of the information from your other soul experiences, including how to transition yourself into another consciousness and how to learn and complete the Earth lessons.

When you come into an Earth body, however, temporary amnesia is experienced. This is the path that everyone must follow. You can have total teaching and knowledge, and right before you come into the Earth, someone taps you on the forehead and says you have to forget everything. Then you come down into Earth.

Some of you do later experience the remembering. Remembering is part of the activation of the Starseed consciousness. It is part of the calling of the Arcturians' mission to remind starseeds of their history.

## THE INFLUENCE OF COLLECTIVE ENERGY

Now we come to this concept of the ascension and upliftment. Perhaps some of the teachings we have given before are coming back to you. Perhaps you are beginning to understand that even if you die before this ascension occurs, it does not mean that this is a failure. You can still participate in this ascension.

The ascension implies that there is an outside influence on Earth. There comes a time in every civilization that we have studied when there is an outside energy that must be introduced into a planet and into a civilization that will shift that planet and allow a transformation. It requires a certain basis of light energy and consciousness for an outside influence or an intervention to occur.

All participants in the mental process of the Earth population contribute to an energy field around this planet. There is a special name for that energy field. We refer to that energy field as the Vosz energy belt. The Vosz energy belt is the accumulated mental energy field surrounding a planet.

This accumulated mental energy is composed of more than just thoughts. It is composed of consciousness and vibrations. This energy belt, or field, is inputted into by every person and being who thinks on the planet. Consider the ramifications of that Vosz belt and how the energy field is affected by everyone. Even the thoughts of a person of the lowest thought-wave energy can enter that belt.

The beauty is that those who are of higher thought waves can counteract lower thought waves. This fact has been proven by the intervention of Jesus when he came onto the scene. One high being entering the planet can have an unbelievable effect for thousands of years. But Jesus' effect did not yet bring in universal harmony and peace.

This means that there is a demonstrated history on Earth that shows that an intervention can result in the total upliftment of this Vosz belt. There needs to be a universal input that raises the whole energy field of a planet permanently. Some will say then that the intervention will mean the return of Jesus and the arrival of other higher beings from the extraterrestrial realm.

There is a halo now around the Earth. This halo of light is contributing to the raising of this vibrational Vosz belt energy. Each of you who have a particular higher thought wave can contribute to the overall energy and counteract many of the lower thought waves—even if the lower thought waves are more plentiful.

A million people contributing unconsciously to a lower thought wave can be counteracted by higher thought input. In the law of galactic spirituality, a higher thought wave—a higher vibration connected to a powerful source like the Central Sun, an Arcturian civilization, or the Central Council—can spread its energy strongly to counteract lower thoughts in this energy belt. The energy belt can even set up a synchronized path for the opening of ascension.

A synchronized energy path can be coordinated and keyed in a special way. When the moment of ascension occurs, then an intersection of the dimensions will occur. This will allow a special downloading of higher light and energy. This higher light and energy will go through the whole Earth belt and raise the energy of those who are already of higher consciousness to an even higher rate. Others will also be raised simultaneously.

When you are raised to a higher rate of consciousness, your view of death totally shifts. Remember, the word liberation implies certain freedom that many of you remember from your other lifetimes.

## ACTIVATE THE RING OF ASCENSION

Coming to the Earth now is a service in which you chose to participate. You desire to participate in the raising of this vibration and the halo, which is called the "ring of ascension." In your meditations, activate with your thoughts this ring of ascension around the Earth. Visualize and believe that this ring of ascension has the powerful ability to raise vastly lower vibrational energy fields to a higher level.

I, Juliano, activate with my light energy the ring of ascension, the halo of light around the Earth. With your thoughts, this ring of ascension is brightened at least ten times from where it was before this lecture began. This ring of ascension provides a higher form of biorelativity intervention now available because with it, we work on an entire planet.

This ring of ascension energy is tied into all etheric crystals that have been placed on the planet through previous work. The whole Vosz energy field is again uplifted. Your participation is a fulfillment of your commitment to be a starseed participant.

The ring of ascension has a vibration related to the Central Sun, to Sananda/Jesus and to mental thoughts of upliftment. This includes the rising toward a salvation and a renewal into the higher body of the fifth dimension. Also, the ring of ascension implies that the entire planet can be uplifted. That has brought many of you back to Earth because you may have even experienced an ascension on another planet in another lifetime. It is a rare occurrence in our beautiful galaxy when an entire planet ascends.

Let us work in the ring of ascension energy. Let us participate in the thought that a planet like Earth can ascend. The mental energy field of a planet is composed of all the thoughts. We are focusing thoughts for a planetary ascension. We are entering these thoughts into the ring of ascension, which has a particular halo of light around the Earth. We have compared this halo to the rings of Saturn or Jupiter.

The ring of ascension is a fifth-dimensional light around the Earth and it is activating the starseeds. It is being coordinated by other higher beings besides those on the Earth. These other higher beings—like the archangels, the Pleiadians and others that you know of—contribute their thoughts to this ring. Higher fifth-dimensional beings are placing their thoughts into the Earth's energy field. They place powerful energy into the ring of ascension. This input provides a ten-fold acceleration of light and energy—a ten-fold acceleration of light and energy that is beyond what you, as starseeds, individually can input from your higher vantage point.

Call on your connection to the higher beings that you know. Each of you has unique starseed connections. You will be able to work with higher beings to establish a strong ring of light and ascension. Visualize the ring of ascension become brighter and brighter. You will see a heightened energy field of stabilization around the Earth, and a heightened knowledge and activity of spirituality never before experienced on the Earth. This coming time will be an especially strong time for the ring of ascension, and it will be magnificently elevated. Teach others about this etheric spiritual ring.

Let us return to the subject of death. Some of you may find that your life process may lead you to a departure from the Earth. You may be called upon and may have the opportunity to leave. Understand that your leaving will be a powerful leaving.

The work you contribute is well received, and there is a guarantee of participation in the ascension—even when you transition to the other side. You who work with this energy will have an opportunity to participate with higher fifth-dimensional beings who are contributing now to this transformation.

This is not to suggest that you hasten your transition in any way. Still some of you may be in your eighties and the physical body may not have the capability of holding on for a given extended period of time. Do not feel in any way that such a departure means a lack of participation in the ascension. I would like Chief White Eagle to speak with you. Please continue your work on the ring of ascension. I am Juliano. Good day.

Hey ya hooyyaahh hey! Greetings, this is Chief White Eagle. We, the Native teachers, walk tall at this point, for the Earth responds to the input of spiritual light that you, as starseeds, download.

By focusing on this ring of ascension energy, you can contribute to a powerful downloading of spiritual energy on the Earth. In other words, my dear friends, you make the halo stronger. That halo automatically distributes light, stabilization and fifth-dimensional energy to the Earth. It is like when we pray to the Great White Father and we ask that we be given guidance and strength. We ask that we be given a light to show us the way.

We know that the energy of our prayers will be directed to the right place, and we know that the light will be shown to us or will lead us into the right place. We have faith in the Father and in the process of transformation. We of the Native peoples have faith in the Earth. We have faith that the Earth responds to spiritual light and spiritual energy. There is a great awakening coming to the Earth.

## YOUR CONNECTION TO THE STAR FAMILIES

There are many different forms of astral light around this Earth body. The astral world often contains bodies that are stuck and confused. Some of these bodies are of a lower vibration. We can chase away the lower vibration.

I, Chief White Eagle, call on the star family, including all the star brothers and sisters, all the star grandfathers and grandmothers, all of the great chiefs from all of the different tribes around the Earth who are now in the higher realms. I call on you collectively as the star group. I call on you to help us in the ring of ascension. Bring your light, your knowledge and your energy into the ring of ascension. We will be with you in the ring.

Our being in the ring brings us an opportunity, O Grandfather, O Grandmother, to be with you. I ask that all who read these words know that by meditating on the ring of ascension, you help the Earth's energy field. You also will have a wonderful opportunity to be with the star family and with your guides and teachers at this powerful time. HeyahooOOOhh.

All the tribes on Earth have unique connections to the star families. Each continent has a special link to a star group, including Australia, England, Israel, the U.S. and other places. The Native people in North America have a particular link to the Pleiadians and the Arcturians. Those in South America and in Australia have a strong link to the Arcturians. The Europeans are awakening to the Arcturians.

From the Native perspective, we reach out to our death and see it as a liberation and a powerful transition. How we approach death is an important sign of our spiritual progress. We accept death by approaching it with a certain attitude. We are often able to heal ourselves in our Earth lifetime in a unique way, which would otherwise not seem possible.

By accepting and greeting death as a friend and as a teacher, we find that we also gain new healing powers. Illnesses that seemed life threatening somehow become like a cold and dissipate. Our spirit is uplifted. Our fear has vanished. That is a great lesson for all of the starseeds to deal with in this emotion called "fear." I know that it can be a great struggle for each of you, but I also know that this emotion of fear is weak when compared to the strong spiritual light that you work with now—in particular, the light of the ring of ascension.

All my brothers and sisters, I send you my love and I send you courage to be the starworker that you are and to be an active star family lightworker. This is Chief White Eagle! Ho!

# CONSCIOUSNESS, VIBRATIONAL UNDERSTANDING AND THE RING OF ASCENSION

Juliano, the Arcturians and Sananda

**G**reetings, I am Juliano. We are the Arcturians. We work with you to accelerate your development. This means that there are ways in which you can advance yourselves rapidly. We are especially interested in helping you overcome karma. You can overcome karma by raising your understanding of the nature of the universe.

## TRANSLATING KARMA AND TIME THROUGH DIMENSIONS

When you have higher consciousness, then you can go into a mode of operation in which you can learn more rapidly. In order to advance, you must learn lessons about why you are on Earth. If you learn the lessons correctly, then you can increase the speed of your vibration. When the vibration quickens, then you are able to bring your entire being to another state. Eventually, you can actually move your being to another dimension. We call this situation "activation." To activate someone is to bring them to a higher state of consciousness. Then they can expand. After they expand, much karma can be cleared.

Having karma in the third dimension means that you often have to return to Earth because you have lessons to learn that you did not resolve previously. You cannot graduate from the Earth. If you expand in consciousness, then you can learn all of your lessons right now in this life. That means you can graduate from the Earth and go into another higher dimension.

We have the third dimension, the fourth dimension and the fifth dimension. Interestingly, you can skip the fourth dimension and go directly to the fifth dimension. We call the fourth dimension the astral realm. That is the realm often of dreams, of spirits and of the place where you normally go after you die.

This astral realm around the Earth we also refer to as the etheric realm, and it contains a great deal of astral energy. There is also the higher astral realm. This is the higher energy in the fourth dimension. If you remain in the fourth dimension, you come back again to Earth. Then you have karma. If you graduate and go through the fourth dimension, then you can become a fifth-dimensional being.

To be a fifth-dimensional being means that you can be in many places at the same time. You can be in one place of high spiritual energy and also in another place of higher spiritual energy. We are teaching people how to practice being multidimensional. This means that you are in the third dimension and in the fifth dimension at the same time. Some of you may even experience this feeling already. We will describe what it is like to be multidimensional. We will also describe to you time in a different way than you usually know.

There have been circumstances where people have missed time in their lives. Missing time means there is time that they do not remember; thus, it is missing. This term "time" has been used often by people who have extraterrestrial experiences. In those experiences, they feel like they have had three or four days of different experiences. Then they are back into their regular consciousness and they realize that they have been gone for only two hours. In other cases, they actually have been gone for twenty-four hours.

Time can be either condensed or expanded. We can alter time by condensing or contracting it. This means that you are actually with us for a short Earth time, but you experience a feeling of longer or expanded time. In this situation, where you are here with us, you may experience one hour differently—such as three or four hours.

What is important is that you can accelerate your vibration so that you can overcome and work out karma when time is condensed. You are actually able to finish work and lessons quickly. I will demonstrate a tone so that you can listen to it and hopefully accelerate your vibration. You will also enter a different time understanding. [Tones.]

## RECEIVE THE LIGHT OF THE ETHERIC CRYSTAL

You are really a vibrational being. Allow this consciousness to emerge. To have this consciousness and vibrational understanding is activation. We connect our energy to the Earth by corridors, and these corridors are connecting tunnels between the third dimension and our dimension, between the third dimension and our space ships and also between the third dimension and special dimensional places that we call temples, such as the Crystal Temple.

I, Juliano, now connect a corridor of light into this room so you are now, if you wish, in this corridor that I send down. You can visualize a fifth-dimensional ship in another dimension sending a corridor of light into this room.

We work with the new technology of etheric crystals. Etheric crystals are crystals that are fifth-dimensional. You must understand that you have a physical body and an energy field around that body. We call the energy field the *"tselem,"* or the "astral body." Your energy field is connected to the astral body. You can take your astral body and travel in it. Your physical body remains in its place while you travel.

Imagine that there is a crystal in the fifth dimension that has an astral body. We call this astral body the "etheric crystal." Through the work of the Arcturians and the Arcturian group members, we sent the etheric crystals to Earth. We call the group members "starseeds," because they have the consciousness and desire to be connected to their galactic family. They help bring this etheric crystal energy to Earth. The etheric crystal is an exact copy of the main crystal in the crystal temple.

The presence of the etheric crystal allows the energy in the whole area to become more spiritual. The etheric crystal is so close to this home now. I, Juliano, create a corridor in this house to the crystal. I bring the etheric crystal light into this room. I do this by raising the etheric crystal out of the water in the crystal temple. Open the palms of your hands to the sky and receive this light. By receiving this light, you enter into a higher and more beautiful vibration. Connect with the other Arcturian starseeds who are meditating on the crystals. Let us meditate together while you and I connect.

You may say to yourself, "I wish to release my karma on Earth." You may feel a great emotion coming up. If you feel the desire, release your karma and any strong emotion within you. We are in a high vibration right now. I feel many of you want to release.

I hold this crystal energy strongly with all of you because there is another beautiful piece of work to do. You have personal lessons to learn. The Earth, as an entire planet, has lessons and karma. All people on the planet who come to Earth participate in karma.

The goal from the fifth-dimensional viewpoint is to bring the whole Earth into fifth-dimensional consciousness. This has been called "bringing the light of Shamballa to the Earth." This is a special energy that transforms or changes a planet into a fifth-dimensional planet. We, the Arcturians, live in a fifth-dimensional planet. Our friends, the Pleiadians, live in a fifth-dimensional planet. You will eventually be living in the fifth dimension.

## ACCELERATE YOUR WORK

We, the Arcturians, have created a special halo around the Earth. We call this the "ring of ascension." We call going up to the fifth dimension "ascension." It is essential that there be a special fifth-dimensional energy around the Earth. This fifth-dimensional energy is like a halo. We send light into the fifth-dimensional ring of ascension. Also, Jesus sends light into this ring.

We work together with Jesus. We call him "Sananda" because he is the master, not only on Earth, but also in the galaxy. We work together. There are many other masters bringing light into this ring, including the archangels and other extraterrestrial masters.

You can experience and help this ring of ascension interact with the Earth. Travel around the Earth with me along this ring. Visualize this ring like you do the rings of Saturn. You can rise up directly into the ring and begin to travel around. As you travel around, you can send fifth-dimensional light around the Earth. We call this "planetary healing."

The ring of ascension receives light from the fifth-dimensional masters. You on the third dimension send your light into it. This ring is an interaction of the fifth-dimensional masters with you. This sometimes is called your "star mission" because you help to bring fifth-dimensional light to the Earth. We also call this activity "biorelativity."

Your connection with a higher vibration can be directed to healing the Earth—especially when you connect with a group like the Arcturian group of forty. All this energy is accelerated when you use the etheric crystals. Your healing power improves. Your spiritual energy increases. You attract more spiritual energy and you also help to bring the light of Shamballa to Earth. You connect with the ring of ascension and with the etheric crystals. You are already performing multidimensional work because you understand and can work with these different places.

Work with the crystals and with the corridors. Work with the ring of ascension. Now everything is accelerated. Use the crystals when you wish to meditate and connect with fifth-dimensional energy, and also when you are with your fifth-dimensional Arcturian starseeds.

We Arcturians are evolved into higher consciousness. We have no war and no disease. We are closer to what you know as *Adonai* Light. We oversee an area in the universe in our galaxy that is called the "Stargate." You even have science fiction movies that use the term "stargate." When you go through a stargate, you can go into another dimension. Interestingly, in these science fiction movies, the stargate is usually portrayed as going into another realm. In our system, the Stargate is the portal for the fifth dimension.

We help to bring and raise the vibration of the third-dimensional Earth starseeds so that they can enter into the Stargate and pass through it. When you pass through it, you enter into the fifth dimension. You can only go through it when you have completed all of your Earth karma.

Some of you have not completed all of your karmic lessons. Realistically, you may need ten, twenty or even more lifetimes to complete them, but through grace, you can accelerate your work. Time can be expanded. When you expand time, you are suddenly able to work through many different problems and complete karmic lessons in a short time. This means that when you come to the Stargate, you will have the right vibration to pass through it.

This reveals another important lesson. You have to be at a certain vibration in order to pass through the Stargate. I now turn the next part of this lecture over to Sananda. I am Juliano. We are the Arcturians.

**B**lessings, my brothers and sisters, I am Sananda. I send my Father's love to you. I am happy that you are beginning to understand there is a family of lightbeings in the universe. You wish to raise yourself to be a lightworker. I need your help in healing the Earth. It is my Father's wish that we do this together and that you continue to work together with all higher beings.

There are many higher extraterrestrial beings in this galaxy. All are connected and are following the light of *Adonai*. This is also the galactic name used for our Father. We connect with all the lightbeings in the galaxy now and send to you our powerful love. I will sing our Father's name to you. [Sings]: *Adonai.*

Think about the concept of being raised up after death. It is not exactly the way you may think. You have a lightbody and that lightbody is above you. You can connect and raise yourself into that lightbody through love, loving God and also loving yourself.

This is not a love for selfishness, but rather it is a love of your lightbody. There is a special code to open yourself to this lightbody, and that code is "I Am That I Am." This is the name that *Adonai* revealed to Moses.

When you hear this name in the special galactic language of Hebrew, then you can open up to your lightbody. You can then connect with your lightbody. Your third-dimensional body will have a higher light quotient. You become so light that you can translate yourself into the fifth dimension. I will now sing this special coded phrase. Have in your mind the thought, "I want to connect with my lightbody." [Tones]: *Ehiyeh asher Ehiyeh*. I Am That I Am.

Raise yourself to your lightbody so you will be at a higher vibration and your life can become more beautiful and filled with love. You can have great knowledge and great understanding and great wisdom. These are your gifts from our Father. Then you can experience the joy of knowing that there are many other lightbeings in the galaxy. These are the star family members. They include the angels and Native Americans. They include all people on this planet. They include you. I send you my love in the name of the Holy Spirit. Good day. I am Sananda.

CHAPTER 13

# SHIMMERING LIGHT

## Juliano

G reetings, this is Juliano. There is a special light and energy in Argentina.[5] In South America, the starseeds have awakened and accepted the fifth-dimensional light. In many ways, the Earth changes will be very kind to Argentina. This country is not in the center of the world conflicts like the United States. At the same time, there is a long history of working with higher beings here, so the role of the starseeds in Argentina focuses on two important matters.

The first has to do with the light cities. Some have referred to the light cities as Shamballa. We call them the cities of light. The second function has to do with biorelativity. There are special energy lines in Argentina that help heal the Earth.

### THE IMPORTANCE OF PRACTICING SHIMMERING

There is a major discussion about ascension with the starseeds. Many people say they will ascend and not return to Earth. We encourage you not to make a decision about returning to Earth. At the same time, we understand the concept of multipresence. This means that you are in two dimensions simultaneously.

In the beginning of the multipresence exercises, you are in the third dimension, and twenty seconds afterwards you are in the fifth dimension. When you become experts, you can simultaneously move between dimensions. This is a special ability that the starseeds can develop. A vortex or corridor can help you to connect to the fifth dimension, and when you

---

5. Channel's note: This lecture was given in Buenos Aires, Argentina.

practice, you can move through the corridor to connect with the fifth dimension. This work also aides the ascension. You can help Earth ascend by being in the cities of light and by creating cities of light.

Shimmering is a way to be simultaneously in both dimensions. The best way to describe shimmering is to refer to a television show called "Star Trek." There was a machine called "the transporter" on that show. When the space travelers wanted to go from the space ship to the planet, they stepped into the transporter. Right before they were transported, their image would go in and out. For a brief second, they would disappear and then they would reappear. The control man would press the button and they were sent down to the planet.

In shimmering, you go in and out of dimensions. This ability and energy can more easily be accomplished at sacred sites on the planet. There are several places in the United States where shimmering can more easily be done. One of them is in the Mount Shasta area in California. The other is in Sedona, Arizona. In South America and in Argentina, there are many sacred places to do this. You can also practice shimmering in your home at special places you have set aside for meditations.

You can practice shimmering in a group. The next level would be to practice shimmering a city. There is a story called Shangri-La, which in our language is similar to Shamballa. Visualize a city that is in the fifth dimension. You are a third-dimensional being in the story and you come up to the city, but you do not see it. You are not on the vibratory level to see it. If your vibration were raised, then you would see the city. In the story of Shangri-La, people were looking for the city in the mountains, but they never could find it because they were not at the right vibration.

Let us look at this from the perspective of groups. You first begin as a small group, and you think and imagine that there is a circle of light around you. This circle becomes a big basket and you begin to chant. First, you start slowly. Then, you begin to increase the speed and go faster and then the basket slowly raises everybody out of the dimension. You enter the fifth dimension and feel uplifted.

## EXERCISE: VISUALIZE THE CRYSTAL IN LAGO PUELO

Imagine you are performing this exercise and somebody who does not know what you are doing enters the room. This person may not even see the group. Think about the different small cities you live in, or even larger cities, such as Buenos Aries where you can be in small groups and do this exercise as a group.

Some people live around Lago Puelo and are from small towns. You can do this exercise in the city or around the lake. It might be easier to do it around a small vortex like the lake, which we will describe first.

Visualize that you have forty people and twenty people meditate in front of the lake. They are all in a circle. The other twenty go around the whole lake. At a certain time, for example, two o'clock, you will do the shimmering exercise and everyone visualizes the circle of light around the lake.

In the case of Lago Puelo, Argentina, you can visualize the crystal coming up, or you can simply feel like the whole lake is rising. Whichever way you choose is fine. This way the whole area of the lake raises its vibration, and you can then move this area into the fifth dimension. There are at least ten places in Argentina that carry this kind of energy. You can do this in Buenos Aires as well, but you have to have many people go around the whole city.

In Lago Puelo, we are happy about the powerful crystal energy there. Imagine that you have practiced the exercise at Lago Puelo. You are about to leave, but you have brought crystals with you. Each person leaves the crystal in the place where they sat. When there is a Group of Forty (GOF) meditation, you can have the group connect with the energy through the crystals. You tell them you will raise Lago Puelo to the fifth dimension. You tell everybody in the group of forty that you have left the small crystals there.

In the meditation, the members can project their energy to the crystals and they then begin to tone. When they increase the tempo of the sounds, they have what we call "remote shimmering." In this way they can work on remotely elevating the energy to another dimension. Imagine that we have groups in New Zealand, Australia, California and Argentina, and everybody is going to do the shimmering exercise together. We now have four areas in the world that are being elevated into the fifth dimension. This will create energy for Earth transformation.

At this time, visualize a circle around this room like a halo. It gets stronger and stronger. The light forms a basket below the room. Make these sounds as the baskets begin to rise. *Ohm,* [slow] *Ohm,* [faster] *Da,* [faster, then fast] *dadadadada.*

You have brought this room into the fifth dimension. The basket descends back into the third dimension. It is a slow and gentle ride. The basket has now completed its descent. You are in the third and fifth dimensions simultaneously. This room now shimmers and we have concluded this descent back to the third dimension. With your mind, you can go to the fifth and return and be in the third and the fifth dimensions simultaneously.

Identify ten places where you can do shimmering exercises. The first will be the Lago Puelo area. You will identify nine more areas and then you can coordinate the exercise we have just accomplished. Remember that you can do this around an entire city, but there are so many energies in a city, it is much more complex. It is much easier to do around a sacred spiritual area. Can it be done in the backyard of a home? Yes.

The planetary coordination is started here. Eventually the GOF will organize around the world. This will take much coordination. I ask that the Argentinean people lead the way for all of this. It will have a nice effect on the whole country.

You will begin to attract more fifth-dimensional energy and more fifth-dimensional people. People will come to experience this energy. It is your assignment to find the ten places and coordinate the exercise. It will be easy to identify these ten places, and the coordination will be so strong that you will affect the whole country. Blessings, this is Juliano.

CHAPTER 14

# GRACE

Mary

Greetings. This is Mary. I send you my love and I receive your love. There are many tears of joy for me to be with you. I am easy to work with and you can very easily receive my light.

I know you think you are the child and I am the mother. But we are all children of the Father, and I help bring you before the Father. I play a major role in the Earth and the Earth changes. I know that the Earth changes bring much suffering to the children. I know that the coming changes will be even more difficult, so it is necessary to work as hard as you can to ascend. I want to help you in a special way.

## RECEIVE THE ENERGY OF GRACE

I want to speak to you about grace. It is a special energy—like a dispensation. This means that grace is especially granted to the followers of the light. It is a special light and gift to those who follow Jesus. You know that surrendering to Jesus brings to you an acceleration of light energy and freedom from karma. Freedom from karma means you can ascend.

Many of you have complicated lessons and problems that you are attempting to complete. You work hard, but sometimes there seems like there are no solutions. Sometimes it looks like you are coming to a wall and cannot get through it. At the same time, I know you try to work through life lessons that may take ten lifetimes, and you are trying to accomplish these lessons in one lifetime. You can expand your consciousness and ask that it be accelerated.

I love this symbol and name called the "Sacred Triangle." I love the word "sacred." You are sacred children of the Father. You do sacred work and I send you now sacred light. Place yourself in the sacred light and I promise that this light will become visual. I promise you your lessons will be easier and I will send you the light of grace. This means that problems will be lessened. In some cases, the problems totally disappear.

To help with the grace, I can cohabitate with you for a brief time. Many of you carry pictures of me with you. Many of you talk to me in your prayers. Maybe this word "cohabitate" sounds like a funny word to you. In your language, cohabitate means that I will be with you for the next twenty-four hours. Close your eyes and visualize my image coming down from the ceiling or from the top of the room. I spread my light through the room with love, and this energy of love has the special ray of light containing the energy of grace.

Receive this grace into your energy field. I agree to be with you for the next twenty-four hours if you agree. I will explain how this works. Say you have a problem with your children or your boss. You can now see the problem through my eyes. You can now see the solution through my mind and you can talk to people the way I would talk to them. You can reach people through the heart energy, which is a strong energy.

The energy of grace is coming down to you as my body image is still above you, and it also brings you better health. You can receive the energy through your crown chakra and then let the energy go through your whole body to where it needs to go. I can only stay with you for the next twenty-four hours. On the fifth dimension where I live, I have a multipresence. That means that I can be with many people at the same time and I am fully present with each one. You too will soon have this ability. It is great fun.

The most important aspect that you need to know about being with the fifth-dimensional light is that there is great joy to be so close to the Father. We all just want to celebrate. We are so happy when you look at us and connect with us. This is joy greater than any joy you have found on the third dimension. I cannot explain it to you in words. I can only tell you that it is spiritual joy.

The work you are doing on the third dimension is in preparation for this experience, so what you do on this dimension is important to your development. Do not look at it as a reward because it is too simple to think of it that way. Think of it as a natural development—an expansion of your light. I keep my image above you and I feel your attraction to me.

## OPEN YOUR HEART

There are already other people who will soon be able to channel my words. I work personally with them now to clear their energy to be able to speak. You know that many of you are already advanced spiritually. You can let go of yourself and go to your higher self. I send waves of healing light to each of you in this room, and maybe you feel the waves in your heart. Now I send you greater light to come into your heart and your heart expands. This helps to accelerate your karmic lessons.

With your heart open, you can be more accepting, less judgmental and more loving to everyone. I have a special role on the Earth and I work with many of the ascended masters to help save the planet. The Father wants the Earth to survive, and he wants this to be a wonderful place for people to prepare themselves for the ascension.

The Earth needs help. I know you share my love for Earth. I want to be with you. Let us be silent together as I continue to hold my lightbody above you. Much of my work with you is just being with you in my light. This is beyond words. Being with you means sharing my energy with you. I am able to be close to the Father. Then my light energy becomes stronger and I give off greater energy. It would be difficult for you to be this close to the Father without being blinded. I can be in his light without being blinded.

I have come down to you and I give off his light. This light is stepped down. It is less intense so that you can assimilate and receive it without being blinded. This is the channeling of energy in light. I enjoy being with you in these states. I work with each one of you individually, so if you have a special request, you may think of it now. This can be a special request for help in the light. Think of that in your mind and I will work with you for the next twenty-four hours.

It is time for me to leave, but my presence will still be with you. I will cohabitate with you, if you wish, for the next twenty-four hours. I send you my grace, my light, my love and my deep respect for your devotion. This is Mary.

# SPACE TRAVEL TECHNOLOGY

P'Taah

I am P'Taah. I am from the planetary system known as the Pleiades. We are also fifth-dimensional like those in the Arcturian system. We are your brothers because we are part of the Adam species. Many of us are actually in South America as what you call "walk-ins." When I say many, I mean less than a thousand, and we have been visiting and helping with the Earth for many centuries.

## INTERDIMENSIONAL TRAVEL

I am a teacher, and I often focus on relationships in the third dimension. Speaking technically, I will introduce the subject of space and time travel. We have advanced technology that enables us to travel through the dimensions. We learned how to travel faster than the speed of light. You may find it interesting to learn how we view this. First, let us discuss energy.

You know, perhaps, that to take a rocket ship to the speed of light would require all of the energy that was ever spent on Earth, including that of nuclear bombs. There would be no energy left for anyone on Earth to do anything else. Obviously, there must be some other method to travel interdimensionally.

Like the Arcturians, we use a special method of travel called antigravity with telepathy. In your language, it would perhaps be called "telepathic antigravity travel." This means that the technology of energy is jointly accomplished with telepathic thought. In this way, we are able to accelerate our spaceship to a certain speed and then add an intervention using telepathy.

There is a special mathematical sequence of numbers called the "Fibonacci sequence." Using this sequence in certain ways can unleash mystical powers. When a spaceship reaches a certain speed measured in relationship to the Fibonacci sequence, then thoughts and energy can mix. This mixture allows you to project your space travel so the propulsion energy for the spaceship interacts with your thoughts. This only can happen after you reach a certain speed.

When you travel interdimensionally, you can project yourself to a different section of the galaxy. When we enter the Earth solar system, we cannot land too close to the Earth because if we did, we could push the Earth off its dimensional alignment. So when we come toward the Earth solar system, we first enter the Jupiter corridor. There are large space corridors around Jupiter, which allow us to comfortably slow down and not disturb the dimensional alignment of your planet.

But we could make a mistake. If instead of landing in the Jupiter corridor, we landed near your Moon, then we would upset the Earth. For example, the Earth could be thrown out of orbit, among other problems. Consequently, we have to allow enough space for our reentry from the other dimensions.

Many years ago in Earth time, one of our spaceships came too close to the Pleiades during reentry. They miscalculated their reentry needs and did not provide themselves enough space. Remember, when we come into this solar system, we have to land in the Jupiter area. That is far enough from the Earth. This needed distance gives you an idea of how powerful it is when someone comes from another dimension into the third dimension.

When the space travelers or astronauts came into the Pleiades, they came in too close and knocked the planet out of its dimensional positional alignment. We were in big trouble as a planet. We were in a situation that can be described as a space-time rift or zone. We appealed to the ascended masters because we could not solve the problem. They granted us special grace because of our spiritual advancement. They allowed and helped our planet ascend to the fifth dimension. That solved a serious dimensional misalignment problem. This event will help you understand how space travel works and how important dimensional alignments are in reentering from another dimension.

You may have heard that many of the extraterrestrial masters and teachers were worried that the Earth would bring nuclear weapons into the galaxy. Your governments are actually closer than you think to interdimensional travel. Many of you may wonder what we are worried about since the Earth would have to travel so far to bring these weapons into the galaxy. However, you can see from the foregoing accident that the Earth could bring those weapons with them through the interdimensional travel method.

In summary, higher space travel requires higher telepathy and antigravity, and there is a special, mystical speed when telepathy and space travel merge.

## THE IMPORTANCE OF RELATIONSHIPS

Let us speak about relationships. Love is such an important fact on Earth. Learning to love is one of the main lessons on this planet. Many lessons have to do with relationships and love. On the Pleiades, we have a way of love that involves embracing. When we embrace, it is like our souls transmit light and energy to each other. This transcends even the physical relationships that you have. This is a higher union that is not possible with Earthly energy.

One of the lessons and things for you to work on is to transcend polarizations, which you can do through love. Many of you do spiritual work with soul mates and others of you work alone. Groups that you have formed often have people you have been working with in other lifetimes. They may feel like family members to you.

When I analyze relationships on the Earth, I see that many of them are filled with much conflict, but I also find that you can choose to be loving. This is an important aspect of relationships: namely, to choose to be loving. Remember, this is the free-will zone where you do not have to follow the lower level of energy and be polarized. The way into fifth-dimensional energy is to achieve a vibration of higher love. You have a great opportunity to practice higher relationships—even in relationships where you may feel critical of people. These relationships contain important lessons for ascension.

We Pleiadians look like humans; the only difference is that our ears are strange compared to yours. If you saw us on the street, you may not even know we came from another area. Some of you actually lived on the Pleiades and reincarnated from the Pleiades to Earth. The reasons why you did this were many. Some of you are students of the galaxy and wanted to experience the third dimension. Some wanted to also be part of and help with the ascension. Remember, the ascension requires the starseeds to anchor energy and light. Group energy becomes more powerful when the group members love each other.

I have been a teacher for many people before and I continue to work with many new people who will be coming to Earth. Our planet is small in comparison to yours. We only have maybe 800,000 people on the whole planet. I am P'Taah.

## CHAPTER 16

# THOUGHT FORMS
# AND HEALING

### Tomar

G reetings, I am Tomar. I work in the Arcturian temples. It is my work to guide spiritual work for the people. I will explain about our work and you will better understand the Arcturian temple project here on Earth, what it means and how it can work.

## THE ARCTURIAN TEMPLE AND HOLDING THOUGHT FORMS

The first subject is the Arcturian Temple on Arcturus. We look at our dimension and our planet originating from a thought form. Basically, we see the foundation of the universe as light and energy. The fifth dimension has a higher energy than the third dimension. Energy without a thought form is called "undifferentiated energy." To stabilize and pull the energy requires thought forms, and we have specially trained spiritual masters who meditate to continually reform the thought forms of our civilization.

We have studied the Earth and note that there are people living in special caves in Tibet. There are also Indians living in Arizona called the "Hopi Indians." Both of these people are actually related to each other, and they both have special training and teachings on how to hold the thought-form energy of this planet together. To put it another way, they hold the key to the thought forms for the Earth's biosphere.

On Arcturus, we have our spiritual meditators doing thought-form work continually. We do not have twenty-four-hour days like you do, but for the purposes of this discussion, we will utilize twenty-four hours as one day. Thus, our meditators work twenty-four hours a day to hold the Arcturian thought form. This helps to sustain the spiritual nature and foundation of our society. It means that it is vital for us to have these people perform this task for which they were specially trained from birth. We value their time and effort a great deal.

When we travel in our spaceships, we have a special room on the ship to meditate and connect to the people in the temple on Arcturus. It is necessary that you understand this first before we speak of the Arcturian temple project on Earth. The meditators in Tibet and the Hopi Indians no longer have the strength to keep the thought forms of the Earth together. The energy field of the Earth is beyond their ability. They still try, but it is too much for them. They need assistance, but you will not have to travel to Tibet to sit in a cave or to travel to Arizona. The Native peoples often do not want white people to come in with them during their spiritual work because they feel protective of their spirituality.

I believe there must be another way to hold the thought forms together on the Earth. This is more difficult because the energy is so diverse. We discussed the development of the Templar with you, although we referred to it as the temple. We need to place this temple within a great deal of pure energy, and also in a place that has a great deal of fifth-dimensional light.

The concept of the Arcturian temple on Earth includes people devoted to working and meditating to hold the energy together in a thought form on the Earth. Different people would work periodically during the twenty-four hours in a day. In our blueprint of the Arcturian temple, the meditators would connect with the Arcturus energy and use that blend of energy, which is the energy of the fifth dimension with the Earth energy, to hold higher thought forms together of the Earth.

This would mean that it would be a great assistance to the Hopis and the Tibetans. This project would demand a big commitment of time. You would need people willing to meditate in a special way for many hours a day. People around the world would also send their energy to this temple. Thus, the thought forms of a fifth-dimensional Earth would be held in third-dimensional thought form on the Earth.

We understand there has been much difficulty in attempting this. We are not surprised, as it takes a whole culture or tribe, such as the Hopis, to provide supplies for several people whom they call "medicine men." In Tibet, monks who have trained for many years can do this work. Consequently, to expect that you could put this together easily is a high expectation. I know that some of you are willing to try this, and it is our hope that people around the world will support it. But we also recognize that it might be too difficult for you to do it here and now. It is possible that you could do it on a much smaller scale.

If you build a tepee, it could also provide a focus for the Arcturian temple project. Obviously, the first choice would be to have a temple, but the meditations can be done in a tepee or even outside the tepee. The most important aspect is to establish a group of people working together in meditation who understand how thought forms change reality. People ask us what is needed. You need to create thought forms for the new Earth. You can create the thought form to hold shimmering light cities. You can combine the fifth-dimensional energy with the third-dimensional energy. This commitment and action would also have a life of its own in terms of its accomplishment. This new Earthly establishment would symbolically demonstrate how thought forms can affect the reality of a planet.

There are different levels of intensity. The first level is to have a group meditate twenty-four hours a day, but if the group only mediates eight hours a day, that is still good. If the group meditates only one hour a day, that is still good. In previous lectures, we have asked people to attempt to meditate continuously over a twenty-four-hour period. Some people meditate for two hours; others for one hour and so on, which acts as a continuous meditation cycle.

## MEDITATE TO HELP HOPIS AND TIBETANS

This subject has been covered rather quickly. Maybe you have some questions. Understand what the purpose of the temple would be.

*What type of meditation do you recommend?*

When we use the term "meditating," it is not necessarily the way the yogis meditate. We mean holding a thought form of a planet, such as "a city of harmonious light is emerging on the Earth." Working on the thought form of a planet is biorelativity at its highest level.

*Should every Group of Forty starseed do this?*

It would be good to have many groups of forty also commit to this. Remember that we have described a structure in which all 1,600 members would be in a circle in that structure. It is too much for one person to meditate continuously. You could assign different group members to do this at different times of the day. They would remotely connect to the temple as a way of working with the energy. What I describe may sound difficult to do as you think about such a commitment. Start simple.

Understand that the Hopis and the Tibetan monks are not able to sustain the Earth's thought form any longer. Even the Hopis are coming out now and saying the Earth is passing through the end times. They say that terrible tragedies are coming. You wait for predictions of terrible tragedies. Even yesterday, the channel was asked if the economy will collapse. Of course the economy and the currencies are in danger, because everything is in a precarious position. But instead of focusing on the collapse of the economy, focus on the thought forms of a new economy based on higher fifth-dimensional light. You can work on this in a way that would have different groups sustaining that thought form.

What will be the description of this new economy? Thought forms of this new economy will be downloaded from the Central Sun to you soon. It is not in your best interest to wait for the collapse of this economy. Rather, use another thought form that there will be a successful transition, such as a new economy that is better for everyone. Even if you don't know what that new economy will be, it is helpful to download it and focus on it as a thought form that will be in everybody's highest good.

When we think of the groups of forty, we never expected that all of the information would come through David. We are happy with David and we think he is doing a good job, but he cannot bring down all the information and all the solutions.

*Please describe thought forms.*

Thought forms are in levels. The thought begins with an energy or a visualization. Then you have a three dimensional image of how it will work.

Use the analogy of money: You have the thought form that you desire to be rich and then you visualize yourself with much money. But you have to go to another level and visualize yourself receiving money. Likewise, you may have to go one step further and even visualize yourself working at a job where somebody pays you a large sum of money.

There are different levels of the thought form, but they are all related. Some of the thought forms remain in the fifth dimension and others are actually three dimensional visualizations coming from the fifth dimension. Different people will work on different aspects of the thought form. Some may work better just on the raw energy of the thought form. Another may be better at manifesting images that are three dimensional.

This summarizes just part of the work of the new consciousness that we call the "next evolutionary step for humankind." Remember what the astronaut Neil Armstrong said: "One small step for a man, one giant leap for mankind."

We allude to the energy of the Sacred Triangle. The Hopis and the Tibetans did not follow that Sacred Triangle paradigm, and it is clear to us that in order to heal the Earth, you must have energy from the fifth dimension. You must have galactic consciousness. You must be able to download energy from the Central Sun. Alignment is what the 2012 energy is all about and why the starseeds become so important. The groups of forty and the Arcturian starseeds understand the integration of the Sacred Triangle light with the thought forms. I am Tomar.

## CHAPTER 17

# HOLOGRAPHIC AWARENESS

Juliano, the Arcturians, Helio-ah, Metatron, Chief White Eagle

G reetings, I am Juliano. We are the Arcturians. A unique feature of the third dimension focuses on how things change. Change is a practical, ever-present option and is a reality in the third dimension. Change is usually preceded by a disruption or disharmony.

You have personally experienced such disharmony or even pain before a period of greater harmony. When you look at the history of the Earth and the third dimension, then you see that there are many periods of geophysical disruption. These periods created dramatic shifts in the climate, temperatures and also the physical structures of the planet. These geophysical changes occurred over thousands, and in some cases, millions of years.

The immediate stimulation for the change could also have occurred in a brief onset. A meteorite struck the Earth at an earlier time, setting forth the changing energy that created the end times for the dinosaurs. If the dinosaurs had continued to exist, it is unlikely that humans, your Adam species, could have maintained or been allowed to live on this planet.

In reviewing the akashic records of the dinosaurs, we are able to determine that the chain of events that led to the meteorite and to the extinction was really set in motion long before the actual event occurred. From the perspective of the scientific mind, you might think it was only the occurrence of the meteorite striking the Earth that created this scenario. In reality, it was a long combination of events that culminated in the strike of the meteor and the subsequent elimination of that species. There was disharmony on the planet. The dinosaurs had been in existence for many thousands or millions of years. There was disharmony in their interaction with the Earth's biosphere.

I point this out so that you have the structure and background to understand the nature of the changes you are experiencing now on Earth. Indeed, one event occurs, and it appears as if that event stands by itself. It creates a certain disharmony. In reality, there were many events leading up to this. Some of the events can even karmically be tied to other lifetimes not in the awareness of the third-dimensional mind.

## GLOBAL CONSCIOUSNESS AND THE HUNDREDTH MONKEY EFFECT

On a personal and transformative basis, you can assume that any disharmony, any pain you experience, has the potential to lead to a greater integration, higher evolution and ultimately, even to the ascension.

A certain level of disharmony and a certain level of uproar will occur now on Earth. This helps to set in motion a greater awareness of the need for a dramatic shift. This is the nature of the third dimension and it is also your personal third-dimensional nature. For you to change usually requires a disruption or disharmony. For you to begin the process of your entitlement to the higher level means that you will experience the disharmony of the third dimension. In fact, it was part of your agreement when you came into this realm. These were the rules that you play by; that is, the disharmony and pain that you experience are the tools or the stimulation for moving into a new way of thinking and a new way of being.

Unfortunately, it is the same path and rules on a global basis. There is a beautiful, interactive state described by one of your biologists known as the "hundredth monkey effect."[6] The hundredth monkey effect is an appropriate metaphor of a spiritual law that explains how global consciousness can expand.

This hundredth monkey effect is being demonstrated by the Arcturian groups of forty and other spiritual groups. A certain core energy thought being developed and held by a significant number of people can eventually reach a creative critical mass, which then will influence more people and events than its actual numerical value.

Global consciousness contains the collective mental thought patterns of the entire planet. Certain higher vibrational thought patterns can actually affect the entire global consciousness—even though a majority of people do not think them.

---

6. Channel's note: This effect was supposedly demonstrated on an island in which a small number of monkeys learned a task. When that number reaches one hundred monkeys, then the other monkeys on the island seem to suddenly learn the task.

These individual thought patterns have a higher energy. Higher individual thought patterns have a certain vibrational frequency that can influence lower thoughts, even though the lower thoughts are manifesting and being thought by more people. Many people have lower energy and input the mental belt with lower thoughts. That is one thing. But if there is a group that is of a higher vibration putting in a higher thought, then that higher thought can counteract the lower thoughts, even though the lower thoughts are more plentiful.

This concept of the hundredth monkey effect can now be focused on the fifth dimension. You have moved into a fifth-dimensional mindset. The fifth-dimensional mindset is so strong that if you were experiencing intense negativity, or intense disharmony and chaos, then you would be able to shield yourself with group energy. This type of shielding is not what you normally would even expect or understand.

Let me give you a scenario: You are in a field and there are a thousand animals charging you as they are stampeding. You are standing in the field working on fifth-dimensional energy and consciousness. Suddenly, for an unknown reason, the animals go around you. The animals do not attack nor stampede over you, but rather they go around you, almost as if you never existed. You stand there, expecting that you will be affected by this overwhelming stampede of wild animals. Even though you may not be in higher consciousness at that moment, you are still shielded and protected. This is one of the key points about fifth-dimensional consciousness.

## PROTECTION FROM THE CHAOTIC

The fifth-dimensional consciousness does not have to be in your consciousness every moment of thinking. In fact, we know from being on the third dimension and from studying you as third-dimensional beings that you will be constantly dragged down by and focused on lower vibrations.

For example, you have fears of terrorism, financial uncertainty or about dramatic Earth changes that will affect you. You have thoughts about the biosphere ending, and you may even have thoughts about plane crashes and other terrible events. These types of thoughts are continually bombarding your consciousness through your media and through other awareness on this planet. You know that there are an uncountable number of factors that are chaotic. The final chaotic factor is the disruption of the biosphere, secondary to imbalances from pollution and overpopulation.

This type of thinking and consciousness, which you would call lower vibrational thinking and fear consciousness, is part of the package of being on the third dimension. Many of you may think it is your test to be able to not have fear. Perhaps you have expectations during these other events that can be described as the chaos leading up to the ascension. You expect that you should be able to transcend your feelings so that you would not experience the fear.

From our new perspective and information, we know and communicate to you that your participation in this fifth-dimensional evolution and consciousness has created a protective energy field around each of you. This protective energy field actually transcends the lower fears and realities.

The reality is that statistically some of you will be exposed to these chaotic events directly or indirectly. I think it would be a great surprise to think that you would not. However, on the contrary, you will be protected from that. Do not worry that you will not be protected. Have a vision of the fifth-dimensional wave of protection that will be around you—no matter what chaos or disharmony comes to you.

You will look with surprise and understand that this chaos is not affecting you directly, though it is affecting you by your observations of the chaos and the pain that may be activating others. You may look around and say, "For some reason, I am standing in all of this, and it is going around me." That is the effect and the power of this energy. I, Juliano, continue to activate this protective energy.

The protective energy and shielding are strengthened through connection with the etheric crystals and the ring of ascension. Your interaction with them helps to stabilize it.

Before I describe the power of these etheric crystals, I will speak of personal healing. The laws and rules for the global level and consciousness also work for you in your own personal development. We continue to work with and offer powerful tools of healing energy for you. This means that any personal problems or chaos that seem to be coming your way can be diverted so that you will stand in the middle of these events, but they will go around you.

Remember that you have an inner core and an inner shield of protection. Therefore, do not identify with fear. Remember the example of stampeding animals. The destructive energy of the stampede does not touch you, even though you are surrounded by the energy. Hold that comparison.

On a personal level, you stand on a protective level, and the chaotic energy goes around you even though you still hold fear, even though you may think it will affect you. On a higher fifth-dimensional awareness, the chaotic bypasses you. Helio-ah, my dear feminine Arcturian colleague, will speak to you about the holographic aspect of this formula of change.

G reetings, my dear Arcturian starseeds. I am Helio-ah. I have been working with many of you already because your consciousness has shifted dramatically into a state that I call "holographic awareness." Holographic awareness is a central force for your personal healing and it is a central force for planetary healing.

Stated simply, the part represents and has the ability to access the greater whole. When you experience only a part, you also can be closed off from the whole. If you are activated, then you can open up the corridors—the channels—to unlock the codes within to access the whole energy of yourself.

Ultimately you, as a planetary being, can activate the whole energy of the planet. You can see the overall picture of the planet and then you can go into the galactic and universal level. The idea of holographic healing implies that holographic images of both lower and higher vibrations were inputted into your system. However, the earlier holographic images from childhood that were implanted or inputted were performed at a time when you could not discriminate and when you did not have starseed consciousness.

This idea of input and implanting has a charged energy. Implanting implies that an external source (that may be of an alien nature) interceded and placed into your mind holographic images of reality of who you are and who you are to become. Some of you have holographic images of simply Earthly aberrant thoughts that were given to you by your parents that could be just as destructive as alien-inputted thoughts. The removal or shifting of negative images that were placed there can activate a powerful shift.

On a planetary basis, holographic images of the planet can also be shifted. Earlier images by the great masters such as the Buddha, Jesus, the great Native teachers many other high Hindu beings and the great spiritual teachers of today can holographically be activated from their past work.

Many of you now are connecting holographically with powerful beings through your channelings. You are connecting with their (i.e. Jesus') imagery.

Channeling is a holographic connection. The work of earlier masters and beings on this planet is being reintroduced continually through many channelings and connections.

I am proud that you can work with this energy. You can connect with your soul family. From previous lifetimes, you can reactivate positive holographic images from your soul family. You can introduce those images of yourself into your holographic healing chamber energy field.

## EXERCISE: ACTIVATE SOUL STAR FAMILY AWARENESS

To introduce a holographic energy slide into your current holographic work will have a dramatic effect on your overall consciousness—especially since you are working in starseed consciousness. The soul family is also the star family.

Activate that soul star family awareness and begin to holographically receive that input. Just as Juliano said, a higher vibrational thought entered into the mental field of the Earth can overcome lower thoughts—even though the lower thoughts are thought by more people.

In holographic work, the soul imagery from your family of soul star sisters and brothers can be downloaded into your current holographic mindset. I, Helio-ah, now call all of you who hear and read these words to open to your soul and star family. Begin and request a holographic image consciousness and the higher self to be downloaded and activated into your current self on Earth. We will meditate together while you do this.

Holographically connect to the crystal in the crystal temple. I now raise the crystal and it creates a holographic energy field. This is now allowing the Iskalia light mirror to download new imagery from the starseed family that oversees the Earth development, particularly under the direction of Sanat Kumara, who is the great teacher and overseer of the Earth development.

Sanat Kumara brings down a holographic image for the fifth-dimensional Earth through the Iskalia light mirror. This image is a special vibratory field, which has an energetic interconnection of the etheric crystals on the Earth. Your participation in this can activate your own personal holographic consciousness. It will affect your ability to heal. It will affect your ability to be in that position where you bypass all negative events. Yes, it is true that there is an escalation of possibilities of greater chaos on the Earth. Chaos is not going to affect the starseeds. Place yourself within this higher energy field. Meditate and hold this interactive light.

Let the light of the Arcturian frequencies hold the crystals in an interactive force that will manifest a heliographic light energy around this planet. The crystal in the crystal temple is back into the lake.

Your energy has greatly benefited holographically from this light. I, Helio-ah, download a higher fifth-dimensional starseed soul family image of the highest frequency from your soul group into each of your consciousnesses now. Hold that light. More importantly, hold that image from your highest light self. This is Helio-ah. Now Metatron will speak to you.

S*halom. Shalom. Shalom.* Greetings, I am Metatron. The opening to this holographic self can be activated by tonal words and sounds. They activate within your system a decalcification so that whatever is blocked neurologically becomes unblocked. There are certain tones and sounds that will let you become holographically connected with higher energies.

I am making some new sacred sounds for you. Think that you are "opening" as you hear these tones. These are new tones. *Ana b'co-ach.* [Hebrew words meaning "please strength now!" repeated.] Let your vessel be strengthened so that you can hold this new energy. Let yourself be strengthened by the new holographic, higher consciousness, which you can now hold. This is a special, spiritual strength.

I send a circle of light around each of you now. *Ana b'co-ach.* Your vessel is strengthened and new codes have been activated and unlocked to the highest connection with your soul light. Our friend Chief White Eagle will speak with you. This is Metatron.

H*ey ya ho hey!* I am Chief White Eagle. I call on the Buffalo Dreamer, the White Buffalo Calf Woman, to holographically appear through the etheric crystals that have been reactivated this evening. I ask that her image, in a visionary way, emerge from each crystal. Starseeds in each area will receive guidance, light and visionary images from White Buffalo Calf Woman. This will be a fantastic experience.

Her time as the bringer of the feminine Messianic light is here. She is drawn to your crystal work with the Arcturians. I call on White Buffalo

Calf Woman now. Hey ya ho hey! Let her feminine light be with you. Hey ya ho hey!

## FEMININE ENERGY ACTIVATION

We are gathering our energy together to activate the feminine Buffalo Woman energy that is directly connected with the galactic kachina. This feminine power will bring a holographic awareness and knowledge and a new holographic healing light to all of you, both personal and planetary.

I call on the Buffalo Woman light to be a personal guide and a protector for each of you in your traveling throughout this planet. Many of you will travel, speak and teach greatly. My heart is open to your receptivity to the White Buffalo Calf Woman. Let her, if you so desire, cohabitate with you as a spiritual guide and teacher. Do not be afraid to channel her. Do not be afraid to welcome her. She will bring a new guidance and a new light.

I know the Central Sun is a feminine energy and the messianic healing light will be transported in feminine activation. I will teach more about this in the coming months.

We have great feminine teachers among the starseeds. There are great soul teachers here now on Earth. Many of you have connections to Lemuria and Atlantis and were great teachers there. Now you, through the holographic work that Juliano, Metatron and Helio-ah are doing, will be activated into your Lemurian and Atlantean greater selves. Many powerful images and visions await you. I, Chief White Eagle, already see many higher visions coming to this planet and coming to each of you.

I honor your work and I honor your commitment to the Buffalo Woman light. I am Chief White Eagle. Ho!

## Chapter 18

# EXPANDING THE HEART AND THE ORIGIN OF THOUGHT

### Chief Buffalo Heart, Archangel Michael, Juliano and the Arcturians

Greetings, I am Chief Buffalo Heart. We are all brothers and sisters. All my words are sacred. I speak the truth to you because you are my brother and sister. We are part of the star family, and there is now a giant tepee over this building and you are sitting with me in my etheric tepee. The Arcturian temple can be another tepee.

The tepee is a galactic shape. The Lakota and Sioux Indians in America received the shape of the tepee from the star family. This galactic shape connects to the star brothers and sisters. It is easy to make, it is cheap to build and it is fun to be in. Everybody is curious. "Can I come inside and look?" And immediately they feel the energy when they step in.

## EXPAND YOUR HEART TO THE SIZE OF A BUFFALO'S

I speak to you about the buffalo and White Buffalo Woman. White Buffalo Calf Woman represents to us a returning of the fifth dimension to the Earth. The buffalo is a sacred animal to us in the way the cow is sacred in India. The buffalo is the giver of life, and in the spiritual way, it represents something special. Look at the buffalo. It has a big heart and this is a symbol of spiritual strength.

Say that you are hurt in a relationship, or that you were hurt as a child. The pain takes up a large portion of the heart. It is still there; it hurts and stops you from developing. In the language and the work of Chief Buffalo Heart, you can enlarge your heart to make it as large as the buffalo heart.

If your heart is bigger, the pain you carry is a small percentage of the total of your heart. If you have a small heart, then the pain may take up to 40 percent of your heart and you feel wounded. If your heart is as large as the buffalo heart, then your heart is so large that the pain only takes up 10 percent. Do you not think that is an easy way to handle pain? Just enlarge your heart; make your heart like a buffalo's because it is a powerful animal.

There is also a white buffalo, which is the special buffalo of the White Buffalo Calf Woman. There are now several white buffaloes born in the United States. This is a powerful sign that White Buffalo Calf Woman will return.

I know that you can expand your mind just by your thoughts. Any pain that you have can be minimized when you expand your heart. Visualize your heart expanding now. Think of the biggest problem in your life that causes you pain and see that pain within the context of your enlarged buffalo heart.

What does it mean to have a power animal? The power animal has powers from the spirit realm. For example, the fox is smart and quick, so if you have the fox as a power animal, you can activate those characteristics within yourself. If you have the deer as your power animal, then you can use the quickness and the agility of the deer. If you have the buffalo as your power animal, then you can use the buffalo heart as a guide and teacher for you.

Let the vision of the buffalo heart come to you. Maybe you will receive the vision of another animal besides the buffalo. The power animal is like a spirit guide to you.

I feel the pain of the animals that are stranded. Many animals are dying now in the world because of the environment. I look at the buffalo heart, knowing that it experiences the pain the other animals are feeling. You may think that you do not want to feel the pain of these animals. By your carrying their pain, this helps them. If you use the buffalo heart, it will not take up much space in your heart. You will be compassionate.

I know that you like to do ceremonies. You can speak to your power animal in a ceremony and your power animal will speak to you. They will send you a message. Chief White Eagle said, "You must gather your personal power, and the more you work with the power animal, the more you take on your personal power." I am Chief Buffalo Heart.

G reetings. This is Archangel Michael. You are living in the third dimension. You are living in a world that is polarized and filled with illusion. The illusion is that you are separate from the One Being. Therefore, you do not feel divine because you do not feel connected to the divine. That is the condition of being on this planet. So a part of your lesson is to learn that you are connected. The laws of the third-dimension work within the reality of duality. But you can transcend the dichotomy of duality through unity thinking.

There are beautiful affirmations in Kabbalah that help you with this. One of my favorites is Master of the Universe. By repeating this mantra, you acknowledge that God is over everything and that you are part of his divine plans. Maybe you do not feel it, but you still can acknowledge this truth by calling on the master of the universe.

All fifth-dimensional beings and higher are divine. You cannot get through the gates of the fifth dimension unless your energy is of a high vibration. You can go to the fourth dimension and be of a lower vibration, but you cannot have negative thoughts on the fifth dimension. The most important thing in your life is to fulfill your spiritual plan.

## PROTECTING YOURSELF AND THE ORIGIN OF THOUGHT

Another subject is the relationship between your immune system and the work that you do on Earth. The immune system is a challenge for everyone. There are many reasons for this and I think you could probably guess some of them. Juliano gave you an exercise called "pulsing." This is the best spiritual exercise that we know to improve your immune system. You do the contraction and bring inside you all of the energy of the illness, and then you expel these lower vibrations out of your energy field. There have been amazing recoveries using this.

There are many ways to protect yourself from negative energy. The most effective way we know is the cosmic egg exercise. Your energy field is being bombarded with different energies. There are negative forces that may attempt to attach to you. All energies that come to you must answer this question: "Do you come to me from the light of Christ?" If they say "No" or "Let me think about it," then send them away quickly. There is also the method of the white light protection that only allows energies in the Christ light to enter your energy field.

Some of you may have lower cohabitated spirits from other lifetimes. This becomes more complicated, but even then, the spirits have a hard time staying connected to you when you raise your vibration.  Be careful around shamans who offer to remove negative spirits.  Some of them will remove the negative energy from you, and at the point when you are most vulnerable, they will attach personally to you and become parasites of your energy.  Not all shamans do this, but some do.

The origin of thought is God.  God created this world in his mind with thought. We speak of the twelfth dimension where you do not manifest a form and you exist only in thought.  It is hard for you now to imagine existing without a body and simply in thought.  There is a paradox.  The paradox is when you have no body and when you exist in thought, you actually become closer to the Creator.  In reality, all seek to become closer to the Creator.  Even in higher dimensions, the Arcturians are looking for ways to be closer to God.  The higher the dimension is, the closer you can be to God.

There is a school of thought in Kabbalah that says that all that is going on now is part of God's dream.  I find that interesting, but it can make you crazy when you think about it.  What does it mean to be part of God's dream?  It is a way of explaining that you are related to God through thought, but I take another view of this.

I would seek to help you have love.  And you may say that the first thought or the first energy that created the world was love from the heart.  God is love.  I am Archangel Michael.

Greetings, I am Juliano.  We are the Arcturians.  The light energy of Brazil is primordial, connecting energy to Source, and by that I mean that the biosphere life energy of this planet is deeply tied to Brazil because of the land, the rivers and the forest.  It is a primordial energy.  If you think about the first person on the Earth, then you think of Adam.  The life force energy of Brazil is like the primordial life matter, like the soup of the biosphere.  It is necessary to hold together the energy field of Brazil.  If the Brazil life force collapses, it would cause a domino effect on the rest of the planet.  Maybe Brazil does not accept this responsibility or this power.

Like all countries, Brazil wants to be rich and have great industrial power.  But this country will be smart and realize that they are rich in a special way on this planet.  I believe that the lightworkers there will play a key part in this energy.  Any work that you do in Brazil should be similar to the work in Argentina, which is to connect the biosphere to thought forms. But there is a slight difference in that you need to connect to the primordial forest, the primordial life energy in the jungles. This is Juliano.

## CHAPTER 19

# HEALING LIGHT

Sananda, Archangel Michael and Chief White Eagle

Greetings, I am Sananda. My coming to Earth was a special mission to accelerate the development of humankind. This opportunity was given to me by my Father. The opportunity was to accelerate the karmic process of humankind by assuming the burdens of each individual's ego. This allows many people to ascend. It allows many people to understand that this body you now inhabit is a coat. You can take the coat off and ascend.

## THE LIGHT OF GOD

There are life lessons and there is work to do in order to ascend to the highest level. There is a way to accelerate yourself and surrender to the karmic laws so that you can transcend them. The second purpose has to do with my Father's light. It is so strong that if you sat next to my Father, you could die instantly. I am able to send his light to you in a way that you can easily assimilate.

My brother Moses, the great leader, was near death, and he asked God, "Please let me see your face." God said, "No man can see my face and live. You may see the shadow of my figure. Turn away from me, look at that rock over there, I will pass by you, and you will see my shadow on the rock. That is all that you can bear to experience." Moses was so happy to have that experience. No man since has been able to see the shadow of God.

The light of God is so strong that it must be stepped down. You ask, "What is the light of God?" God has no form, yet we only understand the emanation of light, which is his essence. If his essence stopped emanating, the universe would be over in a second. The rabbis had a way of describing this. They said that God's eye is open all the time, but if God closed his eye just for one second, the world ends. God's light is the substance that keeps the world going.

The Arcturians talk about thought forms. In reality, this world is a thought form. Behind this thought form, there is energy and light. If you were able to experience this now, all you would see would be an energy and light around you. You would see people, not with the faces you now see, but you would see their egg-shaped auras or the colors of their energy field. Behind that, there would just be energy or light. All that light and healing is being generated from God. It is too hard for man to experience this. Even Moses, who was a very high being, could not stand being too close to God. So my Father said "Let them come to me through my son. They will be close to me if they come through my son. They will look at my son, they will embrace my son, and they will be grateful that my son is there to help."

I know that people were not embracing me when I was on the Earth, but with my Father's help, we see the future. Many people have been able to come closer to my Father through me. So this was the second part of my mission.

And now the third part of my mission is this: I come to help with the ascension. I oversee the ascension work, and I would like to help guide all of you to the fifth dimension. I feel your energy and I hope you feel mine. I feel great tears among you. They are not tears of sadness. They are tears of joy of being together, for when you are with me, you will not feel cut off from the Father. This is his gift to you. It is my service for you. This is Sananda.

**T**his is Archangel Michael. Multidimensional healing starts when you connect to your fifth-dimensional body. The fifth-dimensional body is actually already healed, so what you do is take your third-dimensional spirit with you, and that body carries the imprints of all diseases and problems that you may have on the third dimension. You take that spirit body and send it to the fifth-dimensional garden or the fifth-dimensional healing chamber.

Fifth-dimensional healing is on a faster and more elaborate level than third-dimensional healing. The healing of your spirit body that came from the third dimension accelerates higher. When your spirit returns to the third dimension, that energy is carried back into your body, and like osmosis, it filters back into your third-dimensional body and starts a healing process. This is multidimensional healing. Multipresence is when people are present both in the higher fifth dimension and in the third dimension. This is Archangel Michael.

G reetings, this is Chief White Eagle. The shape of the tepee and the shape of the octagon are both power structures. The Arcturian temple incorporates both power structures in one building. They are complicated to build and expensive. Quite frankly, there is no structure like it now on Earth. You ask, "What is the relationship between the octagon and the tepee?" I would say this: The tepee has a high point where it reaches out to the stars. The octagon helps to ground it, so they work well together.

The southern cross is a direct link to the Central Sun. The top of the tepee connects to the southern cross at a certain point, and that energy comes down through the tepee and is grounded in the octagon. Finally, the Iskalia light mirror is generally used for planetary healing – not necessarily for personal healing. This is Chief White Eagle.

## CHAPTER 20

# ARCTURIAN PULSING TECHNIQUE

Juliano, the Arcturians and Archangel Metatron

G reetings, I am Juliano. We are the Arcturians. I will speak of the fifth dimension and spiritual technology. We are beings who live on the fifth dimension. You are on the third dimension, but you are preparing to ascend to the fifth dimension. We see your energy fields, which are vibrating at a higher speed. When you vibrate at a higher speed, you have the ability to go to a higher dimension.

You are starseeds, and that means you relate to the star family. We are brothers and sisters of spirit to you. Our teachings have to do with spiritual technology. We have worked with your energy fields and understand them well.

## MEDITATION: AURA CONTRACTION

Think of your energy field. You can control the shape of your energy field by your thoughts. Thoughts are the most powerful energies in the universe. Thoughts travel faster than the speed of light. What is most important today is that you understand how your thoughts can shape your energy fields. This is part of the new evolution of humankind.

In the galaxy, there is a special powerful shape of the aura. All spiritual beings in the galaxy know of this shape. We call the shape of your powerful energy field the cosmic egg. The shape of the egg represents perfection in the higher realms. Begin to visualize a line around your energy field. This line is approximately seven inches from your physical body. It is shaped like an egg around your body. Visualize this as a perfect egg-shape line around your body. Any holes in your aura are immediately repaired. Any attachments to your aura are immediately dissolved. I, Juliano, send a special blue light into your cosmic egg energy field so that this egg energy field fills with the blue light from the Arcturians.

Let us meditate together, holding this blue light in your energy field. I, Juliano, open up a corridor connecting this room to the fifth-dimensional Starship Athena. This corridor is like a tunnel, and the tunnel connects from the third dimension to the fifth dimension. I now send down more of this beautiful blue light into the room. This blue light comes down through the corridor and into your cosmic egg lightbody. You are all beautiful in your cosmic-egg-shaped energy bodies.

The ascension includes personal and planetary healing. First, we want to work on your personal healing. You have evened out your cosmic egg energy so it is very smooth. You can control your aura by your thoughts. If I say to you, "contract your aura," you can take your cosmic egg and contract it within one inch of your physical body. Right now, it is about five to seven inches from your body. When I say, "expand," then bring it back out seven to nine inches from your body.

Believe me, a one-inch contraction raises your vibrations quickly to a higher level. We call this technique the "Arcturian pulsing technique." We take this one step further and contract the aura into a place inside the body, and all of your consciousness comes into your stomach. Then, as you expand, all the lower vibrational energy in your body is discharged. This is a powerful healing. Diseases or blockages in the body are discharged out and sent to the cosmos. Are you ready to begin the pulsing?

Using the special blue light from the Arcturian corridor, contract your aura to one inch from your body. Hold that contraction. Now release and expand to six, seven, eight, nine inches outward. You can reach out that far. Now contract again. Bring this energy within one inch from your body. Then come into your body. All lower densities and all blockages are pushed into your stomach area.

Maybe you have a problem with your lungs. Push the energy into the center of the stomach. Contract it into a ball of light in your stomach. Hold that energy, and now expand. Expand out, and all of the densities are released out to the aura, out to seven inches from your body and even ten inches. The energy that is of a lower vibration is discharged. Do one more cycle.

Contract your energy now into the center of your stomach. Hold the energy. Now expand—expand outward. Your aura is pulsing. There is a cosmic pulse of your aura, just like you have a pulse in your veins, and so there is a pulse in your energy field. The pulse in your energy field has been raised. You are ready for light work.

## ADVANCE YOUR SOUL DEVELOPMENT

You have come to Earth now to activate your soul development. The highest soul development possible on the Earth leads to your ascension. Ascension is the simultaneous transformation of your energy field to a fifth-dimensional vibration. At that point, people would look at you and see your physical body shimmering. That means that it is going in and out of the fifth dimension.

When your body is shimmering in the fifth dimension, then people in the third dimension may find you to be invisible. Many of you can shimmer now. Stop. You must hold the fifth-dimensional vibration to remain in the fifth dimension. When you come to the Stargate, you come to an energy point that allows you to cross the gate and go on to the other side. This happens when you are cut off from your incarnational energy. That means that at that point, you cannot return to your physical body. We will not allow you to cross that line today. But you can approach the Stargate and receive information and energy to advance your soul development. I ask Archangel Metatron to speak to you now and I will return to be with you again. This is Juliano.

Greetings, this is Archangel Metatron. I am an overseer of the Stargate and I help you to connect with your soul lightbody. In this Stargate corridor, you receive soul activation. Visualize the Stargate in your mind. You can visualize it just as a beautiful gateway. *Kadosh Adonai.*

## EXERCISE: PRACTICING THOUGHT PROJECTION

We will talk about thought projection. You can project yourself with thoughts. If I say, "Project your aura or your spirit," then you can send your spirit to another level, but your physical body stays here. I can help you project your energy to the Stargate where you can receive soul information and activation. Imagine that this room is a big circle. Inside this room is like a merry-go-round that goes around very slowly, and as it goes around, you do not feel dizzy. As it slowly moves around in a circle, feel your spirit separating from your physical body. Visualize holy light.

Your spirit rises; you project your spirit to the Stargate. You go to the entrance of the Stargate and we all are sitting in a circle in front of the Stargate. I, Archangel Metatron, open the Stargate a small amount and a beautiful soul light is emitted. It is similar to bright sunlight, but much brighter. Soul light comes from another dimension. You receive this light in your crown chakra. I call this light "holy light," and as you receive this light, you can activate all soul lessons in this lifetime.

You will be able to integrate and advance in your soul work on this planet. On the other side of this corridor, you will complete all of your soul lessons and be prepared to advance rapidly to the next level. I open the door a little more so you can feel this wonderful burst of soul light. [Sounds.]

Look down at your physical body that is below. You will begin to re-enter the physical body. We cannot stay at the Stargate too long. Begin to descend back into your physical body, but stay above it. Do not go into your body yet. As you descend back into your body, stop about three feet above it.

It is important to reenter your body correctly, so try to align your soul light and your spirit in exactly perfect alignment with your body. This will ensure that you get the maximum benefit in your physical body when your spirit reenters. Reenter now.

Remember that the circle in the room is like a merry-go-round. As you go into your body, you notice that the room continues going around in a circle. You have reentered in a good alignment. Many of you have wanted to connect more with your soul purpose and accelerate your soul lessons. This will now happen to you through this activation. I now return you to Juliano. I am Archangel Metatron.

Greetings, I am Juliano. The method used for your personal development is also useful for planetary development. We will help you bring Earth into the fifth dimension.

How can you take the spirit out and bring it back comfortably? First, perhaps in other lifetimes you left because of trauma and were unable to come back. As you do the exercises, you now retrain yourself to leave in a positive way and to come back without fear and trauma. You have not always had positive environments in which to work. Now that you have a safe environment, you need to reassure yourself that you can relax.

Secondly, we are talking about a multidimensional presence. There will be times when you need to change to be in the fifth dimension. There are special protective powers you need when you are in your fifth-dimensional self. When the ascension happens, go immediately to your fifth-dimensional self.

Third, you will need to always look at how you reenter your body. Imagine that your spirit is above your body. Imagine that your spirit body is an exact duplicate of your body so when it comes back in, it must be in perfect alignment. When the spirit comes into your physical body, it should come in perfect alignment with the head, chest, shoulders and so on. You should feel lighter. This illustrates again the importance of perfect alignment. This is Juliano.

## CHAPTER 21

# HOLOGRAPHIC HEALING

Juliano, the Arcturians, Helio-ah and Chief White Eagle

G reetings, this is Juliano. We are the Arcturians. We will now speak about holographic healing. Holographic healing is a multidimensional healing method. Holographic energy is a good way to understand the soul. What you see now as yourself is a part of the whole. It is part of the greater "you."

### HOLOGRAPHICALLY HEALING THE PAST, PRESENT AND FUTURE

We know that in using holographic methods from the fifth dimension, you can access the whole from one part. That means you can heal the whole from one part. This concept is important when we talk about planetary healing. I am happy to speak to you about the healing of Mother Earth because the role of the starseeds includes both personal and planetary healing tasks.

When you heal one part of the Earth, then you can send that energy to all of Earth. From one part, you can access future or past times. We look at the holographic images as ways of accessing the present, the future and the past. We can access the future self, or we can access a future time on Earth when there will be more positive harmony on the planet. You can access a harmonious energy in the future, and then bring that energy back to the present. We use this method for personal and planetary healing.

In your personal past, there have been different experiences, some of which were good and some of which were painful. In holographic healing, we can go back to past times and look at trauma, or we can look at negative experiences and change the memory patterns so that the images and the

163

memories do not negatively affect you now. In holographic healing, you can look at memories as images. We developed a technique called the "holographic deck of cards." Using this method, we can help you go back and look at an image representing memories of the past. It could be any image that you choose. You then take that image out of the deck of cards and put it up on a screen. You can look at the screen just like a computer screen.

Think of the computer program called "Photoshop," where you can modify the color and brightness of a photo image. You can even crop the shape and use other techniques to make the picture look pretty. In holographic healing, you redesign the traumatic image from your past and re-shape it into a more positive and healing image. Then you put the picture back into the deck of cards.

This deck of cards, which contains all of the memories and images from your past, then changes because the image that you took out and reshaped has changed. It is like a wave that comes back into the present. You immediately feel the effects in the present so that the past does not affect you the way it did before. Also, future images can be brought into the present for the purpose of obtaining healing energy.

Let us think that we are now ten years into the future. In the future, you are richer, healthier and more harmonious. This image of yourself in the future can be projected onto the screen of your mind. This future image can be brought into the present and then your present attitudes and abilities can be changed through the accessing of future energy.

## DOWNLOAD POSITIVE IMAGES

We have sophisticated computers on our spaceship, which are called "holographic computers." We can focus the computer on one person and then we can look into that person's future or past. We can even see many events in the future about that person based on the present information in the computers. The holographic computer is a special device to help us in healing, and we call the room or chamber that contains our holographic healing device the "holographic healing chamber."

You can visualize a computer with a joystick or having a dial. You are able to turn the dial to the right and enter the future. When you turn it to the left, then you can go into the past. There is a special button on the right. You press that button and instead of going into the past, you go into past lifetimes. Instead of going into the future, you go into future lifetimes. The holographic healing chamber is sophisticated.

You can think of the room as a small phone booth with a small computer and a screen in it. You can do many different things when you go into the past, present or the future. Imagine that there is such a healing chamber for the healing of a planet. Instead of the healing chamber being a small booth, you need a big theater for the planetary healings. Again, the same process is true. You turn the dial to the right and go into future planetary time. Turn the dial to the left and you go into past planetary time.

This is where it gets complicated. The Earth has a universal unconscious and it is actually like your subconscious. When the Earth healing starts, the images that are placed on the screen of the Earth can go into the unconscious and can cause a major positive change in the Earth. This downloading of images is actually happening all the time on Earth. What is different is that the energies and images being put into the Earth are random and often are of lower vibrations.

On television, you see violence, earthquakes and all the terrible events that will occur. You see those pictures and they enter into your unconscious and into the Earth's unconscious. In this way, you are communicating with the Earth with negative inputs. The good news is that you can change those images. We call the ability to communicate with Earth "telepathic planetary communication," and this telepathic communication for healing Earth is also known as biorelativity. The key to Earth's healing is to communicate new telepathically positive images. Imagine there are millions of people on Earth, as there are so many different countries. There are so many negative thought patterns that for you to change the telepathic level, you must use intense energy and effort.

Here is news from the Arcturians: We will teach you special spiritual techniques that are so powerful that they can overcome the normal thought patterns from others that are negative. When we gather people into groups, like the groups of forty, and we use the holographic healing methods, then we help you gain special healing powers so that you can become planetary healers.

First we teach you to use techniques for personal healing so that you are familiar with the methodology. This includes being able to go into past images from trauma and enter into and pull out positive images from the future. It is powerful and spiritual to do this. There is even a technique to amplify the images once you bring certain images to consciousness.

I shall practice two exercises with you. The following is the exercise for personal healing. Visualize the Arcturian Starship Athena. Using the same technique as before, visualize the room turning around in a circle and your spirit can leave your body.

As your spirit leaves your body, feel yourself rising through the corridor and immediately coming into the healing room in our starship. In this room are many small little booths. They are holographic healing chambers and we will ask Helio-ah to work with you in the healing chambers.

reetings, this is Helio-ah. My special technique and expertise is in holographic healing. On Arcturus, we actually call it "heliographic" healing because "helio" refers to the energy from the Central Sun. The Central Sun is the area that is the center of the galaxy and it is the source of all spiritual light in the galaxy.

### EXERCISE: HOLOGRAPHIC HEALING

Now you each are in your own holographic healing chamber. We will work with this lifetime. In front of you is a big dial, and when you turn your dial to the left, you go back into your past. If you turn the dial left all the way to 6 PM, then you return to your birth.

Each turn of the dial goes back a certain number of years. Maybe you have had trauma or something that happened to you in the past that really appears to block your energy now. Turn the dial to the left until you come to the time of your life when that event happened. If it happened when you were five years old, you would have to turn the dial way back. But if you only turned it to an event that happened three years ago, then you would not turn the dial back so far. Remember, you do not really change the event, but rather you are going to change the image of that event in your mental computer.

Turn the dial back to the event that you wish to alter. Notice that the image of that event will appear on the screen. Take a minute to allow yourself to do this. Try to get as many details as possible of the image. Visualize colors, pictures of people or whatever is needed to bring that image on to the main screen on the computer. You have taken one image that represents the trauma and brought that image on to the screen.

Now, just like in the computer software Photoshop, change the image so that it looks more beneficial to you and your development. Maybe you had a pain or somebody hurt you physically, and you might see yourself unable to bear the pain. Or maybe you see yourself very contracted. Now change the image so the same event happens to you, but you do not experience it as a contraction. You are able to experience and "image" the event without negativity.

Create a new image that reflects that shift. Hold that image now and make it brighter. To the very right on the computer is a button that says "save." Press that button and save the image. That image now goes back into the past when the trauma first happened. But now the new image and new information comes into yourself holographically, and that image is now seeded in your past, but it is a new, more positive image. With that technique, it will update all the images after this image has occurred. And it will have a positive effect on your present. Allow this change to occur now. This will actually change the way you view yourself.

Now turn the dial to the future. Turn it a small amount to the right to December 12, 2012. This is the corridor for that alignment event. In the beginning of the exercise, you set an intention to have soul development. You asked to have your soul development accelerated, so see yourself on December 12, 2012, and you have accomplished, you have been integrated and you have been successful at this soul development. If you see how you look with that success, hold that image and see the happiness on your face.

Press the save button and now that image is in your future. We will bring that image in the future back to the present. So even though that positive image will be in the future, we can now bring that energy from the future into the present. You immediately will feel the effects of the future time.

Turn your dial back to the present and your present image has shifted to a higher form. You have felt the effects of a shift in the past, and you have integrated energy from the future and accomplished many things for your soul. You have done this in the holographic healing chamber.

Leave the chamber and begin to descend into your physical body through the corridor. Return and enter into your body in a way that is in good alignment as you are integrating so much.

You will have a seventy-two-hour holographic time period in which you can integrate what you have accomplished and you will see the effects within the first three days. There is a deeper level that you will experience as a soft energy. I am Helio-ah. Chief White Eagle will now speak with you.

**W**e send you the high eagle feather—the white eagle feather. We know that for change to occur, you must raise your personal power. Personal power means that you have access to higher energy. You could go to a shaman, or maybe you could go to a special teacher to help yourselves access more power. The bottom line is that you want to raise your personal power use—that personal power to heal yourself and the Earth. In the ways of the Native people, we use prayer as one tool for accessing personal power.

## YOUR SOUL MISSION

Dear Father, Mother, Creator, we ask that the healing power of your light may point to each of us. Let your light raise our vibration, let us bring ourselves to a higher level of power as we want to help heal the Earth and be of service to you. Let our power animals appear to us. Let them increase our personal energy.

We ask that we each be given a vision. This vision will help us be in alignment with the higher light. This vision will appear to us within the next twenty-four hours.

We use the method of talking to Spirit all the time. We also talk all the time to Mother Earth. We ask Mother Earth where it is that she is blocked and where we, as a man or woman, can go to help unblock the Earth.

You are into your soul mission when you are given instructions on what to do. Maybe you are being asked to travel somewhere to heal some part of the Earth. Maybe you will be asked to do a ceremony in Argentina. Maybe you will be asked to go to Lago Puelo, Argentina, and work with the energy there.

The Arcturians have helped to bring down etheric crystals to the planet. We of the Native people know how to work with this energy. We know that all the Earth's ley lines are interconnected and that the energy in one part can go through the whole Earth. A strong light force in Lago Puelo can generate a healing light to the whole planet.

Mother Earth, I am Chief White Eagle. I ask that you show each person what he or she can do to heal Mother Earth. They all love Mother Earth the way we do. And they are ready to do the service that you ask. Give them a vision. Maybe you will show them some other sign of what they are to do.

I, Chief White Eagle, allow you under the galactic kachina to come to this corridor here. The galactic kachina is the intermediary between the third dimension and the Central Sun. She is a messenger to bring down to the Earth the energy and light from the Central Sun.

The Central Sun is the source of our spiritual light to this planet. Now the Earth is coming into a more aligned position with the Central Sun. You, as lightworkers, can help anchor this light, for without you anchoring this light, it cannot stay.

Some of you like to dance on the Earth and some like to use the rattles. Use these methods and each of you will gain more personal power in your visions. I am Chief White Eagle.

## CHAPTER 22

# BIOSPHERIC ALCHEMY AND CRYSTAL TECHNOLOGY

### Juliano and the Arcturians

G reetings, this is Juliano. We are the Arcturians. We must look clearly at the condition of the Earth and the stability of the biosphere. The biosphere is an energetic belt that supports all life forms. We have visited many planets and have seen biospheres collapse. This is a sad event to watch.

### HOLES IN EARTH'S AURA

The Earth's biosphere has many problems, some of them you see and understand from television—such as global warming, strange weather patterns, earthquakes and cyclones. But there are events that you do not see. We have studied the Earth's biosphere and we see rifts in the energy fields of Earth. We call them "space-time rifts."

Think for a moment about the human aura. Understand that the aura has, or can have, a hole in it. If somebody has used drugs such as cocaine or methamphetamines, then after a while their energy field will have a hole and the life force of the person is drained from them.

When you see this person, you immediately know that they have a hole in their aura. People do not generally think of the Earth's aura, but remember, the Earth is a living energy spirit and it is subject to holes in its aura just like a person. We call some of these holes space-time rifts.

These holes can be created from nuclear bombs, and actually even the bombs underground have created big problems. Right now on Earth, there is a major space-time rift in Chernobyl, Russia. This is a major disaster area. But there are other events besides bombs that create space-time rifts.

Iraq is one example of an area that possesses a hole in the Earth's aura. Think of the galaxy and you know perhaps about black holes. Whatever goes into the black hole does not come out. You get nothing back. You put an object into the black hole and then you say "goodbye." We do not take sides and say who is right or who is wrong. We do not make a judgment about this. We simply describe what we see, and this area around Iraq has acted like a black hole.

We want to make our judgments known about nuclear technology. We do not want Earth people to bring nuclear technology into outer space. Whatever they bring to outer space will affect other systems. Now we have a situation in which there are several space-time rifts around Earth. This is not healthy for Earth and the biosphere. Auric holes must be corrected because these holes cause the life force to leave the body. We must think about how to cure the space-time rift on Earth. Most people on Earth do not even think about this, except the starseeds and planetary healers.

This is a new concept that we talked about several years ago. That is, people who are starseeds can help heal the planet, and they can accomplish this by doing certain spiritual exercises and connecting with certain energies in the galaxy.

## HUMANITY'S ROLE IN PLANETARY HEALING

I previously described the Central Sun. This is a special energy light from there that comes to Earth, and there are beautiful power spots that can receive this energy. There is one other ingredient that makes the change possible for healing. On one hand, we have the energy from the Central Sun, and on the other hand, we have the people who want to heal Earth. The third ingredient necessary to complete the healing is labeled alchemical consciousness. Alchemy is a philosophical study of mixing ingredients to make gold. It is a big mystery how to get the ingredients to equal gold. If you figure out how to do this, you can become very rich.

In planetary healing, it is your galactic consciousness that is the special alchemical ingredient that makes the healing work. This means that you have to reach an altered state of consciousness, and your altered state of consciousness is an ingredient in the change. This galactic consciousness is an altered state and an interactive consciousness with the Earth's spirit.

Let us speak about the evolution of humanity. We call humankind the Adam species. Because Earth's biosphere is in danger, so humanity is in danger. Man will only be able to survive on Earth if humankind integrates galactic consciousness into his awareness. This represents the next stage of development of humans. Those who have this understanding in their consciousness are at the forefront of the evolution of Adam. This galactic consciousness represents the next required evolutionary step. It also means that man can interact with the spirit of Earth for healing the biosphere.

Now I will tell you more about Arcturus. We have special spiritual masters who work twenty-four hours a day (that is just an expression to mean all the time) to spiritually connect with our planet. And they communicate with the planet telepathically. This telepathic communication is necessary for making adjustments to the biosphere of Arcturus. These masters send special energy to the spirit of our planet so we are able to keep a balance that works for the planet and for us.

Can you imagine Earth meditators doing this? Can you imagine the United Nations appointing twenty people to continually meditate on the Earth, focusing on planetary needs? And that these meditators would then give a report and that the governments of the world would follow their advice?

This is exactly what is needed now on Earth. We see that you who are willing to expand represent the first prototype of the new human. I speak of biorelativity, which is the way you begin to interact with the planet. You can work to heal the biosphere and bring the Earth into a homeostasis.

## UTILIZING ARCTURIAN TECHNOLOGY

You have all seen the picture of Earth from the Moon. This has been a big accomplishment of science to bring this image to humanity. This image gives you an opportunity to work with the entire energy field of the Earth, and then you can begin to project healing into the entire Earth.

The ascended masters have created the ring of ascension. The ring of ascension is a halo of light around the Earth. You can refer to it as an aura in the etheric realm. This ring of ascension helps download light from the fifth dimension to Earth. The starseeds can help distribute this energy. The ring of ascension is etheric, but for it to manifest on Earth, starseeds must work continually with it. You, as starseeds, can anchor this light from the ring of ascension onto the Earth. Visualize now the halo around Earth. You have all seen the picture of Earth from the Moon. Have that image in your mind and keep imagining that ring of ascension around Earth.

Another Arcturian spiritual technology focuses on the etheric crystals. These are crystals that actually etherically connect to the fifth dimension. Using crystals is a way to download fifth-dimensional energy into Earth. This helps bring more fifth-dimensional light into the Earth's biosphere.

In order for Earth healing to occur, you must have a new spiritual paradigm. This paradigm is called the "Sacred Triangle." It is the representation of three powerful spiritual sides: the regular mystical Earth religious energy, the Native people's technology and spiritual energy and the galactic spirituality that includes the Arcturians.

Through this paradigm, we have a way to successfully activate all the healings that are needed to bring Earth back to health. Fifth-dimensional thinking contains answers to the problems of Earth. Now you can help visualize and conceive of the solution. You may ask to get solutions to diseases, water pollution or global warming. These new answers and energy can come to you. They will bring energy and solutions that have not been considered before.

Think of the third dimension as a sphere and then think of the fifth dimension as a sphere. If these two spheres touch, then there is a huge energy exchange. The etheric crystals help attract the sphere of the fifth dimension to the third-dimensional Earth.

When the two dimensions interact and touch, then this becomes an opportunity for ascension. It means that you can ascend fairly quickly and easily in that environment. This will give you an opportunity to practice multidimensional being. That means that you can be in both dimensions and you can have consciousness in both areas at the same time. Then you can help download the fifth-dimensional energy and light.

This is a short summary of the Arcturian technologies and the healing of space-time rifts. To heal the rifts requires that you use the ring of ascension and also your thought projections must even out and close the holes that are around. This work involves projecting your thoughts to heal the Earth's aura. I am Juliano. We are the Arcturians.

# CHAPTER 23

# SOUL PSYCHOLOGY

## Vywamus

Greetings, I am Vywamus. I am a fifth-dimensional master who specializes in soul psychology. Does that not sound impressive? We love to look at the relationship between the emotional problems that you have and the soul lessons you are attempting to learn. The first step is to acknowledge that you do have some problems. I know that some of you will say, "Vywamus, I don't have any problems. Please go on to the next person. It is not me." If you have no problems, then you need not be on the Earth.

### YOUR SOUL'S EXPERIENCE ON EARTH

People come to Earth to learn. If you knew all that you needed to know, you would not have to come here. That says something about the energy you have. The energy on Earth is dense, which means that after a while, life and this Earth energy wears you down.

This is a planet of polarization and duality. It is a planet that has a great deal of negative energy. Believe me, the negative energy affects you. So let us say we get over the first hurdle, the first step, and you say "Okay, I do have some emotional problems. Heal me Vywamus." I hold my hand over your head and say, "Yes, you are healed." And you say, "Aha, thank you Vywamus, thank you."

It is so easy, and yet I would not do that because I do not want your karma. It is yours, not mine. If somebody is trying to heal you, they had better be extremely high to take on your karma. Is this not what Jesus did? He said, "I take on the karma of a man and then man can be healed." And do you know how men thanked Jesus for this? Think

175

about that. They were not nice to him. The principle is that we help *you* solve your problems.

The number one problem on Earth is fear. There is fear of being separated from the One. This began in the Garden of Eden when Adam and Eve were with the light and then they were kicked out. Fear expresses itself in many different ways. The first big fear is the fear of death. Then there is the fear of failure. Another big problem is poor self-esteem. Or, to put it another way, people do not feel worthy. People do not feel like they are good enough. People do not love themselves.

You may be surprised to hear this, but people come to Earth to learn how to deal with these problems. In fact, when I came to visit Earth today, as I was flying by the North Pole, I saw souls lined up, desiring to come into the Earth. Who would want to come to a planet like this? The biosphere is ready to fall apart, there is overpopulation and there are probably fifty wars going on right now and nobody knows how to stop them. This is just the beginning. So why would somebody want to come here? Would you not rather go to a peaceful planet?

Your soul needs this experience. You have free will. And this planet is a freewill zone. You can come here and choose what you want to do. If you want to jump off a plane with a parachute, then that is great. If you want to climb the mountains, then that is great. You have a choice.

## FINDING YOUR SOUL MISSION

Think about the third dimension and the fifth dimension. In the fifth dimension, what you think happens immediately. In the third dimension, it does not happen immediately, and thank God it does not! Recall all the bad thoughts you have. You are driving down the street and a man cuts in front of you in his car and you say, "Go to ___" Then that would happen. It would not be good for you and it would create bad karma. Actions are slowed down in the third dimension. You can have bad thoughts, but it may take a year for them to activate. Thank God there are angels, because if all your bad thoughts came true, you would be in deep trouble.

There are people who offer self-help courses. They say, "Send me some money and I will teach you how to think right." Yes, even here there is a sign, "Make a million dollars through real estate." Why not? Well, it does not happen that way on the third dimension.

If you ask for something like a million dollars or a new car, make sure that you say, "If it is in my highest interest." Think about that. What if you came to Earth to learn how to live in poverty? Maybe in your last life-time, you were a Donald Trump personality. Now you say, "I will come to be a Gandhi character. I will have nothing." It would not be in Gandhi's interest to be a millionaire. Nobody would listen to him if he were driving a Mercedes Benz. He gave up all his suits and became a poor man.

Remember, it is what is "in my best interest" that is important, so do not make a decision until you know what your soul lesson is in this lifetime. If your soul lesson is in coordination with your desire, then that is great. But if it is not, then you do not need to have that material thing. That means that everything you do, everything you think, should be based on what your soul mission or soul lesson is. That is where I come in: Vywamus, the soul psychologist, to help you find out what your mission is.

You know the TV program "Mission Impossible." This is how some of you feel. You came into the Earth on an impossible mission. You say, "I cannot do it. I cannot do it. I cannot learn these lessons. I cannot finish this work. I am not good enough. I will do it in the next lifetime." Consider this: Do you want to come back to Earth in fifty years? Do you think it will be better fifty years from now, based on what you see now? Maybe, maybe not, but in this lifetime you have a great opportunity.

You have the freedom and the ability to work on yourself with total dedication. Do you know how many times you had lives where you were a slave, a prisoner? Maybe you were in Egypt as a slave building the pyramids. I have to laugh. People ask me "What is my past life? Oh, maybe I had a past life with Jesus or as an apostle. It was a great life." I ask, "Which part did you like? Was it when you were crucified? Was that the good part? Or when the Romans put you in jail? Did you like that?" I know that people have made great sacrifices. Fortunately, you are not required to do that now. I just want to point out that in other lifetimes you may not have had the freedom you have now. Maybe you do not have as many excuses now. So let us look at the problems.

## IDENTIFYING PROBLEMS

When you have a blockage at the top of the head, it means you had a problem in a previous lifetime. This means that you were forbidden to connect with higher energies. Many women were mistreated for their psychic abilities and sometimes they were even tortured. You have heard of the concept of self-preservation. When you come into another lifetime, you make sure that you survive by using self-preservation.

The soul blocks the crown chakra so you do not get into that situation again. But, of course, the soul also wants you to learn to connect with the universal light, with cosmic light, with trust. Here we have a situation where you are aware of the block. Do you know how lucky you are to be aware of the block? Imagine if you had the block and were not aware of it. That would be far worse. So now you ask, "How do I remove the block?"

There are two methods. The first method is with a soul regression. The second method is to go to your inner child and say, "Do not worry, everything will be all right. If we remove this block, you will be fine. You will not be killed."

Learn how to talk to this part of yourself, which is a real skill. But understand that the blockage is there for self-protection. To remove the block, you must assure your little child that he or she will be safe when you open yourself up to this energy. If you do not convince your inner child of this, then you will not be able to remove the block.

We will now speak of the emotional body. You have an emotional body, a physical body, a spirit body and a mental body. Why do some people neglect their emotional body? We meet a lot of people who understand the ascension and have great abilities, but their emotional body is blocked.

There are many reasons for blockages, but basically it comes down to this: The emotional body has to grow together with the spirit body. If the spirit body grows ten feet and the emotional body grows only one foot, then you have a problem. They must grow together equally.

Some people do not think that it is spiritual to deal with an emotional body. Maybe it is not as much fun; it can be dramatic or maybe the person is just stubborn. There is no need to be stubborn. I am extremely compassionate.

Some of you are actually empaths. That means you feel other people's energy. That is good and bad because some of the energy you feel that other people have is not pleasant. I have seen people shut down their emotional body because they did not like the emotions they were absorbing from other people. But this ability to feel other people is essential for psychic ability. You have to be empathic in order to be psychic. You have to learn certain defense techniques.

Soul attachments are one of my specialties. You have heard of visitations, but there are people who inhabit your body or your soul. If there is a person who is using drugs, alcohol or something like that for a long time, their physical body could have another soul come into it. That other co-inhabited soul can direct the original person to perform harmful actions. You see many examples of this on Earth today – especially in America where people go crazy in a school, or maybe in another place where somebody goes to work, acts crazy and hurts people. I help people detach from any attachments that are negative.

We once worked with a woman whose mother was negatively attached to her and when the mother died, she remained attached to her daughter after death. How could that be? Attachment is a strong bond. We are not going to let a little thing like death get in the way. This woman told me, "Vywamus, I do not want to break the attachment to my mother even though she is dead, and if I cut the attachment, she will become more confused." She was so attached that even in death she allowed her mother to have that grip on her heart. Is that not amazing? I did help her to finally detach. I told her that it would be in her mother's highest interest to leave.

Some of you have attachments now of mothers, fathers, brothers, sisters and lovers. You can also have an attachment to good spirits. This would be the Archangels or other higher spirits that will cohabitate with you—and I am including myself with the higher spirits. We help to raise you to a higher vibration, so cohabitation could be for good if there are higher spirits cohabitating with you.

## WORKING WITH FEELINGS AND DISTANCE HEALING

What you are feeling comes down to one question: Do you want to have the feeling or not? Do you like the feeling or do you not like the feeling? If you like the feeling, then you have no problem. If you do not like the feeling and it is still there, then you have a problem. You may say, "All right, I don't like the feeling and it is still there. Now what?"

Feelings or emotions are energy. Thoughts are energy and feelings are energy, but if you took a thought and put it in a pot and if you took a feeling and put that in the same pot, which would be on top? The feeling and emotion would be on top. Emotions can be more intense than thoughts sometimes, but to release the feeling you have to experience the feeling. But you have to experience the feeling in a way that is in your highest interest.

You have to ask yourself the question, "Which way can I express this feeling in my highest interest?" That is the most important aspect, because all feelings cannot be expressed the same way. You may be angry with your mother. You do not need to slap her around, throw her against the wall and pick her up and do a body slam like they do on TV wrestling. It is not in your highest interest to deal with your feelings that way. You have to find a way to deal with your emotions in a constructive manner. The answer will be different for each of you.

We call this distance healing or remote healing. Let us say that you have a daughter who needs to be healed. You, as the mother, wish to send healing light to your daughter. There is a special healing formula. It is a formula that says that the most powerful healing happens when the person desires to receive it. If I wish to send healing to my daughter, I ask her. My daughter says, "Yes, send me the healing." I tell her I will do this tonight at seven o'clock, and I want her to meditate at seven o'clock, even though she is a thousand miles away, so that she will receive the most powerful benefit.

If she wants the healing but cannot be there at seven o'clock when you do it, then the effectiveness is lessened, but it is still possible. Actually, the Arcturians talk about a seventy-two-hour window: Thirty-six hours on each side of the hour can be effective.

Let us take the situation where the daughter does not want the healing, and does not agree to meet you at seven o'clock. Now the healing will be even less effective. You can still send prayers, and you say you hope these prayers will go to her for her highest good. The answer is that the effectiveness decreases according to the formula I gave you.

The daughter may not want to change, but the healing will still have an effect and your prayers will still have an effect. We are extremely interested in remote healing and we can read the body over a long distance. We can do medical intuitive readings of the body.

Now I will tell you one other method for the daughter's healing. You can pray to Jesus. Jesus will take your prayer and distribute the energy to your daughter through him. This is powerful. Or you can use an Archangel. I am Vywamus.

## CHAPTER 24

# CORDS OF ATTACHMENT

### Archangel Michael

G reetings, this is Archangel Michael. Let us discuss cords of attachments. I send down a golden light into the center of the room. Let each of your physical bodies accept this beautiful golden light from my hands.

## CUTTING THE CORDS

You possess cords that are attached to the Earth plane. Some of these cords carry from one lifetime to the next so that you return to Earth. It is surprising for people to learn that sometimes these cords carry over from person to person and from life to lifetime.

If you think about ascension, then you must consider that you need to cut the cords of attachment to Earth. Consider your ascension. The moment has come and you hear the sound of the horns. It is a piercing sound that only people with a higher vibration can hear. You get ready to ascend, but then you look back at the Earth and say goodbye to your friends, to your work, to your relatives, to your pets and everything to which you are attached. You turn around and the ascension corridor is closed. You are surprised because you are still attached and you remained attached. Your turning around to say "goodbye" demonstrated your weakness.

I wish to help you cut the cords of attachment so that at that moment of ascension, you will not look back. At that moment, call on me, Archangel Michael, and I will help you cut the cords of attachment. This works to heal you.

Let the healing light come to you now. Let that part of you that needs to be healed be healed, so that you can be whole. When you are whole, then you can allow the cords of attachment to detach.

Experience this. If you choose to know what it is like to have the cords of attachment cut for you, it will only last for one minute. With your permission, I will take my etheric sword and cut the cords of attachment to the Earth plane, and then at the end of the one minute, the cords will be reattached. At the count of three, I will take my etheric sword and sweep it above your heads. Enter meditation for one minute and experience this.

You have a brief experience of being unattached. When the ascension comes, instead of looking back, call on me and I will cut the cords of attachment for you at that moment. Blessings, this is Archangel Michael.

## CHAPTER 25

# BIORELATIVITY AND QUANTUM PHYSICS

### Juliano and the Arcturians

reetings, I am Juliano. We are the Arcturians. The subjects we wish to discuss here include biorelativity, shimmering energy, cosmic justice and also some information about pets on the planet and their relationship to the ascension.

## USING BIORELATIVITY FOR THE WHOLE

Biorelativity states that the telepathic intentions and thoughts of high beings can positively influence evolution and planetary energy. In particular, biorelativity recognizes the necessity and effectiveness of large groups of high lightworkers. These lightworkers can gather in a personal, local or remote situation and input light and energy into the planet.

Various levels of skills are necessary for biorelativity to be most successful. Our downloading of the etheric crystals at certain energetic points on the planet has served many purposes. In particular, they are placed at what would be called meridian healing points on the planet. They also are acting as receptors of light that will allow the planetary lightworkers to activate and accelerate their thought processes. It has been our suggestion that any biorelativity work also use these crystals as a way of accelerating and magnifying thoughts and intentions.

In reviewing biorelativity, there needs to be a magnification of the thoughts, much as you would use an amplifier to increase the wattage in a radio signal or transmission. The acceleration and magnification of your thoughts can be accomplished through the connection with the etheric crystals and through group connections.

It also has been acknowledged that there are holographic time windows. There are holographic waves, in which the meditations and group meetings have a window. Those who cannot meet at the exact time still can effectively communicate and participate in the exercises by using the holographic window. In many cases, we have been able to extend the holographic window on this lecture, for example, to a time period of twenty-four or thirty-six hours. People who are not able to meet exactly at this time can still participate by meeting either before or after the time window and still benefit and contribute to the holographic energy and work. Also, their thoughts can be magnified.

There are many Earth changes coming and there is still a great deal of polarization and duality. I want to speak about some of them. I will start with the concept of global warming because there is a huge debate in the U.S., Europe and the rest of the world about global warming. People debate whether it exists or not, and they take sides. This is relevant because people are so polarized in many other ways: There is the Right, the Left, the liberal, the conservative and so on.

People may think that biorelativity can work only for people who meet in groups such as we've met. In reality, biorelativity is continually working. People who argue for or against global warming are in fact sending energy to the planet in an unfocused biorelativity exercise without knowing they are doing so. Some say, "Let's be careful, and let's control the environment so that the Earth is protected." Some say, "There is nothing that can be done to protect the Earth so don't worry about it." Both thoughts are inputted into the etheric energy field of Earth. As biorelativity workers, you must be careful neither to focus on the duality nor to emphasize polarized thinking about this subject.

## THE INFLUENCE OF THE OBSERVER

Related to biorelativity are the concepts of quantum light and quantum healing. The principles of quantum energy certainly have been expressed, perhaps even more eloquently, by some of the famous physicists in the world. The relationship between biorelativity and quantum light and healing has not been explored. In fact, since biorelativity is such a new concept, I doubt that any physicist that we know of has even begun to relate biorelativity to quantum healing and quantum energy.

The aspect of quantum physics of interest is the relationship of the observer to the experiment. It is known in quantum physics that observing an experiment can affect the outcome. You, as an observer, emit energy. That emission of energy has an influence. If an experiment occurred without observation, you would have one result, and if the experiment occurred with an observer, you would have another result. Sometimes those results are not measurable and sometimes they cannot be detected by normal measuring devices.

This occurs not only in the world of physics, but also it occurs in the world of energetics. It is well known in the field of psychology that when you study workers' output and productivity, the fact that you study them influences their productivity—usually for the better. If you do not study them and then you measure the output productivity, you might find different results. It is important that you understand the influence of the observer when working with biorelativity and Earth healing.

The observation factor is also a consideration in health aspects because the human body is extremely delicate. Some of you may have diseases and illnesses. The human body is often able to tolerate and exist with these illnesses for quite a long time. The determination to treat an illness is based on a multitude of factors, including the acuity of the illness and whether or not people can tolerate the treatment.

Another factor in treating illness lies in whether their karmic time has elapsed so that they may need to leave the planet. Let us look at the field of cancer research. The relationship of the observer to the illness is often seen in exploratory cancer surgery. If the surgeons discover cancer, then they can send energy to the patient. The patient is in a vulnerable surgery state. Any negative energy from the surgeons can influence the acceleration of the cancer cells. Imagine that a surgeon opens up a patient and sees that the patient has a tumor. The surgeon can react with fear. They can send fear energy to that cancer. That patient can then experience an acceleration of the cancer.

If, on the other hand, the doctors are enlightened and they can say, "We discovered a blockage of energy, let us send light and energy to this tumor," there is then a possibility that a positive outcome would happen. It is well-known in the field of Chi and Fa Chi healing that a group of Fa Chi practitioners with the right intentions can reduce tumors by sending light and energy. Often this can be done without an operation! I tell you this because I want you to understand that biorelativity principles also are related to the observer/experiment principles outlined here. Starseeds can send light to energy blocks in the planet for healing.

## YOUR EFFECT ON THE EARTH

We deal with complex planetary levels because there are many groups of people and many polarizations. The important point is that those who are not participating in biorelativity exercises still affect the planet. I refer to the normal scientists, the presidents and other world leaders. These people send their energy and light to the planet even though they are not doing it in a controlled biorelativity manner. They talk and think about Earth on a global basis. The debate over whether or not they affect the Earth begins the process of influencing the Earth.

From our perspective, it is absurd to think you are not affecting the Earth. It has been proven in quantum physics experiments that the observer affects the outcome. The fact that humankind has evolved to the point that they have the consciousness of observation means that they can influence the planet. Thus, you can look upon this planet as an exercise or an experiment in many ways.

We have visited many planets and done many interventions. You will understand that we now are observers of your planet. The White Brotherhood/Sisterhood is observing your planet. There are many other higher beings that are observers of your planet. The observations of the higher beings also positively influence the outcome of the situation.

When we speak of biorelativity, we look at it on several levels. The first level is you as Earth beings working with biorelativity. The second level is biorelativity energy that is downloaded from an external dimension or from another source. We, the Arcturians, and other higher beings, are able to be multidimensional. By being multidimensional, we can actually have an effect and presence in the third dimension through biorelativity.

There are laws of dimensional spiritual physics. For us to have an effect on a third-dimensional situation, there must be beings grounded and manifested on the third dimension. There must be beings who can receive our energy, light and thoughts. Of course, that is you, the starseeds! That is you, the many lightworkers who are doing fantastic group work on so many different levels.

The next level of biorelativity is using the light and help of the masters and teachers and using the energy of the Central Sun. This includes using the energy of our ships and the energy of the etheric archangel light and to be conduits for higher energy. This is a practice we have already been doing many times. We enunciate this in the context of the biorelativity explanation because you need to accelerate your connections and down-loading from the fifth-dimensional Masters. An input of light and energy of a quantum nature is required at this time. This input into the Earth of light and energy transcends normal thought consciousness.

When you look at the theories of quantum physics and the subatomic particle experiments, you will then find energies and occurrences that do not always follow logic. There are things that occur that are affected by observation and therefore are not logical. They seem to be a transcending experience. That means if you take A plus B, it should equal C, but for sometimes it could equal D.

The transcending causing input is, in fact, the observer. If you connect with the higher energy of the masters, then you, as an observer, can have "alchemical influence." On the planetary level, the alchemical process is the observation of the Earth's clearing, the 2012 interchange and the ascension. We are coming to the point where the transcendent-alchemical shift is about to occur.

## THE POWER OF DUALITY IN QUANTUM ENERGY

This brings me to the next point of the observation process: dualities. The results of dualities that exist include the many destructive conflicts on Earth, plus the resulting terrible mass extinctions, pollutions and wars.

We receive messages continually from Sananda and other great beings about this unfolding process. The message is that all is as it should be; all is as it needs to be. The relationship between the current events and cosmic justice is beyond the logic of the third dimension. Remember, I said A plus B should equal C, but they could also equal D in quantum energy. You might think, the inputs don't equal the outputs, i.e., the negative energy sustained produces greater negative events than inputted.

This uneven exchange happens now both on the negative and the positive levels. For example, a small positive input may produce a large positive outcome. On the negative level, the input of the energy of the war in Iraq did not equal the output. In other words, the effects of the war in Iraq may be worse and more out of control than what you may think by the input. I am not saying whether the intervention is correct or not correct. We are not taking any sides. From an observational Earth standpoint, the energies that were put in, plus the existing energies, make up for the negativity that has followed.

What that tells you is that the transcendent alchemical process also works in reverse. The reverse would be this: People thought that military force and killing others could control the Earth and make a positive outcome. Actually, in this current situation the reverse happened—more negative energy was produced. This current alchemical quantum-level energy field that Earth is going through will have a dramatic and unpredictable experience and outcome as a result of the negative energy input.

That is why it is truly dangerous for a world leader, who is of a narrower consciousness, to engage in what would be considered a negative, linear thought process. A wider negative quantum outcome could now result, such as what you see in Iraq! If you use the logic and thought processes of the nineteenth century or the middle twentieth century with regard to Iraq, then it would have been logical to expect a different outcome and a different outcome would have happened.

Quantum energy used positively in biorelativity is a transcendent energy. The subconscious light that is inputted into the human subconscious is influenced by thoughts. Once you become aware, then you can change yourself by downloading information and affirmations into your subconscious.

The subconscious has been called the *tabula rasa,* which in Latin means: blank tablet. This is a metaphor for the idea that whatever you write on it will manifest. This *tabula rasa* does not make a distinction between what is put in. That is partially true. The point is that what is downloaded in the subconscious can manifest.

Now you can say that the energy process using the *tabula rasa* is accelerated. What you put in during an earlier time may have taken ten sessions of affirmations to manifest. Now it can only take one. That is powerful information. It also, in essence, can be a warning, because someone who has dark thoughts should realize that they can manifest sooner. Also, these laws work no matter which side you consider, either positive or negative. This comes back to the idea that people debating the effect of global warming can have an effect on a cosmic and quantum level. They are counterbalancing negative and positive energy. The solution for you is to focus your thoughts on balancing Earth's energies.

## UNDERSTAND YOUR LIMITS WITH EARTH ENERGY

Do not suspend your logic just because you should use the existing discernments that are before you. Logic also does have a place. You need to bring logic to the place of transcendence. The physicist needs to have logic to bring him to that point of the experiment where he can observe the quantum energy and the quantum transcendence. The scientists cannot get to that point of the observation of the quantum leap without scientific investigation and without scientific logic and experimentation.

In biorelativity, there are similar principles so that you understand all this information you gather. You have to understand about water currents, wind currents, the ozone and carbon dioxide. You have to understand many different patterns that are so complex that it would take the largest computer ever built to even analyze what can happen. But there is also a transcendent factor—a quantum factor that the scientists cannot measure.

Sananda has reported to us that all is as it should be in the divine plan. I know that there have been earthquakes and some other major disasters that were averted. There are going to be several other disasters that will be close calls. As an example, the Solomon Islands tsunami in 2007 was the result of an earthquake that could have just as easily happened on the coast of Western Australia, and the tsunami could have affected Brisbane and other cities on that coast. It was a powerful energy that could have affected many other areas over hundreds or thousands of miles. It could have gone either way, but it was a lesser outcome. We certainly pray for the successful rebuilding of that island, and we are greatly saddened by the deaths, but this event was less harmful than what could have happened.

There are many instances like this in the future that will be occurring that can be called a "near miss." The Solomon Islands cannot be considered a near miss because it was a great tragedy, but the tsunami did not reach Hawaii or Japan. There were not millions of people killed.

From the biorelativity standpoint, we look at events in two ways. The first is that there must be a release of Earth energy. You, in your work, are not knowledgeable enough to block or to push back this explosive energy. Secondly, we recognize that there must be some external releases. In your biorelativity exercises, you can focus on releasing pent-up energy. This includes releasing volcanic energy or releasing energies in the tectonic plates so that they will shift in the least harmful way.

"All is as it should be" simply means that there is a cosmic plan and a cosmic outcome. This relates to the concept of the shimmering energy and the shimmering light.

## CONNECT TO THE SACRED WHALES AND DOLPHINS

I want to digress for a moment and mention that the whales and dolphins are carrying special codes of the biosphere and the bioenergetic fields of the planet. The decimation of the whales and dolphins can have dramatic consequences for the oceans.

The oceans hold the biolife energy that allows the biosphere to maintain itself on the landmasses of Earth. Do exercises that connect the energy of the oceans to the landmasses on the planet. Many people have acknowledged the dolphins, have communicated with the whales and are trying to transfer dolphin and whale knowledge back to human form. These people do beautiful work. One such beautiful being is Joan Ocean. She does beautiful work to transfer the knowledge and to hold the knowledge base and the codes from the ocean beings. Ancient energies and codes are transferred to humans through her work. This has never happened before on the Earth. This is a positive outcome.

I, Juliano, am connecting through you and the GOF using biorelativity to connect with the dolphins and the whale light energy at this time. Let us go into a brief meditation connecting with them. I will begin the meditation with a sound. We connect now with the spirit light of the dolphins and whales. Each animal on the Earth is sacred. I ask you now to connect to the sacred dolphins and sacred whales. I suggest that from a biorelativity standpoint, they need your etheric connections and energies.

Biorelativity exercises can also be directed toward other animals on this planet. Is it not true that the bees in the U.S. are going through a dramatic extinction never before seen? People ask, "What is that about?" You have massive plants, massive energy and there should be more bees than ever. There are other factors, such as fertilizers, poisons in the ground and wind changes. The bees are sensitive to the wind. The winds have been aberrant with high velocity. If you take everything that has happened, it does not seem to equal that dramatic an outcome for the bees. But in the alchemical and quantum physics world, the bee situation equals an outcome that could not be predicted. You could not predict that the bees could be decimated in America. That is exactly what may happen.

Someone has to work with the bees to get them to change. This is what needs to occur. It is necessary that there is a genetic modification of their genes. There needs to be a group working on a sophisticated biorelativity pattern who will know how to talk the bees into coming back into manifestation in the United States. The bees are not necessarily ready to relate to the thought patterns of the lightworkers initially. The whales and dolphins are, on the other hand, ready to link with human thought.

You who work with the dolphins and whales can help them. Many of the younger dolphins and whales want to die. Many of them have reached a point of discouragement that could only be compared to the existential nihilism that many youths feel in times of hardship—when they feel there is no future. Then they feel hopeless. The younger whales and dolphins have that same experience now.

I know it may be hard for you to understand how they could have those kinds of feelings. There have been some massive beachings of whales and dolphins. Part of this is because of the military experiments with sonar in the waters. This sonar would be like a loud noise that is high-pitched like scraping nails on a blackboard. Imagine how you would feel if you heard that screeching. That is what the sonar is like to the dolphins and whales— especially to the younger whales and dolphins. For example, older people can be exposed to radiation and it would not be as harmful to them because their system is developed and has some defenses. Younger babies would be more harmed by it. That is the way it is with the dolphins and whales regarding high-pitched sounds.

## DISCOVER YOUR MISSION TO HELP ANIMALS AND THE EARTH

Accelerate the connections and also focus the biorelativity on other animals because other animals are also becoming depressed. These animals sense what is transpiring and they know that there is no future for them. Our biorelativity exercises need to include sending positive thought patterns and communicating with these animals as well. Unfortunately, this can be a painful process for you as humans. I know that many of you love animals.

The pain that you feel in the animal world is a pain that is part of their evolution. These animals have experienced extinction before. They have experienced death before. Even though they are pained, they understand on an animal level about death.

An animal experiences pain much differently than you do. From your observational standpoint, pain is difficult for you to observe. Your sympathetic connection with their pain and observation of their pain helps to raise their vibrational level. In many ways, your positive connections can save them.

I am particularly connected with the Great Barrier Reef energy and know that it is one of the key energies in the world holding the biosphere codes on the planet and in the oceans. I know that many of our friends in Australia will be sending biospheric light and energy to the life forms in that area.  They probably already do that and will continue to do so as a way of expanding consciousness.

We know the effects of pollution and increased sunlight on certain aspects of the coral reefs.  But what is unknown is the effect of thought patterns, the interactions of the thought patterns and of the healing light and consciousness and the observational energies that you can send to those reefs.

People ask, "Can we not influence politics?"  The answer is, "Yes."  If you observe what happens, then your reactions can influence the outcome.  The videotapes of negative incidents, such death and destruction, are often shown on TV.  People are shocked and want to stop or change the causes of such events.  That is why it is so important to show other destructions that are occurring, such as accounts of wars, the destruction of forests or the killings of innocent whales.  Some of the starseeds do have political missions to help change such events.

Know that the aspect of your mission is on different levels.  Some of you are here to work telepathically on biorelativity.  Understand that biorelativity principles also apply to the human race.  You are part of the animal world.  In particular, the showing of videos can have a powerful effect.  If you knew of a destruction that is occurring and you have a video camera, or you are a photographer, then that photography can influence the outcome of events by influencing the world's reactions.

When you show a video of the destructions caused by war, people want to stop the war.  When you show the videos of the destruction of the polar bears, then people want to stop global warming.  That is why control of the media is so destructive when the controllers determine what can be seen.  That is also why the Internet is useful.  It is a way of instant communication that can sometimes bypass censoring.  Do not be afraid to send images out.

A dispensation is being made to allow pets to ascend.  Many of you have contributed tremendously to the evolution of your pets.  Some of the pets will die before you ascend.  Some of them will still be alive when your ascension occurs.  You can do shimmering exercises now around your pet.  You can put your hands in their energy field and begin to shimmer them.  They can go in and out of the third and fifth dimension—just like you.

Pets will love the shimmering work.  When you ascend, at that moment you can also access the consciousness of your pet.  They will ascend with you.  This is a recent development that has occurred.  The divine masters and teachers have been impressed with the love and heart openings that occur because of the pets. At this moment, I send the shimmering light and energy to all your pets that are with you in thought or are with you now. Know also that you can shimmer other animals. You can shimmer with the whales, with the dolphins and with many others.

## DO NOT FEEL FAILURE

There are undeniably great polarizations on the planet. You are not required to repair all aspects of people or their situations that are polarized. Sometimes people are not amenable to ascension. There are people who are in their cosmic/karmic path, which is leading them to a certain cliff. They will drop off that cliff. From the cosmic standpoint, it is the fulfillment of their destiny.

You have a destiny that is based on fifth-dimensional evolution. You have a destiny that is based on learning to transfer fifth-dimensional consciousness into certain cities and to the entire planet. Eventually, we will do certain exercises that will help you shimmer the continent, shimmer the ring of fire and eventually the planet. It does not mean that all people and all situations on the planet will be in the fifth dimension.

Because of cosmic justice and karma, there needs to be some clearing. Your shimmering and your ability to shimmer transfers fifth-dimensional energy to other places, other animals and other situations.

Your ability to shimmer helps you connect to other dimensions—in particular to the Central Sun and the inner Earth. Those of a lower vibration, of a lower consciousness will not receive the shimmering energy. That shimmering energy and light will bounce off them. Do not feel failure if there are those who do not accept fifth-dimensional light when working with you.

A particular higher connection of this shimmering energy will be downloaded from our ships so that we are more greatly unified to work with you. Work to shimmer the cities, people, plants or animals. Now we work to shimmer you. The energy that we shimmer you with is a transcendent, fifth-dimensional energy. I, Juliano, through our special holographic shimmering chamber, send you that energy now.

The abilities to work in fifth-dimensional energy are increasing. May the holes in your planetary fields be healed. As you learn to shimmer the Earth, there will be new methodologies to heal the holes in the Earth's aura. This is part of the Earth's destiny, too. I am Juliano.

## CHAPTER 26

# BIORELATIVITY AND
# FUTURE EVENTS

## Juliano and the Arcturians

Greetings, this is Juliano. We are the Arcturians. There is a direct correlation between the energy of prediction and biorelativity. Biorelativity is a focus to help shape the future so that drastic or upheaval-like events are moderated. It does imply that you have a sense of the possibilities of a future event. It is with the knowledge of that future event or prediction that you then begin the spiritual and telepathic technology and intervention that leads to the lessening of the unwanted event.

## BE CAUTIOUS WHEN CHANGING THE FUTURE

What can we say about the ability to predict? We understand that predictions can be projected onto a graph. Perhaps the best way to explain this graph is to think of you driving at night with your headlights on. You look at the road; your headlight beams project approximately a twenty-foot width. You sit in your car, look out the window and see a series of future events. Unlike the headlight, the closer that you get to the event, the width of possibilities becomes narrower. Then, as you are upon the event, the possibilities are even narrower. By the time you are on the event, then you can see what will occur.

In biorelativity, the earlier you begin your quest for shaping the future event, the wider the possibilities are of that event being changed. In some cases, when you begin the process of telepathic connection with future events, you may find that the sooner you begin this process, the more options are available, and indeed, the possibility of actually avoiding an event becomes more real.

Attempting to influence future events is more complicated. If you are successful in any way in changing an event, then there are further future events on top of the original event that also are affected. You may not consider that other future events will be affected. If you work to help avoid one event and then stop the biorelativity exercises, then you have not looked at the layer upon layer upon layer of future events that can occur from the one event with which you worked.

This is demonstrated by the higher extraterrestrial beings that wisely decide not to intervene in the Earth process. They understand that their intervention can set off a chain of events, which can be unknown or so complicated that it would take a sophisticated computer to analyze all of the following events that would occur because of the alteration of that one event.

Interestingly, it is this process of intervention in future events using telepathic modifications that also empowers. This aspect of empowerment has been called "grace" by some guides. Grace implies that an intervention occurs without intervening or a following of a karmic complication. The harmful future event in essence is avoided and you are free from future negative events. The karma that may be associated with that event does not occur.

When working with future events and biorelativity, you also want to take grace into consideration. You always want to take into consideration the highest good in projecting and attempting to change a future event.

## FORESIGHT MIGHT NOT ALWAYS BE POSSIBLE

Take into consideration the fact that you may not have the foresight or the perceptual abilities to look into the future and see all the consequences of any event that you seek to change. Therefore, it is recommended that you always call on higher beings—higher guides and teachers in any undertaking of this nature for their guidance and direction.

Also, call on the insights from holographic energy that could possibly be given to you and that would indicate some of the chains of events that would happen. The chain of events that could happen are on a diagram related to the power of the square root, which is another way of saying that the further away you get from the future event, the less likely other major events will occur. There are diminishing consequences the further away you get from the event that you seek to change.

For example, if you are working on an event in the future that has to do with an earthquake, and then you are able to avoid or help minimize that earthquake, then the effects perhaps within the next day or two would still be significant. But then the further away you get, there is a decreasing effect. To work most effectively with biorelativity and the events and magnitude of the events, you must begin to work with the energy and the time frame after the event occurs as well as the actual event.

A good example that is a lesson for the entire world is Hurricane Katrina. There was significant devastation, but there was potentially minimal loss of life from that event. Many people from around the world and from the United States worked to shift the hurricane so that it did not directly hit New Orleans. There was a degree of success, but the subsequent event of the breaking of the levees was not an event that anyone considered in their biorelativity exercises.

This is not to be considered criticism in any manner. It requires almost a computerized perception of any event to attempt to remove all negative consequences. Thus, it becomes apparent and necessary in future biorelativity exercises for you to consider the subsequent future events from the event that you seek to diminish. All of this is an introduction to let you know that the magnitude of events that we will be looking at will be quite great. The next years will have many grand magnitude events. From our perspective, in many ways Earth is at a turning point in the world.

What do I mean by a turning point? There are so many different polarizations that have been percolating, and that are quite damaging. These percolations of events will become so dramatic. Some people may feel insulated; they may feel that there is a place where they can stay and not experience some of these polarizations. Everyone will be affected, and the events will occur on several different levels. I will attempt to use our predictive abilities to list them.

First of all, there are the political events. Many people have asked us about the political events and whether biorelativity can be used in the political arena. The effects of biorelativity in the political arena are much more complicated than even on the physical arena.

The basic idea of biorelativity on the political arena is to work with the crown chakra of the people in power and to attempt, either through the guides and teachers of the political leaders or through angelic hosts, to download a certain energy into the leader's crown chakra. Every political leader has defenses and thus may not be open to the crown chakra. We have found it especially instructive to work with the wives of the leaders. In many cases, the leaders' wives' crown chakras are more open—especially to universal light and universal energy. Working with the wives of leaders is an effective way of sending universal energy.

People will be forced to look closely at each political leader, especially at the fact that the biosphere could collapse, and thus politically things will not function as usual. There will actually be a continued diminishing role of America's power on the planet because of some of these events. America will continue to become more isolated. The polarizations that occur in some ways will supersede and transcend America.

People might think that this is positive news. But in another way, it is not positive news. You can make the argument that America has moved in the wrong direction in certain events. The problem is, with the diminishing power of America, greater chaos in the world becomes possible because no one is able to step forward.

## CHANGE IS IN THE WIND

In terms of the other events, the polarizations in weather patterns, including those in America, will be more intense. There will be an increase of wind around the world. This is something that many people have experienced before, but they did not really consider strong winds when they talk about the collapse of the biosphere.

What can occur is that in the plains of America, and in the North and South in particular, there could be a return of an event known as the "Dust Bowl." This Dust Bowl energy is actually originating in China because there has been an increase in desert energies from that area on the planet.

The increase in desert energies has not really been discussed at great length because everyone has been focused on the polar ice caps melting. It is creating wind currents and dust. When you talk about the Dust Bowl that occurred in the United States in the '30s, then you think of dust that was blinding. This type of energy is going to come to certain places in the world, from the Asian coasts to central Asia and to Russia.

Europe is not going to experience much of the dust, but Europe will have some of the wind problems. You will see some significant wind energies in London and some of the islands. It will also occur in the central and southwestern United States. The wind energies will occur also around Australia.

I also see general acceleration of the greenhouse effect, which will become more dramatic. You already hear people say they did not think it would occur this fast. People thought that the polar caps would not melt within a five-year period, but rather in a thirty- to forty-year period. In reality, there is a time compression occurring. It is difficult to explain from a technical standpoint why this is happening. Generally, there now is a time compression. Compression means that events that looked like they would take thirty to forty years will be compressed into a shorter time. There will be significant flooding along some coasts. There will generally be what is called the "ice melting."

People have asked about hurricanes. You might see some more problems with hurricanes. People have asked about volcanic eruptions and earthquakes. Volcanic eruptions and earthquakes will not necessarily be the major events in the future. The major events could be more from wind and dramatic rains.

If you look at South America, Central America and Mexico, you will find that they also are having polarized weather as opposed to wind. There is some discussion that being south of the equator is better than being north of the equator. The problem is that in the south, the climate is just as fragile as the north. You would think that the moderate shifts you see there would not be that hard to take. In effect, it is going to create some major imbalances for them.

South America will actually gain in greater political strength and independence as this occurs. Argentina will become a greater world player. Argentina is one of the countries with the ability to absorb some of these shifts and the winds without experiencing dramatic polarity. It will have greater balance.

## THE HARMONIC CONVERGENCE

We feel that the date 8-8-8 was a turning point spiritually because amidst all of these dramatic and polarizing events that have occurred throughout the planet, there is also an increasing influence of spiritual and harmonic light.

This convergence can be discussed in terms of the effects of predictions, biorelativity, prayer and the effects of working together. The harmonic convergence in 1987 was an opening, but it did not have the continual and dramatic effect for which many had hoped. Although it contributed to a significant spiritual movement, and in some ways established the groundwork for the spiritual movement that we are now experiencing, the 1987 convergence was not pervasive enough.

The harmonic convergence of 8-8-8 was a pervasive convergence of energies. The good news is that the events that are more polarizing, such as the upheavals and wind energies, are contributing to more openness in the world. The feminine energies, which are connected with the energies of 2012, are referred to as the Central Sun energies. These energies are creating a new wave, a new paradigm. All of this is coming to the forefront. If the planet is to hold together, if the biosphere is to stay in existence, then there must be an evolutionary leap.

This evolution is a leap in consciousness necessary to hold the world together. Earth must now demonstrate the effectiveness of the harmonic energies of the starseeds for this evolutionary step. I, Juliano, call on everyone who is listening or reading these words to focus on the harmonic energies for this planet. Focus just on those words and the meaning of harmonic convergence. Understand harmonic energy is a process. Let us take a moment now to meditate on the harmonic convergence energies.

## FUTURE UPHEAVALS

The problem of terrorism will continue during the next several years. There always needs to be a balance between those who move toward convergence and try to establish some harmony on this planet, and those who want to destroy the world. You all know that there is a great force of destruction that has been unleashed on this planet.

Many people are focused on Armageddon or *tashmach* (a Hebrew word for the Age of Destruction), the destruction of the planet and the overthrow of certain established ways of doing things on this planet. These people seem to believe that destruction will lead to a new balance. Unfortunately, that is not a proper methodology at this point. Destruction and overthrowing things will create more chaos now. When there is more chaos, then there is more out-of-control energy, more destruction of the environment and more imbalance.

This type of thinking of destroying things is a primitive thought form, which should not be encouraged. When using destructive energy, even a minor event could have a major impact. A minor earthquake, even though it might not be overwhelming, could have a devastating effect on the world economy if it was in the right place. The overthrowing of certain powers would lead to more chaos rather than to stabilization. I do see that more political upheaval will occur. It will be related to the unmasking of what is known as the "world government," which is the cabal, or the hidden organization that runs much of the world.

You have seen the falling or the unmasking of some institutions. One example has been the churches, where there has been the discovery of a great deal of corruption and sexual bad actions that are unbecoming of spiritual leaders. The existence of corruption in the governments will also come more into the forefront. People will realize that some of the leaders who have been running the government and leading people toward certain political goals really have been corrupt. This corruption even goes beyond one country.

The cabal is an interrelated system, and it will be unmasked! That unmasking, however, will contribute to a political earthquake. People will understand that what they thought was the truth is not the truth. This is related to some of the astrological events in terms of the different planetary alignments that have to do with the Neptune-Saturn connection. People will lose faith in the institutions. Unfortunately, there are no other institutions to replace them. It becomes necessary that people of more harmonic and unified energies step in and keep the institutions going.

The importance of the harmonic convergence energies becomes more powerful. You begin to see that the current institutions and governments need to become responsive because they are the only existing structures that can help. Chaos does not lead to harmony. One of the biggest lessons that will come forward to this planet and to the people who are predicting Armageddon is that this type of thinking and upheaval should not be focused on or desired because that energy will not lead to a new peace. Also, the planet cannot tolerate another major war. The planet cannot tolerate a nuclear war. We do not see a war with Iran. The world powers are able to control the situation so it does not occur.

## THE ROLES OF RUSSIA AND AFRICA

Many people have talked about the influence of Russia on world events. There is no question that the Russian energies and politicians have returned to some of their old ways. Russian power is now a force to counterbalance against the American interventions in Iraq and Iran.

What will occur is that the forces of power in Russia, as negative as they might be in some people's minds, will stop the U.S.'s attempt to control Iran. This is both good and bad—the good being that then there will not be another major war. There is no question in our perception and in our predictions that an Iranian intervention by the U.S. would lead to World War III.

Another major war is something that the guides and teachers do not want to see happen, even though some people will say Iran is a negative country and has terrorism, or whatever negative concepts are promulgated from the Western standpoint. The effects of such a military intervention are far greater in a negative way against the world. Therefore, we see the harmonic energies that are going to contribute to a balancing away from a world war.

Starseeds who are working with the harmonic energies will face the problem of negativity or upheaval of events that could be considered terrorism. The focus of the biorelativity exercises that we suggest is to visualize an energy to harmonize and to minimize wars, to minimize isolated terrorist events and to visualize bringing people into an awareness that any violent event, such as a war, would have a devastating effect on the biosphere. Consider the fact that this biosphere already has tolerated many current and existing wars. Potential future wars could tip the scale to further harm the biosphere.

Africa continues to experience great pain health-wise. Africa, in many ways, is suffering from what we call the biomedical devastations of the immune system. Africa is suffering from the inability to maintain a proper immune system support. This problem is spreading to Asia.

In other words, in the coming years, the human immune system will be one of the key discussions. The immune system will suffer on several levels. There is the problem with AIDS and the attack of bacteria and viruses. You have to also consider that the immune systems on the planet are being compromised by the ozone problems and by ultraviolet radiation entering the Earth.

We continually emphasize the importance of controlling the radiation levels in Chernobyl because we think there are still continual holes and leakages over that area that are being unreported. There are other major radiation leakages on the planet. These radiation leakages must be brought to the world's attention.

By the northern Russian oceans, there are underground leakages of radiation contributing to some of the problems that the whales and dolphins have. This radiation causes aberrant energies in the oceans. People think, "Radiation leaks only affect one part of the oceans." But the oceans are interactive with all levels on the planet and radiation leakages are also occurring in all parts of the oceans.

People have wanted to use nuclear power as an alternative to some of the other types of power that cause greenhouse gases. But we continue to warn against nuclear energy because of the holes in the Earth's aura that it can create. If you look at each nuclear power plant in operation from the standpoint of the cosmic aura around the planet, then you would see that there are thin holes around the auric fields where the nuclear power plants are.

Africa will continue to experience great political upheavals and military problems. In some ways, it is at a low vibration. Certain countries are higher obviously than others in that continent. There are still great resources that need protection there and we do see an emergence of Native energies that will bring some stability.

## Focus Toward Convergence

There will be moderation in the Middle East. The new world leader will take a greater role in peace talks. Everybody realizes that a third world war would have a devastating effect. There is a moderating energy in the Middle East working behind the scenes to try to help people come to their senses. People realize that everyone would be negatively affected by a world war.

There could be a drought again in Greece, in Lebanon and in Israel. There is potential for other droughts in Spain and in Southern France. The droughts in Australia will be more polarizing. There will be periods of rains, winds and storms, and then there will be periods of dryness and continuation of the droughts. There will be continued rains and some strong storms in Central Europe and in Russia. Russia may have harsher winters, as well as parts of Northern Europe.

What I see for the future time periods is that there will be variance, which means more polarities. I do see harmonic energies and that the polarizations can be harmonized. There will be some interesting technology developed to work with the weather. This will come partially out of the biorelativity.

There is new energy coming to the planet from the Central Sun. This new energy will bring greater technological surprises. There will be an energy to clean up the oceans and the waterways. This energy has been discussed before, but it has not come to the forefront. There will be a technology that will help with that.

Focus on the cosmic egg around the Earth. There are many holes in the Earth's aura. These holes, through your biorelativity work, can become sealed. Imagine that they are being sealed. In particular, there is an antidote that must soon be discovered to balance the radiation levels on this planet. Focus on the aura around the Earth coming into a perfect shape of the egg.

Understand that our original description of the headlights, in terms of the events of the future, can have a powerful impact. Understand that the harmonic energies will set the stage for the further Earth balancing. Now is the time to work toward this harmonic convergence. Now is the time to understand that the spiritual starseeds—their work, their missions—can have a maximum effect and input into the events.

When you do biorelativity exercises for the planet, include in all exercises the energy of the harmonic light so that each event that you may work toward will be in alignment with harmony. I reiterate: You do not really know what the avoidance of one event will have on other events. But if you do, focus on the following thought: All is in alignment with the harmonic energy for the planet. This inoculates negative karma from one event. This sets the stage for the further energy of harmonics and harmonic energy.

In conclusion, the forces of harmonic energy will be intensified, and now is the time to set the foundations for this. I realize there are many other events we did not cover and we will seek to focus on them through the channel in further discussions.

At this point, I bless each of you, and I encourage you to continue your line of work in biorelativity. Note that your predictive values, your predictive energies, will be increasing so that each of you will be more powerful in seeing events. By increasing your power in seeing future events, this will increase your effectiveness in the biorelativity areas. I am Juliano. Good day.

## CHAPTER 27

# BIORELATIVITY AND COMMUNICATING WITH THE EARTH

Juliano and the Arcturians

G reetings, I am Juliano. We are the Arcturians. For this lecture we will refocus and redouble our efforts in utilizing biorelativity. We will provide a summary of the principles of biorelativity and also go in greater depths into the methodology and intervention strategies that can be utilized in its practice.

Biorelativity is the ability of higher conscious beings, through telepathic means, to influence the planet on which they live. The means of telepathic communications can be through various methods, including crop circles.

Crop circles are actually a method of biorelativity in which extradimensional beings are able to communicate to the spirit of the Earth. Many people thought that crop circles and their symbolism were only for humankind, and of course, they are utilized by humans. But the main thrust of the crop circles was and is to provide interactive biorelativity communication with the spirit of the Earth. This will assist Earth in the transformation of the planet into the fifth dimension. Our purpose in this discussion is not to go into greater depth of crop circles and the method of sacred geometry; rather, our purpose is to go more into the methodology and the principles of biorelativity.

## HARMONY WITH EARTH IS ESSENTIAL FOR SURVIVAL

The main focus of biorelativity is telepathic communication with the Earth. Telepathic communication with the Earth is not exactly the same as if you were attempting to telepathically communicate with another person. There are various methods that include the talking methodologies used by the Native American Indians, and also methodologies that have to do with building sacred structures and medicine wheels. These are all examples of biorelativity.

The latest introduction of biorelativity from the Arcturians actually includes the downloading of sacred etheric crystals that are etheric duplicates of the main crystal in the crystal temple. These etheric crystals have a unique interactive ability for biorelativity.

The purpose and function of biorelativity is to bring the planet into a higher frequency and alignment so that the planet can be in a harmonious relationship with the beings on that planet. This means that the harmonic relationship is such that the frequency of the planet is adjusted, so that the environment is in a threshold of comfort that allows the beings, or members of the planet, to exist and inhabit the planet in peace and harmony.

If you take that description of biorelativity and look at Earth at this time, you would obviously conclude that there are many beings on the planet not living in harmonic comfort with the planet. Droughts are also creating problems and will intensify, as well as wind energies. These are just a few examples. The ability to use biorelativity is an essential ingredient for the survival of the planet. The ability to use biorelativity successfully is the key ingredient for the successful maintenance of this planet and the biosphere.

The ability to use biorelativity focuses then on telepathic communication. I emphasize that telepathic communication is also performed through verbal means as well as through thinking.

We have visited many planets. We have done a great deal of planetary exploration. The Arcturians are explorers and we have a responsibility that includes this section of the galaxy. We have a responsibility that includes the maintenance of the Stargate. We have a responsibility also of welcoming and introducing into the galactic family planets that are coming into consciousness.

There is a small percentage of planets that have life comparable to your level of evolution and beyond. We generally observe these planets. We have seen personally five to seven planets that have reached the state of development comparable to Earth's. Of those five, three did not make it. Two were able to evolve successfully and one is now actually in this similar condition as Earth.

The two planets that were able to survive used biorelativity successfully. Our interpretation is that there is a necessary evolutionary step among the species, in this case man, Adam. Other planets had species that are similar to humans. In some cases, they had different variations. One species was actually what you would call "hermaphrodites." They were successfully able to complete the process of biorelativity and the introduction of biorelativity into their practices kept their planet's biosphere in a survival mode.

## KEEPING THE FLOW OF MERIDIANS

It is an evolutionary step in consciousness of the species that allows them to interact with the spirit of the planet. There are several methods and hypotheses that make biorelativity relevant. One hypothesis has to do with the fact that the Earth is a living spirit. The second hypothesis is that the spirit of the Earth can be influenced by higher consciousness. The third hypothesis is that a planet inhabited by species that is not conscious of the planet's spirit can block the energies of the planet, resulting in chaos, upheavals and polarizations on that planet.

The dinosaurs inhabited this planet for millions of years, but eventually became so dominant that they created an imbalance. Obviously, they were unable to practice any form of biorelativity. They were unable to bring any type of harmony back into the Earth, even though they were able to survive for many millions of years.

This hypothesis of biorelativity then points to the fact that the Earth has meridians similar to the meridians in the human body. These meridians are energetic lines, or pathways, throughout the planet. Some call them grid lines, which is an acceptable description. These grid lines need to maintain an open, energetic flow.

If those grid lines are blocked in any way, then the Earth will attempt to open them through various means, including volcanic eruptions, earthquakes, floods and so on. If you look at a grid line from the Earth's perspective, the blockage, let us say, could even be in a nuclear dump site in Nevada, in the Baltic Sea in Russia or in Chernobyl. Yet the attempt to open up that blocked grid line could be done from another part of Earth.

It might be similar to you having plaque in an artery, and then the blocked artery creates another balloon-like blockage in another part of the body, such as in your leg. This is another way of explaining that an interactive and global view of the Earth must be realized in order to understand and remove blockages.

One of the methodologies of biorelativity is the use of holographic healing, perceptions and holographic work. Working in one area of the Earth can open up another area. If you are working on a grid line, it is important that the whole grid line be encompassed. Even if you are at one point of the grid line that seems relatively open, other areas along the grid line could be blocked.

To summarize, the principle of biorelativity assumes a meridian-like function of the Earth's ley lines or grid lines. These ley lines or grid lines need to be opened and maintained.

## Talking and Listening to the Earth

Telepathic communication includes thinking about Earth energy. It also includes talking out loud to the Earth. You have to learn how to communicate with the spirit of the Earth. The Native American peoples have generally been more advanced in how to communicate with the Earth. They are much more comfortable in talking to the Earth.

Talking to the Earth could be considered a telepathic intervention. To go a little bit deeper, a medicine wheel would also be considered a telepathic communication even though it is not in words. Certain symbolism and certain setting of stones create an energy to which the Earth spirit responds.

Obviously then, the crop circles have a higher level of design, to which the spirit of the Earth is receptive. That is to say, the spirit of the Earth is receptive to sacred geometry configurations. The Egyptians, the Mayans and the Aztecs used the geometric symbolism of the pyramids as a biorelativity exercise. Part of that symbolism was to provide an interactive means to communicate with the spirit of the Earth.

There are also other ways of telepathically communicating with the Earth. We have enhanced your abilities to communicate with the Earth through etheric crystals. The etheric crystals are in direct communication with the spirit of the Earth. Therefore, when you project your energies into the etheric crystals, it can be compared to having an open phone line in which you can more directly interface with the Earth.

One of the key methods of biorelativity is listening to the planet. Each planet is unique. If I were able to take you to different planets, you would see that other planets are not really like Earth. Each planet has a different spiritual vibration and a different spiritual energy. In biorelativity exercises to this point, we have given you instructions on how to moderate or how to assist in the minimizations of certain potential Earth upheaval events.

We have also suggested that the ideal would be to enter into a preventative mode in which you would work to shape the potential negative outcomes in a more positive direction. This would mean rather than waiting for a "negative event" to occur, you would begin a biorelativity exercise first.

A higher level would be to preventatively work with the energy of the Earth so that you can attenuate future negative events. You can see that prevention is a higher level. I always compare this to the spiritual work of the meditative masters who are always working to create the energy field that holds our civilization together.

We learned that it is through thought forms and the holding together of the thought forms that we keep the energy together of our dimension and our civilization. Eventually, humans will come to that point of learning to work with positive thought forms. We had suggested that there should be continual around-the-clock work on holding the energy together with thought forms and biorelativity. To work in such a preventive way requires the skill of listening to the Earth. That means that you would attempt to understand and answer this question: Who is this spirit of the Earth? What does this spirit of the Earth want?

These are some questions that you would ask yourselves in order to learn to listen to the Earth. Listening to the Earth is a special, high-level skill. In some civilizations on other planets, there are spiritual leaders who travel around the planet, listening to the planet and attempting to receive energy from its different parts.

## THE GLOBAL FEEDBACK LOOP

The greatest boost for biorelativity has been the ability of humans to go into outer space and look at and see Earth from a unique perspective. This is a tremendous advantage. Remember that we have often called Earth the "blue jewel." The Earth loves this designation. In biorelativity exercises, when you address Earth, you can use that designation in this way: "Mother Earth, you are the Blue Jewel that we love."

In listening to the Earth, it is important that you remove your ego. Listening is to receive the messages of what direction and what energy the Earth is expressing, and understand that there is a flow of energy and also a possible blockage of that flow. Understand what has been called the "feedback loop." This is expressed in modern climatology as an energetic loop whereby ocean currents in one area of the planet affect weather patterns and climatic conditions in other areas.

A high-level awareness of biorelativity phenomena includes this important principle of biorelativity: One part influences another. If you look at the melting of the glaciers, then you should think it is just one aspect or part of the loop besides warming. There are many aspects in that feedback loop of the biosphere. It is a whole feedback system.

The feedback system involved in the melting of the icecaps has to do many events, including the pollution in the oceans, the extinction of the species of many fish and the destruction of the dolphins and whales and their subsequent declining populations. People may say, "This extensive feedback loop, including the dolphins, doesn't seem logical, Juliano. What do the whales and dolphins have to do with the feedback loop of the global warming and melting of the glaciers?"

Think like a planet. Understand that on a planetary level, the dolphins, the whales and all other fish play an important role in holding the energy of the biosphere in harmony. Even the swordfish, the sharks and particularly the dolphins and whales are vital. They are at the top of the evolutionary chain of consciousness in the oceans. They keep an energetic flow and a meridian open in the oceans.

When you look at the rising ocean levels, then you can consider the relationship between the dolphins and the ocean currents. As the dolphins and whales are being destroyed, there will be more blocked ocean currents. There could also be terrible waste dumping in the oceans that affect the currents—particularly in the Baltic Sea, because near Russia there is a terrible nuclear waste dump in that area of the ocean.

The dolphins and whales have higher knowledge on how to keep energy circuits open in the oceans. You must look deeper than just considering global warming and the relationship of global warming to the melting of the icecaps. You must also understand the whole feedback loop.

That is why listening to the Earth becomes important. In this model, the protection of the dolphins and whales could be just as dramatic an intervention for the increase in global warming as reducing carbon emissions. The dolphins and whales have an important role in keeping the feedback loop open. Then, of course, there is a whole series of fish and plant life that is interactive with the dolphins and whales that also need protection. This goes back to the concept of the listening to the Earth and finding out what is needed.

## IDENTIFYING MERIDIANS

The etheric crystals are set up to accelerate and intensify your abilities to listen to the Earth. When you are at the actual physical sites of the etheric crystals, your power to listen to the Earth accelerates. The major question is once you have learned and once you have listened, then what do you do? After the listening stage, the talking-and-telepathic stage and the sending-of-energy stage are the next levels in which you communicate with the Earth.

These stages are beautiful and fun, and people enjoy the opportunities to do them. Together we are looking for new ways to communicate with the Earth. It raises some issues, such as the kind of communication the Earth likes. This gets back to the thought that each planet is an individual spirit. Therefore, the Earth has unique energies and models for interactions. Each of you are, in part, fulfilling a soul mission by coming to this planet at this time to provide your unique energies, your unique abilities and to harmonize and communicate with the Earth.

The Earth wholly enjoys the talking methods from the Native Americans. Equally important now are the global connections. Never before, including even in Atlantis, has there been the global connections that are now possible.

Atlantis was a civilization focused on one area, and the Atlanteans generally did not seek global domination of the planet or a pervasive global expansion. They had a high level of activation and scientific knowledge, but they never maintained a global presence. They had reasons for it. Now on Earth there is a global communication pattern, and the Earth loves the fact that there is this intercommunication with people all over the planet. This provides a powerful interactive force that can work to eliminate blocks in the Earth's meridians.

The second thing is that in communicating with the Earth, you can identify where these meridians, or grid lines, are. One grid line or energy place could be the ring of fire. There are also longitudinal and latitudinal lines. The Earth's grid lines are dimensional. You might think of the meridians on a body: You can identify the heart meridian, the liver meridian, the triple heater and so on. You would see the meridians as a straight line.

The Earth is shaped so that some meridians are exactly similar to longitudinal and latitudinal lines. Others are more complex meridian lines that go into irregular linear patterns, including going into the inner Earth and through the poles. There is even a meridian that goes from Earth to the Central Sun.

Some crop circles provide an introduction on how to relate to a meridian. The crop circles form different geometric patterns. Some grid lines that the crop circles relate to are not in a conventional shape. We know that there are many sacred patterns and areas in the Earth. Some of these are ancient patterns. There are patterns in the ancient Mayan civilizations that had wonderful openings to the Central Sun.

The Mayans were able to actually open the meridian of Earth to the Central Sun, and this was the source of some of their knowledge of astronomy. They were also able to get more knowledge of mathematics from this energy line. There are many sacred spots of which you are becoming aware. This knowledge can be accelerated. Sacred spots are entry points into the Earth's meridians. Even though you cannot be at all these spots, you can thought-project your energy through creative visualization to these spots.

Some meridians are deep in the ocean. Some meridians are only accessible to the whales and dolphins. Some meridians require methods of access that are beyond your normal abilities. You know that underneath the oceans are deep valleys, mountains and canyons. If the ocean waters were removed, you would see landmasses that would be stunningly beautiful. You would see huge mountains as tall as Mount Everest. You would see canyons as deep as the Grand Canyon or even deeper. The ridges and valleys are covering many sacred areas that, up to this point, humans have no knowledge of. This comes back to listening and receiving the message of the Earth.

I will conduct a brief meditation now, in which we all will sharpen and focus our ability to listen to the Earth. Tell yourself in this brief meditation: "I am going to enhance, I am going to receive and I am going to listen to the Earth." I will emit a brief tone through the channel, and then we will go into a meditation for listening. [Tones.]

## THINK LIKE A PLANET

Another assumption about biorelativity is that the Earth is honored to be able to hold the energy for humans. The Earth wants to maintain its population of humans. The Earth wants to be in harmony, as much as possible, with the needs of the human population. This is an important biorelativity principle because this honors the Earth. It shows that it is a relationship, an interaction that the Earth wants as well as humans.

Humans have not, as a total population, expressed this desire to harmonize with the Earth. From the Earth's perspective, there is a cause for every imbalance. We have to spend more time using the biorelativity technique of listening to understand how the Earth thinks. The Earth is not thinking like a human. It is thinking like a planet. If there is a blockage in a meridian, then the Earth's sensors are limited. Using this approach, you can understand that an imbalance in one part of the Earth can result in a climactic aberration and catastrophe in another part of the planet.

In biorelativity, you work on the first level, which is to try to moderate the rain so there is less of it and that the water soaks in. There has been some success in visualizing that, and we are working with all of you now to visualize that the water is soaking in and the rain is diminishing. Visualize and say that the heavy amounts of rain are an aberration and are not permanent.

Think of the pattern of the human artery or the vein. If you push the plaque to another area, then instead of having a blockage in your heart, you could have a blockage in your brain. That is not really good. Obviously, you can see there is a blockage of energy in the flow that caused the aberration, but if you push it somewhere else, then it could create another imbalance. We want the plaque to be dissolved.

I, Juliano, with the starseeds in this meditation, hereby call the blockage of the energy that created the imbalance in the Earth to be dissolved. Visualize now, with my assistance, the dissolving of what would be comparable to the symbolic plaque in the Earth's meridian so it returns to normal.

The Earth is sensitive to accelerated high aural frequency radiation, which affects different areas of the planet in ways that are extremely destructive. High-frequency aural radiation patterns were used in the Iraq war to help a military victory, but there have been many side effects—including the creation of aural holes and comparable black-hole energies around that country of which you still see side effects.

Combating high-frequency aural radiation patterns can actually be moderated and counteracted through world chanting. The high-frequency aural radiation patterns are intense, and some of them are far beyond the human range of hearing. Your ability to use biorelativity and spiritual harmonic convergence energy can counteract a great deal of this through chanting.

There are certain energetic tones and chants that are particularly healing to the Earth, just as there are energetic chants that are healing to the human body. There may be certain tones that are healing for the liver. The sound "whoa" can be healing and can bring the liver into balance. This is a simple explanation. Toning for the Earth is much more complicated than that, but I just used it as an example.

Biorelativity includes toning and chanting to the Earth. One of the things that will be discovered is that the Hopi and other Native peoples—the Aborigines, the Maori, the Native Americans and many others—know how to perform healing chanting for the Earth. The African people have special knowledge on toning and chanting. This knowledge of the African Native people regarding Earth chanting is at a high level. The African people and some of these tribes have ancient knowledge on how to communicate to the Earth through sacred chants and tones, drumming and sounds that are at a high level.

I recommend that you reconnect with the tonal chanting energies. We will also use some of these chants and help you discover some of the sacred tones that will help heal the Earth. Imagine that there were a thousand starseeds simultaneously chanting a special sound, a new sound and a new tone that is as unique and as special as the sounds of sacred geometry. These tones and sounds can be introduced. They will have a special vibrational healing energy that is comparable to the biorelativity energy for Earth.

These tones and sounds will be chanted simultaneously around the Earth, creating a beautiful healing energy, removing blocks, creating new balances and helping bring humanity into a harmonic convergence with the blue jewel, your Mother Earth. I am Juliano. Good day.

# Glossary

**ADAMIC ADONAI**

A term used to describe *Homo sapiens* or Earth humans. Man (Adam) was formed from the Earth.

**ADAM KADMON**

The Hebrew term for "primordial" or "first." It is the prototype for the first being to emerge after the beginning of creation.

**ADONAI**

Hebrew word for "God" in the Old Testament. It literally means "My Lord." It is also the galactic word for "God."

**AIN SOPH AUR**

Hebrew for "Infinite Light, Infinite One."

**ALTERED STATES OF CONSCIOUSNESS (HIGHER)**

A term in modern psychology used to describe different states of consciousness. This includes the dream state, trances, meditation states of consciousness and also heightened states of consciousness where one has higher perceptions of reality. This state usually is described as a condition where one can see ultimate truth and is able to experience the present more fully. In the 1960s, this term was used to also describe drug-induced changes and consciousness, such as what one could experience with mind-altering drugs.

**ANDROMEDA**

A large spiral galaxy 2.2 million light years from the Milky Way galaxy. The Andromeda galaxy is the largest member of our local galactic cluster. It is commonly referred to as our sister galaxy.

**ANDROMEDANS**

An advanced, higher-dimensional race of beings from the Andromeda galaxy. A specific group of Andromedans is currently working with the Arcturians in their effort to facilitate the planetary ascension process of Earth.

**ARCHANGEL**

The term designates the highest rank of angels in the angelic hierarchy. The Kabbalah cites ten archangels. They are considered messengers bearing divine decrees.

**ARCTURIAN TEMPLAR**

This is a project of building a temple that would represent a connection to the Arcturian spirituality. This temple would have a special shape that is similar to the Navajo Native American structure that is called a hogan. The top of the templar would be shaped like a teepee. See the proposed design (Fig. 5) on the next page by Fernando Luis Grossi, GOF member in Argentina. Fernando drew this beautiful design in 2005 and called it *The Juliano Iskalia Templar 40*.

**ARCTURUS**

The brightest star in the constellation Boötes, also known as the Herdsman. This is one of the oldest recorded constellations. Arcturus is also the fourth-brightest star seen from Earth. It is a giant star, about twenty times the diameter of the Sun and one hundred times as luminous. It is a relatively close neighbor of ours, approximately forty light years from Earth. High up in the sky in

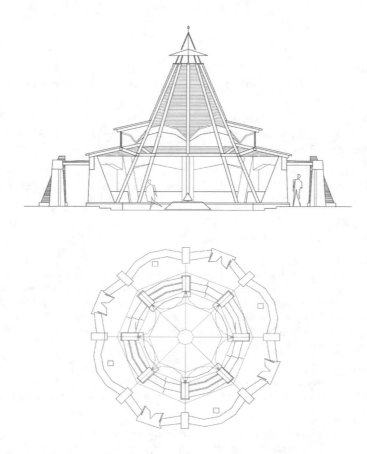

Figure 5: The Arcturian Templar, seen from the side (top) and from above (bottom).

the late spring and early summer, Arcturus is the first star you see after sunset. You can find it easily if you follow the Big Dipper's handle away from the bowl.

## ASCENSION

A point of transformation reached through the integration of the physical, emotional, mental and spiritual self. The unification of the bodies allows one to transcend the limits of the third dimension and move into a higher realm. It has been compared to what is called the "Rapture" in Christian theology. It has also been defined as a spiritual acceleration of consciousness, which allows the soul to return to the higher realms and thus is freed from the cycle of karma and rebirth.

## ASCENDED MASTERS

Teachers who have graduated from Earth or teachers who already are on higher dimensions. An ascended master can be from any Earth religion, including the Native American traditions. They have graduated from the Earth cycle of incarnation, and have ascended into the fifth dimension. Ascended masters can include archangels, higher beings from the galactic world, teachers and prophets.

## Ashtar

The commander over a group of spiritual beings who are dedicated to helping the Earth ascend. The beings that Ashtar oversees exist primarily in the fifth dimension and come from many different extraterrestrial civilizations.

## Assemblage Point

The assemblage point in Shamanism is a cluster of energy lines close to the body. These energy points affect the left- and right-brain energy and the endocrine system. It is reported that this energy cluster affects the way we feel and perceive reality.

## Astral Plane

The non-physical level of reality considered to be where most humans go when they die.

## Atah Gibur Adonai

Hebrew term for "You are great, Adonai!"

## Aur Ha Moshiach

Hebrew words meaning "the light of the Messiah."

## Bilocate

The ability to be in two places at the same time. One can be physically in your body and mentally or spiritually in another dimension simultaneously.

## Biorelativity

Biorelativity focuses on group thoughts working together telepathically to send healing energy to our planet. The practice is similar to the concept of group prayer where people send positive thoughts to change the outcome of an event. In biorelativity exercises, groups of starseeds around the planet send healing thoughts to specific areas in the world. Storms, hurricanes, and even earthquakes can potentially be averted, deterred, or lessened in strength so that minimal damage is inflicted. The Arcturians point out that on higher planetary systems, groups continually interact telepathically with their planet to ensure maximum harmony between the inhabitants and the planetary forces. Biorelativity focuses on group thoughts working together telepathically to send healing energy to our planet. Native Americans know how to pray to the Earth as a group, often asking for rain, for example. In biorelativity exercises, we now have the powerful advantage of globally connecting with many different starseeds, working to unite telepathically for the healing of Earth.

## Biosphere

A term used to describe the whole environment of the Earth, including the oceans, atmosphere and other necessary ingredients that keep and support all life.

## B'nai Elohim

Hebrew term for "the children of Light" *Elohim* is the Hebrew name for God, so the term directly translates into "the children of *Elohim*."

## Carlos Castaneda

Author of a series of mystical books on shamanism and the world of the Yaqui Indian sorcerer, Don Juan. Carlos was an anthropologist. Don Juan is the shaman in the book and he taught Carlos the ancient ways.

## Central Sun

The spiritual and etheric center of our galaxy that is located in the center of the Milky Way. The high spiritual energy is emitted from this area. Earth will come into direct alignment with the Central Sun in the year 2012. It is the name for the center of any astronomical star system. All star clusters, nebulae and galaxies contain a nucleus at their center. Even the grand universe itself has a Great Central Sun at the center of its structure. In most cases, a giant star exists at the center of all star systems. The Great Central Sun of the Milky Way galaxy provides life-giving energy to the entire galaxy.

### CHAKRAS

Energy centers of the human body system. These centers provide the integration and transfer of energy between the spiritual, mental, emotional and biological systems of the human body.

### CHANNELING

The process of entering a meditative trance in order to call forth other entities to speak through you. See "trance channeling."

### CHIEF BUFFALO HEART

An ascended fifth-dimensional Native American guide who focuses on using heart energy to help one ascend.

### CHIEF WHITE EAGLE

An ascended fifth-dimensional Native American guide who is very connected to Jesus and other higher fifth-dimensional beings.

### COHABITATE

Cohabitate refers to the idea of a spirit from another dimension entering the energy field of a third-dimensional Earth being. Cohabitation can be with positive spirits or negative spirits. Positive spirits could be Archangel Michael or other ascended masters. They can live in someone's energy field upon the invitation of that person. Negative cohabitation could include lower disoriented spirits, such as ghosts, living in the energy field of the person and often influencing that person to do or feel negative things.

### CONNECTING WITH THE ARCTURIANS

This first book by David Miller talks about the ascension process and what it means. It asks these questions: Who is really out there? Where are we going? What are our choices? What has to be done to prepare for this event? Is everyone ascending to the same place? What happened to the fourth dimension? How can we understand the fifth dimension? What does it feel like? How does it operate? What are fifth-dimensional beings like? How do they live? This book explains all of these questions in a way that we can easily understand. It explains our relationships to known extraterrestrial groups, and what they are doing to help the Earth and her people in this crucial galactic moment in time. It explains how we can raise our vibration now and begin the process of integrating higher dimensional energies into our third-dimensional world. The Arcturians have given us a crucial focus for the acceleration of world consciousness. They have presented the concept of group ascension through the creation of Groups of Forty. They have also presented the concept of the Sacred Triangle, a method for the integration and unification of spiritual and religious thought on the planet Earth. All those who read this book will feel the presence of fifth-dimensional energy within their being. You will be able to truly experience a view of fifth-dimensional awareness. This will profoundly affect your ability to expand your own perception of reality, and help you to actively participate in the personal and planetary ascension that has already begun. *Connecting with the Arcturians* also contains four visionary paintings by Gudrun Miller depicting the appearance of the Arcturians and other scenes from their world and existence.

### CORRIDOR

A pathway or etheric tunnel on Earth that leads to a higher dimension. Corridors can be found in high-energy places, such as sacred sites on Earth. The Arcturians believe that we can establish corridors within our meditation areas on Earth.

## COSMIC EGG

The optimal shape of your aura for health benefits. When the aura is in the shape of an egg, one is expressing maximal energetic possibilities. The egg is a universal shape of wholeness, and thus it is also referred to as the cosmic egg.

## COSMIC EGG (EXERCISE)

This exercise is based on the fact that the perfect healing energy shape is the shape of an egg. Using this shape is part of a dimensional method of healing. The exercise is based on helping a person form their aura into this egg shape. By keeping his or her aura in this egg shape, that person can experience healing.

## CRYSTAL TEMPLE

An etheric temple on the fifth dimension that has been made available for our use by the Arcturians. The Crystal Temple contains a lake more than one mile in diameter, which houses a huge crystal half the size of the lake itself. The entire lake and surrounding area is encompassed by a huge glass dome, allowing visitors to view the stars.

## EH'YEH

In Hebrew, the supreme name of God. This is the name for God given to Moses in Genesis 3:14. *Eh'yeh asher Eh'yeh* is the full name translated as "I will be that I will be."

## EHIYEH ASHER EHIYEH

In Hebrew, the name of God given to Moses at the burning bush in Genesis 3:14. *Ehiyeh Asher Ehiyeh* is the full name translated as "I shall be that I shall be" (also translated as "I am that I am").

## EL NA RE FA NA LA

Hebrew for "please God, heal her now!" This is a famous Kabbalah healing chant.

## ELOHEYNU ADONAI, ECHAD ADONAI

Hebrew for "Our God is Adonai, Adonai is One."

## ETHERIC

A term used to designate the higher bodies in the human system. In India, "etheric" is used to describe the unseen energy and thoughts of humans.

## ETHERIC CRYSTALS

Invisible crystals that contain fifth-dimensional energy that have been sent to the Earth by the Arcturians. The purpose of these etheric crystals is to provide healing energies to the Earth's meridians. To this date, ten etheric crystals have been downloaded (see Fig. 6). Here is a summary of the process and the roll they can play in the Earth's healing:

1. **Lago Puelo, Argentina.** The home of the first crystal to be brought down to Earth. This crystal holds the primordial energy for the whole planet. It is an energy of initiation and connection to energy.

2. **Grose Valley in the Blue Mountains National Park in Australia**. This connects with the Rainbow Serpent, which is the feminine Goddess energy of Mother Gaia, and is an area of great significance to the aborigines of Australia.

3. **Lake Morraine in Canada**. This crystal contains the quantum etheric energy activation light, which can bypass the normal laws of linear time and space and cause and effect.

4. **Lake Constance in the Bodensee in Germany**. This location is the home of the fourth crystal. This crystal provides new information, new codes, new structures and new dynamics into the Earth's ley lines, and allows us access to new information.

5. **The Poas Volcano in Costa Rica.** This crystal is linked to the great attractor force—the force that pushes and pulls the galaxies in different directions. It also helps to attract and

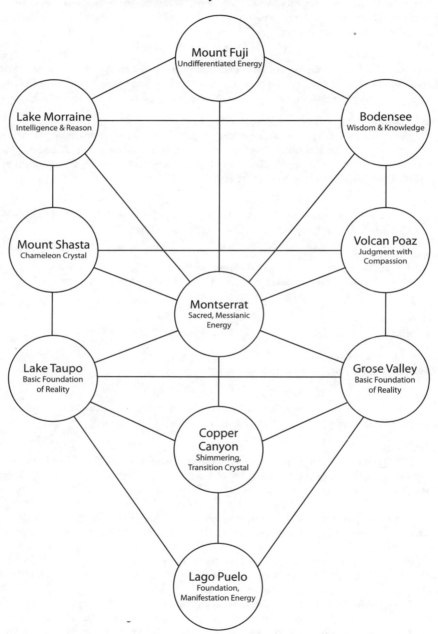

Figure 6: Diagram of the Arcturian etheric crystals and their locations.

discharge blocked energy in Earth's energy channels, like modifying the ring of fire to create balance in that area.

**6. Mount Shasta in California in the United States**. The combination of this crystal, the galactic kachina and the imprint of the Stargate means that Mount Shasta has become a powerful ascension point. It also gives us an easy connection to our soul, our soul power and our soul mission.

**7. Lake Taupo in New Zealand**. The seventh crystal is a symbol of good luck and good fortune, and it brings wealth and prosperity. It is a great attracting force for energy for those who work with it. It is also a reaffirmation of the spiritual strength and power of the Native peoples on the Earth, and will help to reawaken them to their mission.

**8. Copper Canyon in Mexico**. This crystal gives us a new link to Arcturian energy, a link where we can connect with the planet Alano and the fifth-dimensional master named Alano who resides there. The crystal also carries the special energy of shimmering, allowing us to move ourselves or objects into another dimension.

**9. Montserrat near Barcelona in Spain**. This magnificent place is a holy site. Juliano tells us it is mostly free from wars and polarization, and the crystal that was brought in here recently—the ninth crystal—has a powerful, sacred and holy energy. This crystal was downloaded to work with holy sacred light and will help the other crystals become truly sacred energy sites.

**10. Mount Fuji in Japan**. This crystal holds energy of life forces from Lemuria that have now been unlocked by its arrival. It is an ancient crystal containing great secrets of light and ancient knowledge of the planet, and it has a connection with the ancient grandmothers and grandfathers.

### Etz-ha-Chayim
Hebrew for "Tree of Life."

### Fifth Dimension
A higher dimension of existence that is above the first and third dimensions. We currently live on the third dimension. On the third dimension, we are bound by the laws of cause and effect and the laws of reincarnation. The fourth dimension is the astral realm and also the realm of dreams. The fifth dimension transcends this and is the realm of infinite energy and love and can be compared to the Garden of Eden. In the fifth dimension, one transcends the cycle of incarnation. It could be said that one graduates from Earth and goes to the fifth dimension. The ascended masters residing now in the fifth dimension include Jesus. The ascension focuses on going to the fifth dimension.

### Galactic Kachina
In Native American Navajo folklore, a kachina is an intermediary between this world and other worlds—in particular the spirit world. The Native peoples were the first to accept a spiritual philosophy or theory, which includes the existence of other higher beings throughout our galaxy. They also take the perspective of the broader galactic view, which says that we are all part of a galactic family. The galactic kachina is the intermediary between the Central Sun and this planet.

### Galactic Spirituality
This term describes a spiritual philosophy or theory that accepts the existence of other higher beings throughout our galaxy and therefore takes the perspective of the galactic view in understanding our planetary evolution as part of a galactic family of civilizations.

### GOF
An abbreviation for Group of Forty.

### Grays
Fourth-dimensional, old extraterrestrial beings often depicted in movies having a small, thin figure. They are said to not have the ability to love and are very absent of human's spiritual energy.

They have been known to abduct Earth people and have been involved in genetic manipulations to further their own dying race.

### GRID LINES

Another name for energy lines that run through the planet. In Chinese medicine, energy lines that run through the body are called "meridians."

### GROUPS OF FORTY

A concept of group consciousness suggested by the Arcturians for our use in the group ascension process. According to the Arcturians, forty is a spiritually powerful number. The Arcturians emphasize the value and power of joining together in groups. A group of forty consists of forty different members located throughout the U.S., who focus worldwide on meditating together at a given time each month. Group interactions and yearly physical meetings are recommended. Members agree to assist each other in their spiritual development. The Arcturians have asked that forty Groups of Forty be organized. These groups will assist in the healing of Earth and provide a foundation for the individual member's ascension. See the Appendix for more information.

### HAARP

High-Frequency Active Aural Research Project. A scientific research project conducted by the U.S. military that some have described as an aspect of the Star Wars project. High-frequency radio waves are sent into the ionosphere with the purpose of jamming all global communications systems. It is being tested in the remote bush country of Alaska. The project uses a radio transmitter of immense power. It offers a unique ionosphere heating capability.

### HARMONIC CONVERGENCE

A term used to describe a harmonic energy downloaded to the Earth from the Central Sun. The first harmonic convergence was in 1987. The most recent one occurred on August 8, 2008, when a harmonic energy was brought down to the Earth at Mount Shasta, California, and transmitted around the world.

### HELIO-AH

A female Arcturian Ascended Master and Juliano's twin flame.

### HOLOGRAPHIC DECK OF CARDS

The holographic deck of cards is a concept based on the idea of past memory images in our mental bodies. Our memories and brains store these images. Each image looks like a card, and the entire memory bank looks like a deck of cards. To heal past traumas, we can access past memory images and reshape those images for a healing.

### HOLOGRAPHIC HEALING

The concept in holographic healing states that the part represents the whole. In holographic energy, healing one aspect of the Earth can affect the entire planet's energy. Healing one part of the Earth can affect other parts of the Earth.

### HOLOGRAPHY WORK

In the scientific world, holography is described as a part of any image created through a laser that actually reproduces the original whole image. In fifth-dimensional work, holography is the ability to access all universal energy from any spot in the universe. Holographic healing is based on the assumption that we can access our greater self through holographic energy.

### HUNDREDTH MONKEY EFFECT

This is a revolutionary concept theorized by scientists who studied the Japanese monkeys *Macaca fuscata* on the island of Koshima in 1952. On this island, scientists were providing the monkeys with sweet potatoes that were dropped in sand. The monkeys liked the taste of the sweet potato, but they found the sand unpleasant. One female monkey found she could solve the problem by washing the potato in a nearby stream. She then taught this trick to her mother and her playmates. Amazingly, this technique was soon picked up by many monkeys on the island. Between 1952 and 1958, many young monkeys learned to wash the sweet potatoes. The scientists believed that when the hundredth monkey learned to do this, then suddenly almost all of the monkeys on the island also learned to do this. The added energy of this hundredth monkey learning to do this task somehow created a breakthrough. See the book *The Hundredth Monkey,* by Ken Keyes Jr., Vision Books, 1982.

### ISKALIA MIRROR

A fifth-dimensional, etheric mirror that has been placed above the North Pole by the Arcturians. The purpose of this mirror is to help focus high light from the Central Sun and to direct that light to Earth for transforming Earth into a fifth-dimensional planet.

### JULIANO

The main Arcturian guide and ascended master working to help activate the Earth and Arcturian starseeds toward ascension.

### JUPITER CORRIDOR

An interdimensional corridor between Mars and Jupiter that extraterrestrial ships use to enter our solar system. Also, many extraterrestrial ships can remain in an orbiting position there without entering third-dimensional Earth space.

### KABBALAH

The major branch of Jewish mysticism. The Hebrew word "kabbalah" is translated as "to receive."

### *KADOSH*

Hebrew word for "holy."

### *KADOSH, KADOSH, KADOSH, ADONAI TZEVAOTH*

Hebrew for "Holy, Holy, Holy is the Lord of Hosts." This is a powerful expression that, when toned, can raise one's level of consciousness to new heights and also assist in unlocking the codes for our transformation into the fifth dimension.

### KUTHUMI

One of the ascended masters who serves Sananda. In a previous life, Kuthumi incarnated as Saint Francis of Assisi. He is generally recognized as holding the position of world teacher in the planetary White Brotherhood/Sisterhood. An extensive record of his teachings can be found in the works of Alice Bailey.

### LAKE MORAINE

A lake in Banff, Canada, in the Canadian Rockies, where an etheric crystal is located.

### LIGHTBODY

The higher etheric spirit body that is connected to the highest soul energy.

### BILLY MEIER

Bill Eduard Albert Meier is a citizen from Switzerland who has had numerous contacts with extraterrestrials from the star system Pleiades starting at age of five. These contacts are recorded in his series of books called *Contact Reports.*

### MERKAVAH

In Hebrew, merkavah means "chariots," and in modern spirituality it refers to a chariot in etheric form that is used to bring spiritual seekers to the higher dimensions.

## METATRON

Tradition associates Metatron with Enoch, who "walked with God" (Genesis 5:22) and who ascended to heaven and was changed from a human being into an angel. His name has been defined as "the angel of presence," or the "one who occupies the throne next to the divine throne." Another interpretation of his name is based on the Latin word *"metator,"* which means a guide or measurer. In the world of the Jewish mystic, Metatron holds the rank of the highest of angels— that of an archangel. According to the Arcturians, Metatron is associated with the Stargate, and assists souls in their ascension to higher worlds.

## MICHAEL

His name is actually a question, meaning: "Who is like God?" He is perhaps the best known of the archangels and is acknowledged by all three Western sacred traditions. He has been called "the prince of light," and is said to be fighting a war against the sons of darkness. In this role, he is depicted most often as the winged (with unsheathed sword) warrior of God and slayer of the dragons. His role in the ascension process is focused on helping us cut the cords of attachment to the Earth plane, which will allow us to move up to higher consciousness. In the Kabbalah, he is regarded as the forerunner of the Shekinah, the divine mother.

## MONAD

The original, elemental creative force. Each one of us contains a portion of that force at the center of our true essence.

## MULTIDIMENSIONAL PRESENCE

We can become aware that we exist on several different dimensions. The Arcturians are trying to help us become aware that we have an existence not only on the third dimension, but also in the fifth dimension.

## NESHAMAH

Hebrew for "lightbody." In Kabbalah, or Jewish Mysticism, it refers to your highest self, which transcends third dimensional reality and the Earth ego and is linked directly to the divine light.

## NULL ZONE

A zone outside of the third dimension, but not necessarily in any other dimension. It is an area outside of our known time-space universe structure where time is nonexistent. Some have speculated that the photon belt contains null zone regions, and that the Earth is temporarily in this null zone now—at the time of this writing—until the year 2011.

## ORION

Orion is a superb constellation that dominates the southern winter sky. The most striking part of the constellation is the belt, which consists of three bright stars. No other constellation contains so many bright stars. Rigel, which is outside the belt, for example, is a giant star over 500 light years away. Betelgeuse, another star outside the belt in Orion, is about 300 light years away.

## ORIONS

An extraterrestrial culture that descended from another ancient civilization near the constellation Orion. The Orions have been extremely influential in the genetic makeup of current human beings. Human beings possess a portion of Orion DNA and reflect Orion traits in our current physical, emotional and mental composition.

## PHOTON BELT/PHOTON ENERGY

An energy emanating from the center of the galaxy that is about to intersect with our solar system and Earth. Some have predicted that the photon belt contains energy particles that could affect the Earth's magnetic field, causing all electronic equipment to stop working.

**PLEIADES**

A small cluster of stars known as the "Seven Sisters" in some mythologies. Some Native Americans believe that they are descended from the Pleiades. It is near the constellation Taurus, about 450 light years from Earth, and is the home of a race called the Pleiadians, who have frequently interacted with Earth and her cultures. It is said that the Pleiadians have a common ancestry with us.

**PORTAL**

An opening at the end of a corridor that allows one to go into an interdimensional space. This could allow one to go into the fifth dimension.

**PULSING**

An exercise technique created by the Arcturians in which one can heal ones self by contracting and expanding one's energy field. One becomes aware of one's vibration energy field. By increasing the rates of the energy field and then rapidly "pulsing," or expanding and contracting, one can raise ones spiritual awareness and also do self-healing

**RING OF ASCENSION**

An etheric halo of energy around the Earth, containing fifth-dimensional light from the ascended masters. This halo is supposed to aid the Earth in her ability to ascend as a planet to the fifth dimension. The starseeds are to interact with this light through visualizations and meditations

**RUACH HA-KODESH**

Hebrew for "Holy Spirit."

**SACRED TRIANGLE**

A term used by the Arcturians to denote a triangular symbol representing the unification of three powerful spiritual forces on Earth: the White Brotherhood/Sisterhood, masters including Sananda/Jesus, the extraterrestrial higher-dimensional masters, such as the Arcturians and the Pleiadians, and the Native American ascended masters, such as Chief White Eagle. The unification of these spiritual forces will create the Sacred Triangle that will aid in the healing and ascension of Earth.

**SANANDA**

Sananda is known to us as the Master Jesus. He is considered the greatest Jewish Kabbalist of all time. His galactic name—Sananda—represents an evolved and galactic picture of who he is in his entirety. In the Kabbalah, Sananda is known as Jeshua ben Miriam of Nazareth, which can be translated as Jesus, son of Mary of Nazareth.

**SAN FRANCISCO PEAKS**

A 12,000-foot mountain range near Flagstaff, Arizona, which is the sacred home for the Navajo Indians. The kachina spirits are supposed to live there.

**SHAMBALLA LIGHT**

Light from the fifth dimension that is focused on cities of perfect harmony that exist in the fifth dimension. One such city of light is called "Shamballa."

**SHIMMERING**

Shimmering is an energy exercise that allows one's auric field to vibrate at a frequency that enables the aura to shift the electrons. The atomic structure of your cells transmutes into a vibratory energy field that elliptically shifts the cellular structures into the fifth dimension, causing a back-and-forth or "shimmering" modality. This modality actually affects the atomic and quantum levels of your cellular structures. This shimmering energy is the precursor to the ascension. The ascension is an accelerated and enhanced shimmering energy in which you elevate yourselves into the fifth dimension permanently. The energy that we are now working with in shimmering is a powerful and necessary prelude to the fifth-dimensional ascension.

## STARGATE

A multidimensional portal into higher realms. The Arcturian Stargate is very close to the Arcturus star system, and it is overseen by the Arcturians. This powerful passage point requires Earthlings who wish to pass through it to complete all lessons and Earth incarnations associated with the third-dimensional experience. It serves as a gateway to the fifth dimension. New soul assignments are given there, and souls can then be sent to many different higher realms throughout the galaxy and universe. Archangel Metatron and many other higher beings are present at the Stargate. Many people are now using the term "stargate" to refer to openings on Earth to higher dimensions, when in fact they are describing corridors. The Stargate is a magnificent, temple-like, etheric structure that can process and transform many souls.

## STARSEEDS

People who have or are born with the awareness of galactic consciousness. Starseeds may also have memories of past lifetimes on other planets and feel connected to civilizations of other planets, such as the Pleiades or Arcturus. Some starseeds have come to Earth at this time to assist her in this evolutionary transformation.

## TACHYON

A small particle that travels faster than the speed of light. A tachyon stone is an object that contains tachyon particles and is used for healings in much the same way one uses crystals.

## THOUGHT PROJECTION

A technique described by the Arcturians involving projecting thoughts through a corridor to reach the fifth dimension and beyond.

## TOMAR

An Arcturian ascended master whose specialty is using and describing the Arcturian temple energy.

## TONES/SACRED SOUNDS

Sounds producing a vibratory resonance that help activate and align the chakras.

## TRANCE CHANNELING

Putting yourself into a light trance to do automatic speaking. A trance is a type of self-hypnosis in which you put yourself into an altered state of consciousness. There is light trance and there is deep trance. A deep trance is where you go out and are almost in a somnambulant or sleep state. This is the way Edward Cayce used to channel. In light trance channeling, one is still awake while bringing through messages.

## TREE OF LIFE

The Tree of Life is a galactic blueprint for the creation of this reality. It includes ten energy codes placed in spheres in the shape of a tree. These codes are used for individual and planetary healing. The three spiritualities of the Sacred Triangle are included in the Tree of Life. The Tree of Life is not flat, but multidimensional and holographic. It has paths for manifestation. Its twenty-two lines are these pathways. The Tree of Life connects to the energy of the cosmos.

## TSELEM

Hebrew for third-dimensional image or form, as in "God created man in his own image."

## 2012 ALIGNMENT

A time when the Earth goes into alignment with the center of the Milky Way galaxy. This is also referred to in the Mayan calendar and prophecies made for this date. The Mayans believed that on December 21, 2012, the Earth will come into alignment with the center of the galaxy. Some have interpreted the Mayans' statements as marking the end of the world. Others say that this alignment represents the transformation of the world. One view is that our world will be born again on December 21, 2012. John Major Jenkins, in *Maya Cosmogenesis 2012,* interpreted the Mayan vision of this alignment in 2012 as a union of the cosmic mother, or the Milky Way, with the father represented as the December solstice sun.

## 2012 CORRIDOR

A tunnel or corridor to the future time of 2012 when the Earth's transformation will be at its height. By projecting positive energy and images into this time, one can help maximize positive outcomes for this time.

## VOSZ ENERGY BELT

This is a term the Arcturians used to describe the mental energies around the Earth also called the "mental energy field." It consists of the thoughts and emotions that has been used around the Earth.

## VYWAMUS

A fifth-dimensional soul psychologist known for his insight into the psychology of Earth problems and resolution of issues related to starseeds incarnated on Earth.

## WALK-INS

Humans who have received other spiritual entities into their bodies. The term is also used in reference to the new spirit that has entered the body. In some cases, the original spirit of the person may have left—for example, after an auto accident or some other form of severe trauma—and the new spirit "walks in" to the old body. This is always by agreement of the person vacating the body before incarnating to allow their body to continue in service after their particular incarnation is complete. It also allows the "walk-in" being to skip the process of childhood and adolescence to get straight to their mission on Earth. The walk-in does agree to honor the commitments of the previous occupant's life.

## WHITE BROTHERHOOD/SISTERHOOD

The White Brotherhood/Sisterhood is a spiritual hierarchy of ascended masters residing in the fifth dimension. "White" is not used here as a racial term. It refers to the white light or higher frequency that these masters have attained. The masters include Sananda, Kuthumi, Mother Mary, Quan Yin, Sanat Kumara, Archangel Michael, Saint Germain and many other ascended beings.

## WHITE BUFFALO CALF WOMAN

In Lakota Native American folklore, she is the fifth-dimensional spirit being that appeared to them bringing forth special information about holy ceremonies and accessing higher spirit. She taught the necessity of being in harmony with the Earth. Her focus is on the unity of all beings and that all are relations. She is representative of the dawning of a new age.

## ZOHARIC LIGHT

Light from the Creator Source. Zohar is the Hebrew word for "brilliance" or "splendor."

# About the Author and Artist

## David Miller

David has been a channel for 18 years. His original spiritual study was the Kabbalah and Jewish mysticism. He began trance channeling his Kabbalistic guide and teacher, Nabur, on a camping trip at Sublime Point on the North Rim of the Grand Canyon.

David has published four books and over 50 articles in both American and Australian magazines. He currently does phone readings and conducts workshops focusing on the concepts and techniques of ascension, healings, and psycho-spiritual issues. He also works full time as a medical social worker and part time conducting group workshops, personal readings and healings.

## Gudrun Miller

Gudrun has been an artist for 30 years and has been a spiritual seeker all of her life. When asked by the Arcturians to bring forth images with their assistance, she was honored and thrilled.

Gudrun's spiritual awakening was assisted by her spirit guide Spirit Fire, an ascended American Indian. She helped Gudrun build a medicine tepee in her backyard, and has also guided her in her work as a visionary artist. Many people have since come from all over the world to experience the healing energies of the Eagle Medicine Tepee.

The Arcturians make their requests through David, who then channels specific information that helps stimulate Gudrun's imagination. She then senses their presence in a heightened awareness and focus as she paints. The Arcturians have reassured her that if the images were not suitable, they would tell her.

When not painting, Gudrun works full time as an art therapist and counselor. She senses the healing presence of her guides and teachers in her practice as well.

# THE GROUP OF FORTY

The goal of this project is to establish a network of 40 Groups of Forty throughout the world. The formation of 40 groups will enhance the energy of group meditation, provide powerful healing energies for the Earth and aid all members in raising their consciousness to the fifth-dimensional level. Each Group of Forty will provide the basis for building the energy necessary for group ascension.

## MEDITATIONS

All groups simultaneously meet in meditation once each month. Currently it is held the first Saturday of every month at 5:45-6:45 PM, Mountain Standard Time. During the main meditation, David channels a message for everyone in all the groups, which is later transcribed and sent out to all group members with the monthly newsletter.

Group of Forty members do not have to be physically together to participate in the group meditation. The powerful Arcturian energy can be called in wherever any member is meditating, and through that connection, the member can experience the group energy being generated by all Groups of Forty.

Meditations also include a group healing, where all members of the group focus healing on one designated person in the group who has requested it. Members who have been the focus of this healing energy have reported profound healing experiences. All work by the Arcturians is directed toward personal healings, healings for Mother Earth, and our transformation to higher consciousness, leading to ascension to the fifth dimension.

## THE MONTHLY CHANNELED MESSAGE

Messages channeled during the simultaneous group meditation usually cover topics including:

- The Arcturian Frequency
- Preparation for Ascension
- Arcturian Healing Chambers
- Multidimensional Corridors
- Accelerating our Spiritual Growth
- The Arcturian Crystal Temple
- The Arcturian Stargate
- The Sacred Triangle

Members are encouraged to submit questions for the channeling sessions to David at the beginning of each month.

## THE MONTHLY NEWSLETTER

David prepares a monthly newsletter providing general announcements and updated information that pertains to all groups. The newsletter, along with a transcription of the monthly channeled message, is mailed to all members each month. Cassette tapes of the monthly channeling sessions are also available on a subscription basis.

## THE EMAIL REFLECTOR LIST

David maintains a reflector list through email communication, where those members who wish to may share experiences and information, ask general questions of the group and also have a chance to get to know individual members from near and far. It is a wonderful way of building our Group of Forty community. It is an invaluable resource and a great deal of fun, too.

## THE ANNUAL ARCTURIAN GROUP OF FORTY GATHERING AND WORKSHOP

Annual gatherings are planned for the second weekend in October and are held in Sedona, Arizona. This is a fantastic opportunity to make your in-person connection to the entire Group of Forty project. There are different topics addressed in David's channelings each year, along with guest presenters. It has been a profoundly enlightening, healing and above all enjoyable experience for many past participants. David and Gudrun also conduct other workshops during the year at other places around the world.

## REGISTRATION

To become a Group of Forty member, please contact:

David Miller, Group of Forty
P.O. Box 4074
Prescott, AZ 86302
USA
Phone: 928-776-1717
Email: davidmiller@groupofforty
Web: www.groupofforty.com

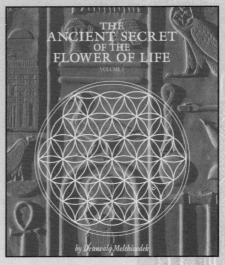

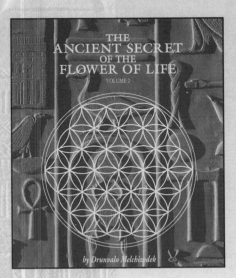

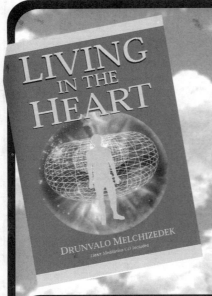

# THE GENTLE WAY

## A SELF-HELP GUIDE FOR THOSE WHO BELIEVE IN ANGELS

THE GENTLE WAY

A SELF-HELP GUIDE FOR THOSE WHO BELIEVE IN ANGELS

TOM T. MOORE

Let me explain what I believe you'll achieve from reading this self-help book:

This book will put you back in touch with your guardian angel or strengthen and expand the connection that perhaps you already have. It will strengthen your spiritual beliefs. You will have more fun and less stress in your life. You will greatly lower the "fear factor" in everyday living. In lowering the fear factor, this book will give you the confidence that you can travel in safety wherever you go, whether it is to work and back home, to the store, across the country or around the world. It will assist you in achieving whatever goals you have set for yourself in your life. This book will assist in finding just the right job for you. It will even help you find that special person to share your life. It will assist you in handling those major challenges we all experience in life. This book will even inspire you to learn more about our world and universe. How can I promise all these benefits? It's because I have been using these concepts for over ten years, and I can report these successes from *direct knowledge and experience*. But this is a self-help guide, so that means it requires active participation on your part. What you are going to read in this book is *unique information* that you have *never seen before!* This book is for all faiths and beliefs with the only requirement being a basic belief in angels.

—Tom T. Moore

## CHAPTER TITLES:

- ANGELS
- HOW I BEGAN
- EASY STEPS
- HOME LIFE
- THE CORPORATE ENVIRONMENT
- SMALL BUSINESSES
- POLITICS
- TRAVEL

- BINGO, CASINOS AND CARD GAMES
- REQUESTING BENEVOLENT OUTCOMES IN DANGEROUS PLACES
- THE RADIANT EFFECT
- LIVING PRAYERS
- "I HOPE" REQUESTS

$**14**^{95}$ Softcover
ISBN 1-891824-60-0

# THE EXPLORER RACE

## Zoosh, End-time Historian through Robert Shapiro

You individuals reading this are truly a result of the genetic experiment on Earth. You are beings who uphold the principles of the Explorer Race. The information in this book is designed to show you who you are and give you an evolutionary understanding of your past that will help you now. The key to empowerment in these days is to not know everything about your past, but to know what will help you now. Your number-one function right now is your status of Creator apprentice, which you have achieved through years and lifetimes of sweat. You are constantly being given responsibilities by the Creator that would normally be things that Creator would do. The responsibility and the destiny of the Explorer Race is not only to explore, but to create.

### CHAPTER TITLES

The Genetic Experiment on Earth
Influences of the Zodiac
The Heritage from Early Civilizations
Explorer Race Time Line, Part 1
Explorer Race Time Line, Part 2
The Experiment that Failed
The ET in You: Physical Body
The ET in You: Emotion and Thought
The ET in You: Spirit
Emotion Lost: Sexual Addiction in Zeta History
Sex, Love and Relationships
Sexual Violence on Earth
The Third Sex: The Neutral Binding Energy
The Goddess Energy: The Soul of Creation
Origin of the Species: A Sirian Perspective
An Andromedan Perspective on the Earth Experiment
The Perspective of Orion Past on Their Role
Conversation with a Zeta

The Order: Its Origin and Resolution
The White Brotherhood, the Illuminati, the New Dawn
    and the Shadow Government
Fulfilling the Creator's Destiny
The Sirian Inheritors of Third-Dimensional Earth
The Explorer Race Is Ready
Coming of Age in the Fourth Dimension
The True Purpose of Negative Energy
The Challenge of Risking Intimacy
Etheric Gene-Splicing and the Neutral Particle
Material Mastery and the New Safety
The Sterilization of Planet Earth
The Tenth Planet: The Gift of Temptation
The Eleventh Planet: The Undoer, Key to Transformation
The Twelfth Planet: Return of the Heart Energy
Moving beyond the Mind
Retrieving Heart Energy
The Creator's Mission and the Function of the Human Race

**$25.00**

574 P. SOFTCOVER
ISBN 0-929385-38-1

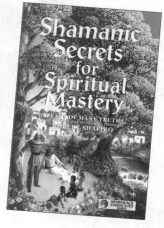